Psychic Deadness

Psychic Deadness

Michael Eigen

JASON ARONSON INC.
Northvale, New Jersey
London

This book was set in 10 pt. New Baskerville by Alpha Graphics of Pittsfield, New Hampshire and printed and bound by Book-mart Press of North Bergen, New Jersey.

Library of Congress Cataloging-in-Publication Data

Eigen, Michael.
    Psychic deadness / by Michael Eigen.
        p.   cm.
    Includes bibliographical references and index.
    ISBN 1-56821-735-8 (alk. paper)
    1. Death instinct. 2. Death instinct—Case studies. 3. Self-
destructive behavior. 4. Self-destructive behavior—Case studies.
    5. Psychoanalysis. I. Title.
    BF175.5.D4E37   1996
    155.2'32—dc20   95-24825

Manufactured in the United States of America. Jason Aronson Inc. offers books and cassettes. For information and catalog write to Jason Aronson Inc., 230 Livingston Street, Northvale, New Jersey 07647.

To all who strive to make this world
a place the heart can live in. *

---

* This dedication is inspired by Edward Dahlberg's, *Can These Bones Live.*

Come from the four winds, O breath,
and breathe upon these slain,
that they may live.

Ezekiel 37:9

Contents

Acknowledgments

I wish to thank the editors who published some of these chapters in journals and books while this work was in progress: Jerome Travers, Mark Stern, Otto Weininger, Nathan Schwartz-Salant, Chris Farhood, Jay Greenberg, Stephen Levine, Emmanuel Ghent, Stephen Mitchell, and Martin Rock. Writing a book like this becomes more tolerable when one feels there are people who want to read it. Working with psychic deadness is, at best, difficult, and it helps to have lines of communication "out there."

Many people have asked me to speak on this subject—too many to mention. But please know that I am grateful for these opportunities and that I think of you. The good words of many colleagues—including Jessica Benjamin, Mark Epstein, Marion Milner, Art Robbins, Jeff Seinfeld, Adam Phillips, and Harold Boris—have fueled faith in work that thrives in dark nights. Members of my seminars and my patients provide daily bread—the challenges and the stimulations that nourish life. So do my wife, Betty, and my children, without whom none of my books could have been written.

Thanks again to Jason Aronson, who has published books of mine for a decade. His response to my work is immediate and forthright, and I appreciate that. This book begins our second decade and I'm proud to be included on a list that includes many bold and imaginative areas. The production and editing of this book was aided by Judith Cohen and Adelle Krauser. Norma Pomerantz, as usual, was helpful in administrative tasks, and Michael Moskowitz helped to get things going.

Introduction

Many individuals today seek help because they feel dead. A sense of inner deadness may persist in an otherwise full and meaningful life. Deadness can be related to emptiness and meaninglessness, but is not identical with them. I have seen individuals who are filled with emotions and meaning, but somehow remain untouched by their experiences. They remain impervious and immune to the potential richness of what they undergo. They complain of a deadness that persists in the midst of plenty.

Sam, described in Chapter 12, "Primary Process and Shock," changed careers from science to writing in an attempt to break through his deadness. He felt that science exacerbated an inner deadness and hoped poetry and fiction would help him come alive. To his chagrin, he learned that one could be dead as a writer too. He had girlfriends and emotions galore. When he wrote, his being was saturated with meaning. He made his writings bristle with the aliveness he wished he had. His work came alive, but in his person the deadness continued. He gave to his writings what he wished *he* could have.

Sam's life was not a horror story. He lived a good life blessed with many advantages, physical health, mental gifts, and talents. His parents cared for him, tried to nurture him. Sam felt they overdid it. He pictured his mother as sexually seductive and his father as a raging baby, although they were both professional people who showed competent and well-meaning faces to the world. They tried to do a good job with Sam too. They could not realize what a toll the daily breakdowns of their "official selves" took on their children, or if they realized this, they were helpless to stop.

Sam's was not a case of successful parents being uninvolved with the children. It was more a case of successful parents wanting to be successful with their children too. They poured themselves into their children like they poured themselves into their work. However, the children were not able to deal with the flood of feelings that the parents poured into them. Sam's parents tried to give him all the nourishment they wanted themselves. It was as if Sam were their proxy. They gave him what they wanted—or some version of what they imagined they wanted. In their minds, Sam was getting *everything* they wanted to get. Most of all, he was getting *them*—vastly nourishing, giving, caring parents. Sam was getting the childhood and parents they had always wanted.

They tried to give Sam more than life could offer. Thus they lived beyond themselves emotionally, and broke down throughout the day. They could not be supernourishing beings. His father yelled so loudly at daily frustrations that Sam cringed with contempt and terror. His mother tried to cajole and seduce Sam out of his bad feelings. She could not tolerate his fear and hate. She needed a happy and successful child, one who thought the world of her. Her husband's rages were more than enough for her to deal with. Her child should give her pleasure. To deal with a child's destructive urges seemed overwhelming: she tried to love and soft-talk them away. She was frequently depressed and weak. Her dreams of a perfect family were shattered, although she kept hoping things were better than they were.

Sam learned the hard way and early that he would have to take care of himself emotionally, but he was not a very good substitute caretaker. He felt more depleted than nourished by his parents' attention and lacked the psychic equipment to genuinely process their and his turbulence. He became smart and adept at scanning states of mind and developing verbal formulas for them. But the better he became at figuring out what others or he were feeling and why, the unhappier he felt. He could not buy happiness by becoming successful or smart or talented or caring, no more than his parents could.

A sense of deadness developed as he grew into adulthood. At first, he could not believe it was there. He felt so much and had so much in life. How could he, who was so alive, so full, be dead? Yet the deadness did not go away. It became persistent, and he monitored it. He put a mental barium tracer on it and could locate it virtually at will. In time, he did not have to look for it. It was in the background, spoiling his experiences. Against his will and outside his conscious control, he deadened himself as a form of self-protection, a shield he wished he did not have. He came to therapy for help in freeing himself from self-deadening processes.

Sam is one example of a successful person feeling deadness in an otherwise pleasurable life. Mr. Y., described in Chapter 3, "Goodness and Deadness," is another. Like Sam, Mr. Y. lived an apparently good life from childhood on. He was a good student and athlete and was well liked by his peers. Unlike Sam, he felt his parents were too restrained in their display of attention and feelings, although they were proud of his accomplishments. Whereas Sam felt his parents were overinvolved with him, Mr. Y. felt his were underinvolved. They cared for him, but were low keyed and reticent. They expected him to be the competent person he was. Sam grew up in a steamy and stormy emotional atmosphere, whereas Mr. Y. described a temperate, orderly one.

Mr. Y. enjoyed his relatively easy life. People gravitated toward him, and things went his way. He was a "nice" guy, good at what he did. But he had long been aware of a lack of passionate intensity, and as time went on, his tepid emotional life increasingly bothered him. For many years, the challenges of work and relationships kept him busy. But as he grew in status and position, his inner deadness grew in importance too. It was easier to advance in work and make new friends than to meet the deadness he feared could derail him. By the time I met him, he was beginning to feel that if he did not do something with the deadness within, nothing else he did would be worthwhile.

People who meet Sam or Mr. Y. would not guess they are dead. In certain regards, they even seem enviable. Neither Sam nor Mr. Y. lacked friends or opportunities for self-realization. Not all people who have gone dead are so lucky. On the other end of the scale is Deborah, who looked like a corpse and is described in Chapter 1, "Psychic Death." She was living a horrible life and looked horrifying. No one would envy her. She seemed almost beyond help.

Deborah was raised by professional parents in the suburbs, who alternately doted on her and attended to their careers. Deborah experienced extremes of parental attention and self-absorption, a mixture of emotionality and vacancy, of too much and too little. Many children are subjected to such a regime. Why did it take such a toll on Deborah? Are there more Deborahs, perhaps in less extreme form, than are realized?

Deborah's very presence was a critique of a world that could produce her. Her corpse-like body seemed a cruel finger pointing at a world that did not know what to do with children. Her visage and bearing signaled meaningless, useless suffering without end. And yet she *was* looking for help. In spite of the death that possessed her, she was trying to find someone to help her or, perhaps, someone to help her help herself. However, she was dangerously near the edge and was sliding. It was a real question whether she could find help before the end.

Lucy was someone in between (see Chapter 10, "Counterparts in a Couple"). She found it difficult to partake of the pleasures of life, but she did feel deep joy. She felt joy in her children, her art, her husband. But she also was depressed and was even more than depressed. A deep deadness threatened to suck up her existence. It often seemed that the deadness in her being was her most intimate companion. For many years, she felt most herself and knew herself best when she hid in the center of her deadness. She spent many sessions raging against her deadness and crying, but she never felt more at home than when she crawled into it and disappeared. In a way, she valued deadness more than life.

We will see that, for someone like Lucy, deadness is not something that will go away. It is a very real counterpart to her existence, a part of her life. We can trace it back to a suppressed, sometimes depressed mother and a guilt-inducing father. But her deadness has become a habit, a way to soothe, if also torment, herself. It has become second nature. Over the years, Lucy learned to use deadness as a source of nourishment. It would be cruel and wasteful for therapy to try to eradicate her deadness, her most intimate complaint and friend. But therapy can help aliveness grow. What emerges is not an end to deadness, but a new and better movement between aliveness and deadness, a rhythm or oscillation. The psyche cannot do away with its states, but it can grow to make more room for them.

The above sampling of individuals plagued by deadness suggests that the sense of deadness varies in form and background. It can cripple an entire life or only part of a life. It occurs in individuals who have been overstimulated or understimulated or a combination of the two: parents can erratically overstuff or deprive a child of emotional transmissions. Often a parent, especially the mother, has suffered depression, although it is not clear that this must be so. In any case, understanding the background of psychic deadness is not suffi- cient to ameliorate it. For example, Mr. Y. and Deborah had been in various forms of analysis for years and had extensive understanding of their psycho- social backgrounds and personality patterns without obtaining relief of their deadness. On the contrary, self-deadening processes increased over time for both of them and, in Deborah's case, dangerously so.

Some patients do benefit from catching on to how they shut down in face of pain. The shutting-down process can sometimes be caught in the act. Pa- tients can be helped to connect shut down with distressing moments. Repeated failures in relationships and work, a wounding rejection or loss, frightening emotions that become destructive: many kinds and combinations of precipi- tants are possible. Often the therapy relationship becomes a kind of labora- tory, in which varying states of deadness–aliveness can be tied to what is going on between patient and therapist as well as in the patient's life.

Nevertheless, understanding and practicing better response patterns do not do the trick with many individuals. Their deadness tends to overwhelm under- standing and resolve. For some individuals, whatever they do to help themselves gets lost in the deadness. Something more or else is needed, and no treatment formulas may do.

In many cases, the growth of knowledge must be coupled with adequate emotional transmission by the therapist. The emotional tone of the therapy can be the most important element. Yet an atmosphere that works in one case may not in another, even when the background of both seem similar. In the end, nothing may save the patient and therapist from working to discover what the patient is looking for—that is, the precise combination of psychic nutri- ents, responses, attitudes, and tones required for a given individual, or even a given moment, so that a person can begin to open and the deadness may lift.

Although theoretical and clinical formulas may add to the deadness, the vast reservoir of theoretical ideas and clinical wisdom can be used as stimuli or probes or resources to sensitize one to issues and concerns in a given case. If theory is useless or even harmful without the "right" clinical tone or touch, one's tone and touch can become more finely nuanced and richly communicative if informed by a background of theoretical groping.

There are so many psychological schools and theories today that it is useful to describe briefly the tapestry of ideas that inform my clinical intuitions. Thus the first part of this book "Theoretical Soundings," is devoted to sketches of major theorists who have had the most to say to me about psychic deadness. These chapters are not meant to be exhaustive, systematic explications. Rather, they are soundings. At times they become dialogues, reveries, arguments, questions—part of a search to bring someone's thought to its limits, a search for what can be useful or enlightening or sensitizing. To an extent, a walk with any theorist is like walking the plank. Sooner or later we reach the end of the walk for now, with nothing left but the leap into the ocean of life.

The second part of this book, Clinical Probes, portrays attempts to be in the ocean. It explores clinical realities with a variety of patients and brings out in detail what it is like to immerse oneself in work with psychic deadness and related problems. What happens when deadness lifts or fails to lift, and a person opens or fails to open? In these chapters patient and therapist struggle with factors that maintain psychic deadness, as they try to find and support whatever in a person seeks life. Some of these struggles are related to larger social realities as well as deeply personal ones.

THEORETICAL SOUNDINGS

The major theorists I write about in Part I are Freud, Klein, Bion, and Winnicott. These are authors I have wrestled with for many years and who themselves have wrestled with problems related to psychic deadness. Each of these authors has threads to pull that go in many directions, open many vistas. One cannot readily get to the bottom of their work: one exhausts oneself before exhausting them. After being immersed in the work of these authors and the terrible clinical realities with which they deal, popular representations of their thought seem appalling. At the same time, these authors have played a role in generating some of the most interesting recent writings on psychic deadness (Boris 1993, 1994, Emery 1992, Green 1986, Grotstein 1990a,b).

Other major writers that have been important to me include Lacan, Reich, Jung, and Kohut. But limits must be set, and I have chosen for discussion a sampling of writers among those I use most, all of whom burrow deeply and fiercely into the deadness that many individuals bring to the consulting room today.

Freud

Freud often seemed more interested in why psychoanalysis failed than in why it succeeded. In an amazing three pages, written near the end of his life, he flashes a kaleidoscopic array of images of therapeutic failure, clustered around an obscure inability or resistance to change (1937). He writes of people whose libido is either too sticky or mobile, too slow or quick, to change objects, so that the growth of relationships is stillborn or short-circuited.

He characterizes another group of individuals by an attitude that shows "a depletion of the plasticity, the capacity for change and further development." He says of this group that "all the mental processes, relationships and distributions of force are unchangeable, fixed and rigid." He associates images of "inertia" and "entropy" to this state of being. He notes that although once he thought of this inability to develop as "resistance from the id," he now envisions something more pervasive, if obscure: "some temporal characteristics are concerned—some alterations of a rhythm of development in psychical life we have not appreciated" (1937, p. 242).

In yet another group of individuals, Freud has the impression of a "force which is defending itself by every means against recovery" (1937, p. 242). This force is something more than a sense of guilt and need for punishment. For Freud, it is traceable "back to the original death instinct of living matter" (1937, p. 243).

Regardless of the questionable scientific status of Freud's concept of a death instinct, its poetic and heuristic power is striking. He no longer attributes widespread masochism, resistance to recovery, or even neurotic guilt to permutations of the pleasure principle. The fact that many people cling to suffering leads him to imagine a darker desire, wish, drive, or instinct: a pull or even flight toward death.

To be sure, Freud's work had always envisioned some push–pull of forces. Even on a bare neurological level, he early envisioned old brain excitations inhibited by cortical functions. Excitations had to be modulated, dampened, controlled, channeled, insulated: a barrier was required to regulate the flow of internal–external stimuli and to protect against untoward surges and excitatory flooding. In his later writings he continues to refer to a tendency to tone down stimuli, even reduce stimuli to zero, a kind of on–off double movement in the psychoorganism: aliveness is increasing–decreasing at the same time toward its maximum–minimum.

By the end of his life, the image of a psyche that could not change, that fought recovery, that succumbed to inertia and entropy, that was mired in useless suffering, that zeroed itself out, became prepossessing. His conceptual equipment may or may not be up to the task required by self-cancelling/nulling processes, but his writings circle around phenomena critical for us today. He focuses our gaze on an array of self-deadening processes and makes us wonder what we can do with them. Chapter 1 focuses on aspects of Freud's life and writings that give us a sense of what we are up against when we attempt to lift the deadness.

Ferenczi

Almost as soon as Freud wrote of a death drive, Ferenczi (1929, p. 104) was quick to add that "aversion to life" can arise as a result of "signs of aversion or impatience on the part of the mother." He emphasizes the effects of early trauma in cases where life seemed impossible. Yet, one ought not oversimplify and polarize Freud and Ferenczi, pointing to Freud's emphasis on drives and Ferenczi's on the quality of care. Such a stark contrast would be unfair and misleading. Both writers have extremely complex and searching views of what makes a decent life possible.

Indeed, Ferenczi feels that, because of the weight of the death drive in infancy, maternal care is all the more important. The child needs support in carrying him or her over into life. "The child has to be induced, by means of an immense expenditure of love, tenderness, and care, to forgive his parents for having brought him into the world," lest he succumb to the destructive undertow. Ferenczi depicts a state of affairs in which the parents must ally themselves with the life force of the infant, lest it slip into the nonbeing to which it is so close. A good deal of weight is placed on the parents' responsibility to mediate the infant's journey into life, but the rewards also are great, since "tactful treatment and upbringing gradually give rise to progressive immunization against physical and psychical injuries" (1929, p. 105).

Ferenczi's work forms an important part of the background given new turns by Klein, Bion, and Winnicott. Each of these authors digs deep into processes that constitute "aversion to life." I mention Ferenczi now because he stands as a beam of light, explicitly emphasizing the importance of the analyst's love in counteracting destructive forces. Freud seems to take this role of the analyst for granted, and writes more of the ins and outs of the patient's difficulties in loving. He does not emphasize how the analyst's difficulties in loving contribute to the destructive force in treatment.

Nevertheless, Ferenczi's experiments teach us that love is not enough. Tender, tactful care in the treatment situation does not always yield good results. Sometimes therapist love stimulates greater destructive urges (see Chapter 13, "Being Too Good"). What if spoiling tendencies are so great that they overwhelm the forces of good? What about situations in which goodness incites more intense destructive frenzies? What if the individual lacks the capacity to use another person for growth, and therapy is about how such a capacity becomes constituted? What does a therapist do if therapy is unusable by an individual who nevertheless is (possibly literally) dying to be helped?

Klein, Bion, and Winnicott, each in their own way, closely examine what might be happening when destructive forces annihilate the possibility of seeking and obtaining help and what might be needed in order to be able to use another person for growth purposes.

Klein

Klein focuses on ways in which internal object relations organize and modulate the death drive, the *destructive force within* (Klein's phrase, 1946, p. 297). For Klein, anxiety is most essentially annihilation anxiety, a signal or expression of the death instinct, and psychic deadness or motionlessness is a defense against the anxiety that means the death instinct is operating (see Chapters 2 and 3). In a way, deadness is a defense against death.

In Klein's work, libido tends to function as a defense against death work. Love circulates in the psyche in the form of good feelings/good objects, which try to offset bad feelings/bad objects. The psyche develops a kind of fantasy pump, attempting to use fantasies of good objects (with good affects) to counteract bad ones. The model makes use of respiratory/digestive/circulatory images. Bad affects/objects are expelled; good objects/affects are taken in. But things are never so simple, and the reverse also happens (e.g., bad in-good out), along with other possibilities and combinations.

In a way, Klein pinpoints processes within the psyche that replicate the mother's function. Freud notes that an elemental function of the mother is to respond to the infant's distress and to make it feel better. The mother, among other things, is an affect or mood regulator, taking the edge off destructive spins. Ferenczi sees this as a basic function of the therapist: the therapist's loving care helps the patient over destructive agonies, including and especially those maintained by early, persistent, or cumulative trauma. For Klein, there are internal psychic processes that operate like a mother, attempting to wash bad feelings away with good ones.

Internal attempts to regulate bad feelings can run amok. Too much splitting and projection of bad objects/bad feelings can thin the personality through dispersal, so that one passes from rage/dread through progressive phases of deadness. On the other hand, filling or stuffing oneself with good objects/good feelings can be deadening too, especially if one uses good feelings to seal oneself off from one's spontaneous affect flow and the natural impact of events.

Klein is a kind of specialist in showing the consequences of different ways that the psyche deals with the death drive. She traces movements of destructive urges throughout the psychic universe. For her, deadness is an epiphenomenon or defensive outcome of ways that the psyche tries to work with destructive anxieties. In Chapters 2 and 3, "The Destructive Force" and "Goodness and Deadness," I examine how far her account can take us and where it seems to leave off. As with Freud, it pays not to dismiss her writings, even if the conceptual status of a psychobiological death drive is doubtful. Her detailed focus on the dynamics of destruction makes her work relevant for our clinical and social concerns today.

Bion

Bion intensifies the stakes darkly implied by Freud's "force against recovery" and Klein's "destructive force within." He writes of a "force that continues after . . . it destroys existence, time, and space" (1965, p. 101, see Chapter 6,

"Two Kinds of No-thing"). This is a ghastly vision or construction. Can such a force be possible? How can x destroy existence and still go on working?

Bion tends to use affect rather than drive language. He does not use formal concepts such as life or death drive, but speaks of enlivening–deadening processes. How does the psyche deaden itself? What is the dread of aliveness that can ruin a life? In some individuals, the psyche seems to undo itself, work in reverse, reduce itself to nothing. Can such extreme self-damage be reversed? Can one who has died come alive?

Bion is less interested in polemics than in discovering what psychoanalysis is and what it can do. The formal status of a destructive force is less important than its function as a marker, a way to note, focus, and trace destructive processes. The notion of a force that goes on working after it destroys existence stands as a barrier against underestimating the horror of self-nulling processes. Whether the cause is genetic or environmental, once the destruction of personal existence gathers momentum it can blight any help extended to it. What can a clinician do in the face of such total negation?

Chapters 4 to 6—"Bion's No-Thing," "Moral Violence," and "Two Kinds of No-thing"—present variants of nulling processes that Bion charts. The idea of a self-cancelling psyche is chilling, but Bion helps us tag some of its workings, so that we can extend the range of what we can do.

Winnicott

Winnicott's work is a kind of biography of the sense of aliveness as it unfolds in infancy and throughout a lifetime. He depicts different forms that aliveness takes at various developmental phases. He charts waves of aliveness.

In Chapter 7, "The Area of Freedom," I organize concepts that Winnicott uses to depict aliveness around an experiential navel he describes as "the chosen area" where "there is no room for compromise" (1964, p. 70). I call this navel Winnicott's "area of freedom" since feeling free is at the core of the movement of his thought. The waves of aliveness that flow from Winnicott's point of no compromise or area of freedom evolve through his writings on transitional experiencing, object usage, unintegration, madness, and the incommunicado core. His writings add successive layerings to what it feels like to be alive, how precious core aliveness is, and how fragile it can be.

A most awful deadness arises when violence is done to the point of no compromise. Winnicott's writings about the evolution of aliveness have, as background, a clinical concern with individuals who feel terrible deadness and unreality arising from violence done to the area of freedom. His work repeatedly takes up the thread of what is needed for individuals to be alive in a genuine and viable way. As his work unfolds, he explores what interpersonal attitudes and nutrients are necessary conditions for the growth of aliveness and what conditions lead to deadness.

Winnicott's work joins Bion's, as both depict ways that aliveness can be too much for people—either oneself or others. Bion's emphasis is on ways the psyche is too undeveloped (embryonic), deficient, and/or malevolent to support its own aliveness. Winnicott, in addition, emphasizes an *external factor,* an incapacity in the Other to support the child's aliveness. He feels that so much depends on the quality of response that the destructive aspect of aliveness meets.

The destructiveness inherent in aliveness is so important to Winnicott that he credits it with the very creation of the sense of externality. The external world becomes alive and real if it survives one's destructive aliveness. The Other becomes real and alive by surviving the impact of one's aliveness. Winnicott is extremely sensitive to how the inherent aliveness of the infant/child can break the parent down.

The aliveness of the infant/child can be very threatening. A parent may rejoice in the baby's aliveness, but also be envious, afraid, enraged, and smothering. A parent may not be able to take the full force of the baby's aliveness in all its forms and may need to tone it down, modulate it, even spoil and deaden it. For Winnicott, much depends on how the parent comes through the impact of the baby's aliveness. Whether and how the Other survives destructive onslaughts becomes crucial for how the world will be experienced, and perhaps whether there even will be a world.

To what extent can a parent come through a child's onslaught relatively intact? To what extent does he or she become retaliatory, "gone," collapse into reactive fury or spiteful/fearful withdrawal, or become suffocating? Winnicott does not believe in a psychobiological death drive, but is concerned with the deadness that results from the failure of innate aliveness to create/discover a sense of Otherness or externality, a world to live in—a world that can tolerate aliveness. To put it dramatically, there can be no Other if no one survives one's impact. The evolution of one's sense of aliveness depends partly on the quality of responsiveness versus retaliatory reactiveness of one's milieu.

Winnicott tries to convey his meaning with a grim, yet apt example:

> You will see what I mean, and allow for oversimplification, if I refer to the way in which one of two worlds is waiting for the child, and it makes all the difference which you and I were born into.
> One: a baby kicks the mother's breast. She is pleased that her baby is *alive* and *kicking* though perhaps it hurt and she does not let herself get hurt for fun. Two: a baby kicks the mother's breast, but this mother has a fixed idea that a blow on the breast produces cancer. She reacts because she does not approve of the kick. This overrides whatever the kick may mean for the baby. The child has met with a moralistic attitude, and kicking cannot be explored as a way to place the world where it belongs, which is outside. [1970, p. 287]

This does not mean Mother must always go along with or give in to the child. Not at all. Mother will feel the whole spectrum of aliveness herself. She will be annoyed, hate the baby, feel boundless joy and peace, fatigue, and hell. But this is not a fixed, moralistic, life-despising attitude, but an alive stream of feelings, including an adequate responsiveness to the baby's needs.

There is a point at which "destructive aliveness of the individual is simply a symptom of being alive" (Winnicott 1968, p. 239). To what extent can we survive, enjoy, tolerate, and use each other's aliveness? For an individual who is used to being dead, a therapist's aliveness may be horrifying. Part of the art and luck and skill in working with psychic deadness is discovering what combination of aliveness–deadness is manageable and eventually usable by a person.

CLINICAL PROBES

To enter the consulting room with a fixed idea is akin to the second mother Winnicott describes above (1970, p. 287), who fills her baby with anti-life moralism, rather than allows for an alive moment-to-moment flow. We cannot say exactly what therapy is or what it can do, any more than we can say exactly what a person is: both are subject to processes of discovery. The theoretical soundings we have taken do not provide rules or recipes. There is no guarantee that if we follow a, b, and c, that then x, y, and z must happen. People are more baffling than that, as are the intricacies and intangibles of the clinical encounter.

Our theoretical soundings are part of a broader journey of clinical sensitivity. Thinking sensitizes us to nuances of feelings, to imaginative possibilities. But we keep coming back to what it is like being with a particular person at a particular time. We keep dipping into the impact someone is having on us, the sensations, feelings, imaginings, and thoughts that grow from mute impact.

In the second part of this book, I describe impacts that patients have had on me and my struggle to process aspects of those impacts. This is especially difficult when an impact is deadening. But if one stays with a deadening impact, one begins to experience different sorts of deadness. One begins to note varieties of deadening processes, as our eyes get used to seeing shadowy forms in the dark.

My work tends to be an impressionistic–expressionistic, evocative psychoanalysis, one in which subject-to-subject impact speaks. The clinical probes in Part II emphasize growth of the capacity to tolerate the build-up of experiencing, and the breakdown or inability to jumpstart this capacity. The problem can be horrifying when the experience that threatens to keep building up is some form of deadness.

In some of the chapters, such as Chapters 16 and 17, "Disaster Anxiety" and "Winning Lies," society becomes the patient, since individual deadness involves a violent process and violence runs through the social fabric. Violence is not only an attempt to enliven the self: it also deadens the self and often is part of self-deadening processes. Thus the clinical study of deadness is also a small attempt to make social life better.

Each clinical encounter touches further nuances of psychic deadness. Each chapter turns the kaleidoscope a bit to see what deadness can contribute to growth or how it swallows existence. In Chapter 10, "Counterparts in a Couple," we discover a deadness that is part of psychic binocular (multi-ocular) vision, part of our doubleness or multiplicity, part of the over–undertone of experiential resonances. In Chapter 12, "Primary Process and Shock," we discover a deadness that is a hole or a blank where the primary processing ability should be. Chapter 14, "In Praise of Gender Uncertainty," explores relationships between deadness and gender identity difficulties, which can become life-threatening without help. Chapters 13, 15, and 16—"Being Too Good," "Emotional Starvation," and "Disaster Anxiety"—show ways that the deadening impacts that life has on patients spill over into therapy and are transmitted to the therapist's supervisor and, through the supervisor, to the therapy field in general. As the chapters unfold, the importance of psychic deadness and related phenomena takes on new life and meaning. We develop a better sense of what we are up against, of the sorts of materials with which we work. Our appreciation of facets of psychic deadness grows as we keep dipping into it, as we keep opening to it.

It may be a truism that no two therapies are identical, no two snowflakes the same. But it is a truism with dramatic consequences. Chapter 18, "Boa and Flowers," brings home how high the stakes are if we fail to find the precise set of therapeutic experiences that an individual may need. When we work with intractible psychic deadness, we are working with our own capacity to evolve. I heard somewhere of a kind of baby bird needing to peck its mother in a certain spot in order to elicit an adequate maternal response. It strikes me there are certain patients who keep pecking away at the therapeutic field, trying to elicit the as-yet unknown responses needed for their development.

The rage of a psychically dead person can be terrifying. Yet I cannot help feeling that his or her fury is an attempt to peck or stimulate the evolution of a missing capacity in the therapist and in the therapy field. This book is an attempt to help peck that capacity into being. Patients and therapists who must deal with persistent deadness are partners in a psychic evolution that is very much alive.

REFERENCES

Bion, W. R. (1965). *Transformations.* London: Heinemann.
Boris, H. (1993). *Passions of the Mind.* New York: New York University Press.
———— (1994). *Envy.* Northvale, N.J.: Jason Aronson.
Emery, E. (1992). On dreaming of one's patient: dense objects and intrapsychic isomorphism. *Psychoanalytic Review* 79: 509–533.

Ferenczi, S. (1929). The unwelcome child and his death instinct. In *The Selected Papers of Sandor Ferenczi, M.D: Problems and Methods of Psychoanalysis,* vol. 3, pp. 102–107. New York: Basic Books, 1955.

Freud, S. (1937). Analysis terminable and interminable. *Standard Edition* 23: 216–253.

Green, A. (1986). *On Private Madness.* London: Hogarth.

Grotstein, J. (1990a). Nothingness, meaninglessness, chaos and the "black hole." I: the importance of nothingness, meaninglessness and chaos in psychoanalysis. *Contemporary Psychoanalysis* 26:257–290.

—— (1990b). Nothingness, meaninglessness, and the black hole II. *Contemporary Psychoanalysis* 26:377–407.

Klein, M. (1946). Notes on some schizoid mechanisms. In *Developments in Psychoanalysis,* ed. M. Klein, P. Heimann, S. Isaacs, and J. Riviere, pp. 292–320. London: Hogarth, 1952.

Winnicott, D. W. (1964). The concept of the false self. In *Home is Where We Start From,* ed. C. Winnicott, R. Shepherd, and M. Davis, pp. 65–70. New York: Norton, 1986.

—— (1968). Comments on my paper, "The Use of the Object." In *Psychoanalytic Explorations,* ed. C. Winnicott, R. Shepherd, and M. Davis, pp. 238–240. Cambridge: Harvard University Press.

—— (1970). Individuation. In *Psychoanalytic Explorations,* ed. C. Winnicott, R. Shepherd, and M. Davis, pp. 284–288. Cambridge, MA: Harvard University Press, 1992.

PART I

THEORETICAL SOUNDINGS

1

Psychic Death

The sense of being dead has become a popular clinical theme. More people than in the past now seek help for feeling dead. Although feeling dead is a central complaint of many individuals, it is not clear where this deadness comes from or what can be done about it.

There are many variations of psychic deadness. For some people, deadness does not consume much psychic space. It is a circumscribed counterpole or subtheme in a fuller, richer existence. It comes and goes or nags in the background. At times it becomes prepossessing, and one wonders, with a chill, what one would do if it swallowed existence, if it became all there was. One waits for it to fade and usually it does. It moves along with a variety of moods and states of being.

Some people have pockets of deadness that are relatively constant. They become used to living with areas of deadness. They wish they were more alive, that life offered more, but they make do with their portion. If life is decent enough, a bit of deadness is not too much to pay for satisfactions. One adapts to being less than one might be, to feeling less than one might feel. One talks oneself into imagining one is about as happy as one *can* be, as happy as one is *going* to be. One more or less succeeds in believing oneself, since one fears (rightly) that things could be worse.

For some people, the sense of deadness is pervasive. They describe themselves as zombies, the walking dead, empty and unable to feel. An extreme example of massive deadness was an anorexic-bulimic woman, Deborah, who passed through my office several years ago. She weighed under eighty pounds and looked like a corpse. Her bones were like piercing icicles that stung and ripped me apart.

I wept upon hearing her story, a familiar one but yet a story shocking in its outcome. Deborah's parents were successful professionals. There was a history of neglect, a mixture of over- and understimulation, the usual story of emotional poverty in a luxurious setting. Overeating–vomiting–starving parodied the too much–too little that characterized her life.

Deborah's parents both indulged and deprived her. They catered to her fears and pushed her aside. At times it seemed as though she had two sets of parents: one that spoiled her and catered to dependency and another that required her to be healthy and independent and to act as if she did not need them. Deborah was left with a double imperative: she could not live without her parents, and she should leave them alone.

Each time Deborah sought help, she got worse. Her therapists tried to foster and support her independence, but her dependency needs were too great. One therapist in college was so stimulated by her neediness that he began an affair with her. Deborah relished, yet feared their closeness. The outcome was devastating. When he backed off and became colder, her sense of forlornness intensified. Ordinary therapy did not fill the hole in her being

After college Deborah drifted in and out of therapy and in and out of jobs. She felt helped by some therapists more than by others. The therapy situation itself was tantalizing and frustrating. It offered the hope of contact and elicited longing, yet at the end of sessions, therapist and patient parted. Hope and longing went unfulfilled. Intense neediness met a void. No amount of transient contact seemed adequate. The very structure of therapy annihilated the desire it elicited.

Having an affair with a therapist made things worse; not having an affair also made things worse. Contact was overstimulating, and lack of contact was too depriving. In time, Deborah found an analyst with whom she could stay. They worked many years together. He was a highly respected man in the field, one of the best. Yet it was during this treatment that Deborah's downward plunge accelerated and seemed to become irreversible.

Her analyst ended up refusing to continue treatment with her, apparently horrified by the turn of events. He told her, she said, that had he known what was going to happen, he would never have started with her. How could he have known? Who would have known?

Once more the pattern was repeated: a promise of too much and then the drop through the hole in the bottom of the universe. Perhaps any therapy would have been a promise of too much for Deborah had a dual attitude toward it: therapy solves nothing and ought to solve everything. The wish for therapy to be more than it is can be overwhelming. Part of Deborah's tragedy was that she found an analyst who was good enough for her to want to be with. His very goodness overstimulated her. She wanted more from him than he could provide. His skill and caring heightened her unfulfilled longing, and at some point her whole system shut down. Therapy could not support the intensity it fueled.

Yet Deborah continued to seek help. This must mean that she believed change was possible, hope was alive, but it also could mean that she was stuck in a pattern, a sort of sticky free fall, like a pinball bouncing through therapy slots until movement stopped and the game ended.

Therapy was a chronic part of her life; she clung to it, then dropped it, over and over again. Some of her therapists did the same with her. To some extent, she regulated the dosage of therapy she was able to take. She usually left therapy before it or her feelings overwhelmed her. Was she better off dipping in and out? Staying in may have killed her.

Normally therapists like it when a patient comes more often, stays longer, and works more deeply. One assumes that dedicated work leads to better outcomes. In Deborah's case, the attempt to work more intensely broke open a hole in her psyche. She became numb and far away from herself. Her life got caught on a trajectory that moved from deadness to deadness. Therapy no longer was life calling to life, but a magnet drawing out depths of deadness.

What can be said about such psychic deadness? How can we meet it? We do not know why a person like Deborah falls so far out of life, while another similar to her pulls out of it and builds a satisfactory existence. Deborah vanishes through a hole in her psyche, while another finds a way to swim in the emptiness. At times it seems as though a toss of the dice determines whether the hole one falls in supports life or not.

FREUD

Freud's work is rich with ambiguities, contradictions, and complexities. Freud may say there is no death in the unconscious, yet he writes of unconscious death wishes. By unconscious death wishes he usually means that *I* will live forever, but *you* will die. The unconscious acts as a magnifying machine. My hostility toward you becomes absolutized in the wish for you to die. Common speech bears witness to this passion in the phrase, "I wish you were dead!"

The Freudian world is one of high (or low) drama. The "I versus you" runs deep in Freud's picture of psychic life. The Freudian ego originally reacts with hostility to the external world. Externality creates discomfort. The ego tries to avoid it, to wish it away. From the outset one escapes, even annihilates reality. The you is partly an enemy from the beginning.

The Freudian you follows the track of pain. Pain is Other, alien, not-I. Wherever pain is, you are. If pain comes from inside the body, then the inside of the body becomes Other, not-I, something that is happening to me, an alien, hostile, or indifferent you.

The boundary of I-feeling shifts. I-feeling tends to identify with pleasure and react against pain. One tries to set pain outside one's boundaries: I try to exclude pain from *myself*. Pain may be the most intimate fact of existence, but I make believe it is a stranger.

Above all, death—that stranger of strangers, other of others, alien of aliens— wells up from my body, seizes me, takes me away. Processes that constitute me and support my life are also enemies. Death wipes meaning out of life. In the middle of a beautiful experience a voice mocks, "What good is it? You will be a corpse someday."

People live with an eye glued to death; in Deborah's case, with two eyes. Deborah's knowledge of death swallowed her up. She became a parody of death, a living corpse. Perhaps she imagined she could control death by aping it, by becoming its proxy. Perhaps she wanted to stuff death into people's (her parents') faces to show them the lie they lived. She became in her body a haunting critique of self-absorbed luxury, a physical image of psychospiritual starvation.

In Freud's writings there are death symbols as well as sexual symbols. An obsession with dying ran through Freud's life and work. Freud's attempt to reduce death anxiety to castration anxiety was never fully convincing.[1] Libido theory could not wish death away. Death kept popping up in its own right, and finally Freud legitimated it in his theory by declaring death an instinct or drive.

In *Beyond the Pleasure Principle* (1920) Freud writes of a death instinct that is initially turned inward. There is a drive toward death from the beginning, and there are many facets to this faceless drive. Freud emphasizes the conservative principle of instincts, the tendency to regress to earlier states, to repeat a position. The logical conclusion of the slide backward is zero. The earliest state is no state at all, zero stimulation, zero complexity.

In semi-biological, physical terms, Freud depicts organic life becoming inorganic again, because the inorganic state was original, the point of departure and point of return. Life sustains its complexity only so long and then collapses. Cellular units are bound together and then fall apart. The binding of any sort of unity is precarious, subject to unbinding.

Life feeds on death and death on life. Life deflects death outward for a time. Ambition, the will to power and mastery, sadism, and destructiveness, are some indications of variable life–death drive fusions. Life holds death captive, directs its attention toward objects, makes death want things, persons, places, positions. It is as if libido attracts death's interest, fascinates death, busies death with

---

[1] Through much of his psychoanalytic career, Freud gave a certain primacy to castration anxiety in clinical neuroses. Perhaps he felt that if it were possible to "resolve" castration anxiety, one would not be pathologically afraid of death. Thus he tended to filter death anxiety through castration anxiety. Yet death retained a certain autonomy (e.g., going on a train journey as a death symbol or the third woman in "The Theme of the Three Caskets" [1913, pp. 291–301]). Even after Freud introduced the death drive, castration anxiety exercised a privileged position: "I believe that the fear of death is something that occurs between the ego and the superego. . . . These considerations make it possible to regard the fear of death, like the fear of conscience, as a development of the fear of castration" (1923, p. 58). In the last decade, Freud still gave centrality to castration anxiety, yet wondered whether the death drive did not play a crucial role in the individual's inability to change. The full relationship between castration fantasies and the death drive has yet to be worked out.

diversions. The deception, masquerade, and rerouting take effort. Systems wear themselves out by the work of sustaining themselves. One dies, in part, from exhaustion.

Yet it is not enough to speak of inertia, collapse, or the wearing down of systems. If death is a drive, it exerts force or pressure in a certain direction. When the life drive does not bind the death drive, the latter unties sentient unities. Psycho-organismic being is dismantled, broken apart, reduced to chunks of inorganic material. Death is more an active breaking down than a passive falling apart.

It is tempting to dramatize Freud's vision with mythic language and phrases from everyday speech. We speak of life or death as taking or losing hold or its grip. We speak of life's victory over death or death's over life, as if the two were gods eternally wrestling, at war. We say death or life wins or loses. Freud also uses the language of struggle, combat, tension, and difficulty. When an individual dies he is in the grips of a process that has won out. From Freud's point of view, it is doubtful that there can be such a thing as an easy death or an easy life.

An individual like Deborah makes one feel the force of Freud's death drive. Deborah is a symbol and embodiment of death. One *feels* death working in her. One feels a dark force taking her more and more out of life, sucking life dry. One feels a negative process working even after life loses the battle.

It was not only Deborah's body that lacked flesh and fullness; her psyche had undergone an enormous reduction. There was not much left of her. Perhaps she never had been too full a person, but I have no doubt that there was more to her, that there were more possibilities. Death had eaten away almost all it could eat away. The shell of Deborah—a bundle of reflexes—persevered. She moved from office to office looking for therapists to feed the death within or to miraculously stop it. She could not die before the death inside her devoured every crumb of potential aliveness in every corner of her being. It was as if she had to stay alive until there was nothing more for death to eat.

Deborah's life is carried away by something deadly that accelerates over time. Does Freud's formulation adequately depict the death momentum? Is it enough to say a drive toward tensionlessness won out? Aren't there explosive tensions in inorganic matter? Explosive processes seem to be part of the universe. What would a tension-free universe be like? Would a tension-free universe be a process-free universe, no universe at all?

Deborah's life is a silent scream stretched over time. It is an explosion that no one can hear because it occurred and goes on occurring in a place where no Other is. Deborah explodes in a vacuum. No one hears Deborah cry. She does not hear herself crying, yet quiet crying of her insides continues. All the loudness has gone into her visual appearance: her skeleton rips the eyes of the Other, tears the Other's heart. The more she vanishes the more full of impact the place where she was becomes. The blackness she leaves behind or falls into is not tension free, but a heightened, condensed, blank, magnetic-like field increasing in force. What processes govern this force? What can be said about the black hole consuming Deborah's life?

MAXIMUM–MINIMUM

It is important to note that notions of maximum–minimum states are part of the fabric of Freud's writings. For Freud the primal trauma is flooding, a maximum state of excitement. Freud pictures a system that can generate more stimulation than it can handle.

A *one is too much for oneself* paradigm can be applied to many facets of psychophysical being—neurological, sexual, social, emotional, and cognitive. Freud posits mechanisms that dampen and regulate the psycho-organism's tendency to become overwhelmed. A stimulus barrier offers resistance to the promiscuous streaming of excitations. Psychological defenses resist the rise of libidinal promptings. Freud's picture is always of systems with double or opposite tendencies, one offsetting and regulating the other.

In an informal fashion, one can speak of being overwhelmed or flooded by energy, stimuli, drives, emotions, ideas. At such moments, filter or containing systems break down or are inadequate. One may enjoy the flood, but one may only be able to take so much of it and no more, or it may be too dangerous to begin with. In response to massive flooding, one may massively shut down. It is as if the psycho-organism short-circuits, turns off, being unable to bear its sensitivity. The blankness of too much is replaced by the blankness of nothing.

Instead of too alive, we have too dead. Which is the greater anxiety in Freud's work—the dread of aliveness or the dread of death? The Freudian ego lives this double anxiety. There is no end to the permutations. When one is dead, one fears aliveness; when alive, one fears death. There are sublime moments of aliveness when there is no room for the fear of either life or death. There is a deadness that fears both life and death and a deadness that fears neither.

There are two tendencies—toward maximum aliveness and toward total deadness, toward building up and tearing down, toward increasing tolerance of energy and complexity, toward a zero point of sensitivity and stimulation. For Freud all life is made up of these two tendencies, summarized under the rubrics of Eros and the death instinct, a doubleness that marks all psychic products. Whether or not one likes Freud's double instinct theory, issues related to the theme of psychic aliveness–deadness cannot be wished away.

A QUANTITATIVE FACTOR

The play of aliveness–deadness runs through Freud's work. He is concerned with the raw presence–absence of sexual energy, its rise and fall, reroutings, rechannelings, its fate as it meets with internal–external obstacles and resistances.

As his work developed into "official" psychoanalysis, with an emphasis on conflicts between and within psychic systems,[2] and between psychic systems and the external world, his interest in sheer presence–absence and in the strength–weakness of raw sexual energy persevered. Remarks on *psychaesthenia* and *actual neurosis* are sprinkled throughout his work.

For Freud, psychaesthenia is a condition marked by low sexual vitality, by weak life energy. Freud believes there is a physical contribution to this psychological depletion. Perhaps the individual is congenitally endowed with less vitality or perhaps energy loss is tied to the actual damming of libido. In so-called actual neurosis, the damming of libido results in anxiety rather than depletion. Freud suggests that masturbation or the use of condoms could reflect or provoke psychaesthenia, actual neurosis, or mixtures of the two. Physical actions have psychological effects and vice versa.

Libido sluggishness/blockage can reflect/lead to states of low/high psychic arousal (variations of minimum–maximum states). Either depletion or anxiety may be dominant, may seesaw, or be mixed indistinguishably. Individuals can feel helpless when faced by either extreme. One can fade out via depletion or be obliterated by anxiety.

Perhaps sluggish or blocked sexuality is different for individuals with a low or high energy endowment. When more sexual energy meets a barrier, more tension is created, which is reflected in a higher anxiety level. Low sexual energy may be more readily pacified by inner–outer barriers and yield to inertia or weakness. The idea of an innately low–high fixed quantity of energy, interacting with inner–outer barriers–openings, can be used to describe a wide variety of conditions.

Freud's work is a tantalizing mixture of phenomenological description and insistence on a quantitative factor beyond phenomenology. The two levels of discourse often interact and fuse. One *feels* the quantitative factor in everyday life. How much energy one has from moment to moment and over time, how alive or wasted one feels: one is on intimate terms with one's level of energy. One *feels* rushes of energy, its waxing and waning. Now one is uplifted by the flow of energy, now one is flooded, cast down, or feels too little energy ("no wind in one's sails"). Such terms as "drifting," "stagnant," "flow," and "flood," are among the plethora of ways in which language spontaneously gives a running account of our felt pulse, our energic moods.

There is no obvious fit between the felt quantitative factor—how much or how little energy one feels—and the fixed quantity of energy beyond conscious-

---

[2] Since many readers associate conflict *within* psychic systems with the development of ego psychology, it is useful to point out that it is an inherent part of Freud's thinking: e.g., eros/death drive as id forces, ego as hallucinatory and reality tester, superego as persecutory and inspirational. See my book, *The Psychotic Core* (1986), for selected portrayals of Freud's intrasystemic complexities.

ness that fuels psychic systems. High-energy individuals can suffer massive depressions and depletion, while low-energy individuals persevere. When the hare, when the turtle? All combinations and reversals are possible. Freud's writings are a meditation on the plasticity–fixity of psychic life. The hidden snake of energy takes myriad forms—now evanescent, now intractable.

The idea of a fixed quantity of energy variously distributed through psychic subsystems informs Freud's depiction of thinking–feeling splits in hysterical and obsessional states. In obsessive states, ideas are substituted for affects; in hysteria, diffuse emotionality is substituted for ideas. Maximum thinking–minimum feeling, maximum feeling–minimum thinking: both the form and intensity of neurosis depend on how much energy is where.

The variable fluidity–fixity of energy bounces in and out of different boxes of time, uniting–dividing different developmental moments. For example, hysteria is more advanced because it is genital; obsessiveness is more primitive because it is anal. Yet Freud likens hysterical emotionality to the diffuse and global affective storms of infancy, whereas obsessive thinking marks an advance in interiority. A rise in energy can increase tightening or explosiveness, so that hysterical–obsessive operations, so radically different, slide into each other or shift positions in a broader field.

TOO LITTLE–TOO MUCH: A NEED FOR INTENSITY

Emptying out feeling, emptying out thought, emptying out energy versus hyperfeeling, hyperthinking, hyperenergy: going through extremes is an important part of life. Extreme states add intensity, diversity, and richness to living. The poet William Blake celebrates this aspect of life in his aphorism, "Enough or too much." Winnicott's patient implied this when he eschewed the midway path in favor of a "blend that includes both extremes at the same time" (1986, p. 133).

Blake and Winnicott's patient express a hunger for intensity. We need to feel and think intensely. Intensity nourishes us, waters our bodies and beings. To go through something intensely and enjoy the afterglow is akin to or better than an infant's good feeding and sleep. Extremes of intensity (empty–full, radiant–dull) fuel wonder, awe, and curiosity.

IMMOBILITY

It is not the presence–absence of duller or more heightened states that vexes Freud so much as when something is off with the movement between or through them. Individuals who run through states or objects too quickly and easily, who have too much mobility of libido, may not be affected by what they go through.

Nothing sticks or builds. They have a lot of experiences, but do not deepen or grow through them.

Even more disturbing is too little movement. Freud notes in certain individuals "a depletion of the plasticity, the capacity for change and further development" (1937, p. 241). More forcefully, he notes that in these people "all the mental processes, relationships and distribution of force are unchangeable, fixed and rigid" (1937, p. 242).

Freud's image here is death, the immobility and rigidity of the corpse. When Freud wrote this he was an old man, soon to die. It is easy to think that Freud's writings surged with fluctuations of libido theory when he still felt wind in his sails. Jung implies as much (1943, 1945) when he suggests that Freud's psychology is most apt for the first half of life. Freud's daily walks through the city, his summer hikes in the country are an indication that he enjoyed vigorous movement well into his sixties. As his mobility decreased, the image of death came to occupy a greater place in his work.

It is not that deadness wasn't important to Freud earlier. As noted above, Freud had been keenly aware of the ebbs and flows of energic moods, of being now more alive, now more dead. However, he tended to understand deadness as the loss or weakness of life energy, not as the positive work of death. Deadness was a sort of *privatio bonum*, of too little libido, whether constitutionally, the result of changing inner–outer conditions, or through energy drain connected with conflict. He was more concerned with the fear of death or the loss of aliveness than with death as a force working in personality, especially a force working against change. It was not until Freud's last two decades that death achieved explicit, formal, conceptual status as a major actor on the psychoanalytic stage. It was, of course, always a part of Freud's associative flow and informal usage.

As age and illness took their toll, the display of fireworks from Freud's libido theory slowed down. The slippery, sliding fluid, the electrical dance of libido that sprayed vast arrays of symptoms, character scenarios, and cultural productions was rendered immobile, fixed, and rigid by death work. Death work was responsible for the personality's inability to develop.

For Freud (1937, p. 242) "a kind of psychical entropy" in old people and "a certain amount of psychical inertia" (fear of change, reluctance of the libido to enter new paths) at any age are normal. What struck him was the depth and insistence of an inability or refusal to change that went beyond age and usual hesitation. The individual's wish to grow met an impasse, an unbudgeable x. Change or growth or development stopped. The source of the blockage was deeper than ego or character. It seemed to come from the very foundations of personality and faded into the depths of the individual's prehistory.

In his later life, Freud writes of a "force . . . defending itself by every possible means against recovery and which is absolutely resolved to hold on to illness and suffering" (1937, p. 242). This force has "different and deeper roots" than ego–superego resistances. The intensity and pervasiveness of the sense of guilt and need for punishment (for instance, superego punishing ego for libidinal wishes), far from explaining immobility, are an example of it. Why should guilt grind personality to a halt? Why should the need for punishment have such extravagant effects?

One imagines that therapy would mobilize enough personal elasticity to enable work with guilt and punishment. What Freud noted was that in certain individuals, elasticity itself is in question. A kind of psychic rigor mortis sets in. The need to punish the wish for pleasure does not account sufficiently for the enormity of stagnant rigidity. Pleasure does not seem to be the bottom-line motivater of personality in such cases. The personality seems driven by unpleasure. It is the death drive or unpleasure principle that gives such force to guilt and punishment.

Freud implies that inelasticity is rather widespread. He writes of a masochistic core in many people that is linked with the negative therapeutic reaction and sense of guilt. Throughout most of his career he saw such recoils against life as reactive prohibitions against libidinal strivings. Now he threw in the towel, admitting a darker, primary force, with roots in "unspecified places." The darker primary force was anti-life yet built into life: "the original death instinct of living matter" (1937, p. 243).

The important structural change in his theory is that resistances to change or growth or cure or development do not originate primarily from the top down (superego against ego against id) but from the bottom up. The unbudgeable rigidity that Freud points to is rooted in the very foundations of psychic life and in the very nature of matter. Freud (1937, pp. 240–247) notes that his entire life's work must be reinterpreted in light of this revision.

No amount of psychoanalysis can wish immobility away. The play of immobility–mobility is a structural given. Moreover, if "the concurrent or mutually opposing action of . . . Eros and the death-instinct" (1937, p. 243) makes up the phenomena of life, death work goes into the making of psychoanalysis as well. Freud is more concerned with why psychoanalysis does not work than why it does.

"For the moment we must bow to the superiority of forces against which we see our efforts come to nothing" (1937, p. 243). Yes, for the moment, a moment stretched over time. Yet, as we stare into the darkness, our eyes see shapes and movements previously unnoticed. Death work is not uniform. There are many death worlds. A person like Deborah goes from death to death. She experiences many sorts of death in one lifetime, many variations in the death her lifetime is.

FREUD'S SENSITIVITY

Was Freud's death drive sour grapes, the revenge of an old man on youth? Was it the outcome of aging processes, illness, a world war, the death of a child? All these factors may have contributed to the growing significance of death in the later Freud.

Freud is exquisitely and agonizingly sensitive to the waxing–waning of energic moods. He is hyperaware of shifts in energy states on a daily and hourly basis. Freud's theoretical interest in the flow of energy dovetails with his sensitivity to energic moods.

Freud's sensitivity to somatic shifts covers a variety of states. He possessed a *coenesthetic/interoceptive/proprioceptive/kinesthetic* sensitivity that magnified his cardiac, respiratory, and digestive sensations. He could alarm himself with a catalogue of shifting somatic symptoms, so much so that he was convinced he would die in his fifties. His letters to Fliess (Masson 1985) are quite open about his somatic/sensory anxieties and moods.

His sensitivity included an array of psychic sensations. He experienced psychaesthenic depletion, sexual damming and anxiety, hysterical emotionality and diffuseness, and obsessive passions. He had a talent for tolerating and complaining about manic-depressive swings in creative work. He had an intuitive conviction that mood shifts played an important role in creative processes. He could be mentally active and try out hosts of possibilities in a trial-and-error fashion, but he also was gifted with an ability to wait. He seemed to have an innate respect for shifting emotional states and moods, a belief in their alternation or periodicity in larger rhythms of development.

Freud's sensitivity to rhythm led him to think that death work probably involves "some temporal characteristics," "some alterations of a rhythm of development in psychical life which we have not yet appreciated" (1937, p. 242). We do not know what Freud had in mind, what alterations of developmental rhythms he might have charted. Had Freud lived another twenty years, what would he have found in the death drive? What would his dynamics of immobility look like?

MOVEMENT BETWEEN

Let us bring together some of Freud's expressions of immobility, strung together from a telling two pages in *Analysis Terminable and Interminable* (1937, pp. 241–242). Adhesiveness of libido, a depletion of plasticity and the capacity for development and change, psychic inertia and entropy, something unchangeable, fixed, and rigid, a force against recovery: Where does such immobility come from?

By 1937 Freud no longer localizes this anti-development force in the ego. The notion of localization is called into question. The anti-growth force does not have any specific locale. It pervades the psyche, depends on unknown fundamental conditions in the mental apparatus, and works in unspecified places. It is part of the individual's inherited equipment and so antedates his historical struggles. Since we cannot map this force in terms of its psychic coordinates, the "distinction between what is ego and what is id loses much of its value" (1937, p. 241).

To describe the anti-growth force in terms of its immobilizing effect is not strong enough. Entropy implies increasing disorder. To speak of entropy and inertia is to suggest a psyche working in reverse, not only not growing but also undoing growth. Can we speak of a psyche undoing itself? What sort of process eats itself up, nulls itself, nulls everything?

There is something transpersonal in a force field that wipes everything out. An analyst may feel attacked or poisoned by the patient's anti-growth tendency. The analyst may feel unable to move or breathe; therapy may feel suffocating. How can one endure this?

A force field that wipes everything out also wipes out the analyst's sense of his own anti-growth tendency. An analyst who cannot sense his own anti-growth tendency may become overly absorbed or polarized by that of the patient. The analyst loses balance and perspective; anti-growth is everywhere. The patient's and analyst's anti-growth tendencies fuse and suck the life out of the situation. Analyst or patient may fight or withdraw to salvage some semblance of individuality, but the amorphous pull to oblivion is not assuaged easily. It is important that the analyst find his own anti-growth sense. Focusing on his own anti-growth tendency, paradoxically, makes room for the patient's.

Countertransference literature is filled with reference to the analyst's use of his paralysis, weakness, contempt, and fear-rage. The analyst struggles to stay alive, to maintain a viable psychic existence, but the odds are against it. At times the best one can hope for is that the entropy/inertia/inelasticity—the constant wipe-out—forces one to stare at limits of one's capacity. Intense, persistent, and heightened experience of incapacity may spur movement at the edge, at limit points, always with a certain unpredictability, as the song goes, "on a wing and a prayer."

What is unnerving is not simply that the patient is stuck, but that he or she seems to be falling into the stuckness. Images of quicksand, suction, black holes, of drifting and vanishing beyond the pull of human gravity prevail: all movement seems to be aimed at taking one further and further outside existence. The ability to move here and there, to zigzag, to correct one's position is lost. In life, one movement corrects another. One tries this, then that. A slow-motion film of Matisse drawing a line shows his hand oscillating, although the line seems straight. A film of a baseball player making a great catch shows his glove tracking the ball, correcting one movement with another. Such moment-to-moment estimates escape the naked eye. Yet it is precisely the lack of open-ended searching and zeroing in on a target (a new line, a good catch) that makes the patient's fall out of existence so lethal and heavy.

In the fall out of existence, one movement does not seem to qualify another. There is simply the leaden fall. A momentum quietly builds that cannot be deflected. The patient's whole life gradually becomes built around insidiously mounting lifelessness. By the time she came to my office, Deborah's existence was consumed by details of taking care of herself: strategies for physically getting through the day, hour by hour, moment by moment, were all that was left, and they were fading. The monotonous oneness of her concern was deadly. She had become a macabre proxy for the total care she always wanted and failed to break from.

Freud earlier wrote of an "alteration of the ego" that made personality growth difficult (1937, pp. 238-240). By this, in part, he meant the defensive deformations that the ego suffered, so that the ego treats recovery as a danger and analysis as an enemy rather than ally. Now Freud locates a deeper source of resistance to recovery, not in the ego but in "some alterations of a rhythm in development in psychical life" (1937, p. 242), an alteration that makes the distinction between ego and id relatively useless (1937, p. 241). This alteration characterizes the foundations of psychic life. It cannot be localized, pinned down. It is structural and atmospheric; it taints the very "space" and "air" in which the psyche moves and breathes. It means something more than a deformation of the id or a warp in instinctual life.

Freud pins the warp not in place but in rhythm. The focus here is not psychic topography, but timing and movement. The music of the psyche is off. *A rhythmic rather than a structural warp is crucial.* A rhythmic warp results in structural alterations. Structure depends on rhythms (as well as the reverse).

One wonders what psychoanalysis would look like had Freud chosen time rather than space as his organizing analogy. He did what was expedient. Space is more accessible than time. The idea of psychic space enables one to locate motivations and capacities, to speak of the psyche as if it had containing or structural properties (see Freud 1940, p. 145 for an elaboration of the use and meaning of mental space, see Matte-Blanco 1975, Part IX). One can make spatial diagrams; yet, when facing bedrock resistance to change—an apparently immutable force against recovery, an unyielding rigidity—the idea of psychic space reaches a point of diminishing returns. The idea of psychic space is fruitful as long as Freud can use it to stage libidinal dramas. Space was the place of movement. When movement ceased, space was useless. What could space teach us about a world where movement stopped? What could space mean in a world without movement?

Is it odd to say that time begins where space leaves off? Philosophy and common sense teach that space and time go together, and they do. However, in psychic reality one may leap into time after space dies. In average life, space and time constitute each other. A person moves and rests, goes about the business of living, takes space-time interweaving for granted. If psychic movement dies and space falls away or hardens, a person may cling to time to escape the grave of space. The psyche does not die evenly. Space may die before time.

For Deborah, time was still more alive than space. Time haunted her. She was going to die. She was already quite dead. Yet temporal anxieties stirred her. She did not have much time left. Would she die before she lived? Would it be over before she had a chance? There was nothing left for her but the care of her dying body, yet time pressured her. Time was dreadful. Perhaps she would come alive in time! Perhaps there was still a chance for a moment of sensitivity, a time of heightened aliveness. There was no body or place left for this to happen. If it ever would happen at all, it could only be *in time.*

She might be saved in time. Time might redeem space. A moment of renewal might bring her body back, spread through space. A good moment, a heightened moment, a moment of aliveness could warm existence, thaw space. The likelihood was that time would die while she was still alive. It would be eaten by death work, the way that space was. Still, time nursed a bit of hope. Deborah's great cynicism and despair were tied to space, but time's badly clipped wings had not dropped her entirely.

WINNICOTT

Winnicott fights against deadness in his writing. He wants his writing to be alive, to be moving. He says explicitly that he wants his concepts to convey movement, process, paradox and not to deaden (Eigen 1992a; Rodman 1987, p. 42). His "transitional experiencing" and "use of object" notions express movement between persons, between dimensions of self, between worlds. He did not want to fight deadness in his office only to die in his writings.

Winnicott is concerned that his writings not simply convey ideas but also evoke experience. Writing creates/discovers/opens experience. It is the edge of what is happening, not merely a report of what has come and gone. Winnicott's work is an adventure in psychoanalytic imagination, the creative self in action. Above all, he wants to convey a sense of creative aliveness, to be alive when he wrote. To an extent, he uses writing as Kafka did, to "crack the frozen sea within." At the same time, he tries to speak from the place of aliveness, to let the sense of aliveness speak. Winnicott is always digging into an experience and opening it up.

Speaking and writing are forms of movement. Words pop out of nowhere, out of an implicit sense or feeling or premonition, now more gut, now more heart or head. They spill or fly into the air or across a page, sometimes agonizingly slowly and sometimes too rapidly to keep up with. At his best, Winnicott links clinical experience with clinical writing. A creative thread runs through both.

It is important to say this because so much psychoanalytic writing has been dead and deadening, a disease. If psychoanalysts are as dead as their writing, for what can a Deborah hope? A dead analyst may calm an individual who is beset by throbbing impulses, but an anhedonic spirit melds with Deborah's fall out of life, scarcely creating a ripple of deadness.

The *movement between is* the important moment in Winnicott's writings. I would add the *movement through.* To move between or through experiences, to let an experience build, to go through something: this is what Deborah can *not* do. Deborah's *between* or *through* is not working.

Deborah had an affair with a therapist, but it fell flat. Impulse led nowhere. The affair collapsed, and Deborah was alone, deader than before. The shock of having and losing led to weakening and eventually to the collapse of impulse. Her learning was that impulse led to deadness. There were little moments when impulse lived, when she was propelled into contact, but they did not last nor did they amount to anything. They were not strong or full enough to warrant the pain and emptiness that surrounded them. Deadness was a relief until it took on a life of its own.

. Her affair with her therapist was doomed from the outset. She and he knew it would come to nothing. It would be good to say that she lived it out anyway, but neither he nor she fully *lived* it. The impulse that drove her had failure written on it. It happened, but not with all her might and being. She floated through it, more ghostlike than impassioned. She did not love him, nor he her. There were no illusions of desire. They fell into it and did it. The pull, the undertow drew them in. They sank into it, and after tasting the sensations, he pulled out. Exploitation? Abuse of power? It would be good to say that they went with the flow, but there was not much flow. Neither party got much out of the experience: there was not much experience to get something out of. The hole was already there, and they fell through it.

Impulse led to death. But no impulse was death as well. There was marking time, treading water, sinking, trying to stop sinking. Over the years there was less and less except for sinking, and finally, only the sinking was left.

Deborah's affair with her therapist was a more condensed version of what happened or failed to happen with her "boyfriends." She never really had a boyfriend. The rhythm that goes into making a relationship was not there; that is, the rhythm of relationship was not there. Nothing grew or built on itself. There were moments of almost contact, but no hits. She could not get *into* things or be swept away. She could not let life play on her, uplift her, lift her out of herself. To have glorious moments one needs to be able to move between states, between selves, between worlds. The rhythmic movement between self and other never quite evolved or took hold.

By the time college ended, Deborah sensed she was in trouble, but had no idea what the trouble was. She still was hoping things would right themselves, that therapy would help, that life would come to her aid. She never thought her life would become as bad as it did. She always thought that she would pull out of it, that *something* would happen. As time went on, the entropy-inertia swelled until little was left outside it. A brittle yet tenacious rigidity made it impossible to flow or float or fly. Deborah's life sank like a dead weight.

She brought the sinking weight to my office and cried, "Catch me, catch me! Stop the dying!" I reached out, but she stared and demanded what behavior recipes I could offer. I could offer my mind, heart, and soul, my strength, my ability—but no recipe. I was not enough for her.

She wanted what I could *not* offer, something that I wasn't, something I didn't have. She left after our first few weeks of sessions. In such a short time, there was such a deep impression—on me, not her.

Winnicott counsels that it is important to recognize limits to therapy and that there are people who cannot be helped. He wants therapists not to hate themselves too badly because of failure. Failure is part of living. There can be no therapy without failure. It saves time and energy to know who cannot be helped, since it enables us to give more time to those who can.

Yet it is important to try to work with a Deborah, if she wants to or stays in therapy. Does one know who may be helped and how? I have helped Deborahs on occasion. And there have been Deborahs with whom I thought I failed, only to find out years later that our work had been valuable. One may need to sink a long time into the limits of capacity, into what cannot be done, for bits of movement to begin, for unexpected openings to occur. What would have happened if Deborah gave me a chance? Would it have been her most horrible experience of all, or would *something* have happened?

By her leaving before we started, she stopped my potential movement toward or away from her. I/she could not get in or pull out. There would be no movement at all. I would not have the chance to let something build, or to fall with her, or to sink together. I would not have the chance to withdraw, intrude, abandon, die out, come back. My chance, my freedom to move between states was stifled, killed off, aborted. I would never get the chance to find out how bad we could be together. I would not find out how she might murder me. I would never get to dip into the ways I could not take her, how unbearable being with her could be.

There would be no finding out, no chance, no opportunity, no loss, no failure, no learning. There would be no time. Perhaps not getting a chance, not having time, was the experience Deborah meant me to have. I was to taste a bit of her death. Perhaps my job was to somehow begin to metabolize the unmetabolizable—the death of time, the death of promise.

She could not move from one state to another, from world to world, self to self, self to other, and back again. Yet I could move in and out of death. I could sink and rise. I could let her state and world touch me, her monomanic sinking, dying, falling, fading. I could sink, die, fall, fade. But there is a rhythm that takes me in and out of these states, a flow between states, a flow through states. I *do* get something going through worlds of deadness. I get something in the fall. Something sticks, grows, a blind appreciation of what we are up against, what we are, what we can go through. The bottom is as important as the top.

Deborah's inability to move between top–bottom or in–out must be taken in by someone, be given some gestation process. For Deborah to be helped, the impossible must happen: the indigestible must be digested, worked over, processed. Perhaps better, movement between the digestible–indigestible needs to get stimulated and sustained. That no one knows how to do that is precisely what must be lived with.

A NOTE ON BIG BATTALIONS:
WHERE DOES PROCESSING START?

It is an oddity in Freud's work that he enjoys sticking pins in human narcissism, yet lobbies for ego control and mastery. Freud saw psychoanalysis as mortifying the Western ego, a Copernican revolution in which the ego is no longer master in its own house. His writings abound in instances in which instinct, like an impish, irrepressible child, sticks out its tongue at ego, evades control, makes ego flop on its backside, is clown more than crown. Yet Freud admires Michelangelo's Moses for the intensity of ego's victory over instinct. The hallucinatory, anxious, conflict-ridden ego is also the site of the still small voice of science, the light of consciousness. The clown is hero; the hero is clown. Yet Freud is quite serious in his admiration of ethical, esthetic, and scientific achievements in which the ego makes the most of its equipment, does not succumb to inertia-entropy, channels instinctual drives, and pushes past its deformations.

Near the end of his life Freud writes that the business of analysis "is to secure the best possible psychological conditions for the functions of the ego" (1937, p. 250). This is a more tempered view than the war cry, "Where id is, let ego be." The wish for ego mastery and dominance is chastened. It is enough for ego to have room to function. The jungle grows quickly; ego's achievements are fragile. Death work undoes the culture it helps build. Yet there is still in Freud the tone of struggle, warfare, the blood of the warrior. Analysis secures the best possible conditions for ego, as it might secure a beachhead or fortify a strategic position. Analysis is not immunization from life. Positions can be overrun and achievements reversed. One does the best one can with the materials at hand.

Our modest battle to secure the best possible conditions for functions of the ego is a fight against odds: "it seems as if victory is in fact as a rule on the side of the big battalions" (1937, p. 240). "Hostile forces" have the greater share of energy. Freud, partly, has in mind instinctual drives, especially death work. But the ego is not only besieged from without. It is its own enemy. The ego inflates–deflates, hallucinates, splits, adopts critical perspectives, seeks truth, mixes truth and delusion. Now we side with ego, now with id; now with one ego function, now with another. We move back and forth between positions.

The ego is partner, not only fighter. We enter into partnership with processes that constitute us, support us, undo us. We try to get to know what we are made of, perhaps over many millennia. What is the It or Thou or O that we are part of, that we stand out from, that we feel within us and around us, that we fight with, that we immerse ourselves in? What sort of beings are we? Of what are we capable?

Freud's vision is not only one of battle between and within psychic elements but also of union. The psyche is one fabric. There is connection, nourishment, and support between psychical divisions. A sense of connection–division characterizes psychical work. What is most alive in Freud is his portrayal of a flowing psyche, x turning into y, interchangeability, polarization, one thing becoming–standing against–standing for another. Equivalence, interchangeability, reversal, polarization, all manner of mixtures and antagonisms: Isn't this what draws us to Freud, this restless flow of energy, affect, and meaning?

For Freud this flow is fundamental. He felt he never did better than his "dream book" (1900), in which he portrays primary process work, wriggling displacements, condensations, incessant reshuffling of forms expressing unconscious concerns. As his sense of the plasticity of psychic life developed, his work depicted myriad reversals and substitutions: reversibility of affect (e.g., love ↔ hate); substitution of meaning for affect, meaning for meaning, idea for idea, idea for affect, affect for idea; reversibility of persons (I ↔ you); reversibility of tendencies (active ↔ passive); reversibility of direction of tendencies (toward the self ↔ toward the other). Freud had one eye on mobility, another on barriers. The psyche was alive with pulsating movement. Yet the flow met inner–outer resistances, had its own inertia, stickiness, backflow (regression), and finally emptied into the river of death. Perhaps the emphasis on structuring tendencies, ego integration, and mastery kept analytic attention too riveted on dichotomies between free and bound energy, drive discharge and realistic delay, wish fulfillment and disguised rerouting, impulse and control, irrational–rational, pleasure–unpleasure. Not enough credit was given to what *primary process flow* achieves, the *work* it does.

Freud overemphasizes the contrast between pleasure and pain and places primary process work firmly on the side of pleasure. In the end, this dichotomy broke down. A psyche fundamentally devoted to pleasure could not explain the pervasiveness of pain in human affairs. Nevertheless, Freud's work possesses resources that contribute to revisualizing what primary process does. *Primary process works on the pain it tries to wish away.* Even the wishing away of pain *can* be a first approach to working with it.

On the one hand, primary process may try to cushion or rid the psyche of pain, reroute pleasure around pain, or try to circumscribe and limit pain. It searches out pain and begins to weave webs of meaning around it, a psychic wound-licking, cocooning, secreting pearls around irritants. Even as it tries to delete pain, it acts on it, does something to or with it, alters it. Primary process begins the transformation of pain.

Freud (1920) calls attention to cases in which primary process focuses relentlessly on pain. Mythic images and literary narratives give the fact of suffering privileged emphasis. Dreams are filled with catastrophic moments. Repetitive painful dreams, like the traumatic war neurosis dreams Freud notes, suggest that the psyche is up against more pain than it can process. Pain breaks through the cocoon of wishes, shatters pearls of meaning. There is a breakdown in the psyche's ability to begin the processing of pain.

Mastery of pain is too much to expect. But perhaps primary process can bite off bits of painful impacts, rework painful injuries in fragmentary ways. Reworking of pain is always partial. One cannot make savage wounds go away. But little by little, primary process can absorb more of the impact, keep turning shock around, make room for the shock. Growth of even a little digestive capacity goes a long way.

Sometimes primary process effectively shrinks a painful mass, like a psychic radiation treatment. The images, fantasies, primitive narratives it secretes can partially break up and dissolve the pain on which they act. At times the subject may so enjoy exercising primary process capacity that the painful moment takes second place to the thrill of using one's equipment intensely and fully. A poem may be more important to a poet than the pain that occasioned it. The *self* a patient finds while speaking about injury can alter one's experience of what injury is.

On the other hand, primary process may never catch up to the sense of injury. Sensitivity to wounds may always be steps ahead of processing ability. The growth in ability to *live* with this assymetry is a kind of wisdom. One learns to give pain time. It takes time for pain to diminish enough for processing to begin nibbling at it. The seasoned personality is steeped in time.

Primary process is attracted to wounds. It begins the binding and processing of wounds. It not only attempts to sneak pleasure past forbidding eyes but it also tries to heal. It tries to right the psyche, to make one feel better and actually *be* better. The double tendency to avoid and to work over pain is implicit in primary process. On the one hand, there is shock, blanking out, numbing, turning off, getting rid of, wishing away, trying to substitute pleasure or fullness or oblivion for pain. But there is also recovery, nursing wounds, producing images and proto-narratives that coat, lubricate, and begin breaking down and metabolizing chunks of horror. We turn wounds into dreams, poems, religions, art, laws, and social institutions. By feeding injury into dream work, primary process begins the endless task of making something of suffering, of working with pain through images, of discovering the joy of symbolizing what cannot be endured.[3]

---

[3] For alternative, related portrayals of the work that primary that process does, see Ehrenzweig (1971) and Bion (1970). This theme runs through my earlier work (Eigen 1986, 1992b, 1993, 1995) and is part of a strong imaginative current of psychoanalytic writers (e.g., Matte-Blanco 1975, 1988, Milner 1957,1987, Noy 1968, Rycroft 1968).

Primary process does its work in better and worse ways. Primary process itself can be wounded and be unable to work well. Something can go wrong with
the psyche's ability to process injury from the outset. If primary process is damaged, it cannot properly begin the task of processing catastrophic states. It is
part of the catastrophe. The images and proto-narratives it feeds the psyche
lead nowhere, perpetuate damage, and lam movement.

Primary process tries to right itself, to heal itself, but may not be able to do
so. It may become preoccupied with signaling its own damaged state, its own
blocked processing ability. If it does not get help and is left to its failing
devices, its images and proto-narratives can become ever more damaging to
itself and the psyche generally. The image-making process becomes part of a
process of injury, a vicious spiral of imaging damage that acts in such a way
that more damage results. This spiral can reach a point where images of damage are less symbols than they are instances of the damage itself, momentary
glimpses of the damaging process in progress. In extreme instances, the damage is so severe that images are no longer produced or are inaccessible, and
the individual begins to vanish as the wound closes over him or her.

This is the sort of trap into which Deborah has fallen. Her psyche has closed
in around her, has failed to support her. Primary process is not processing. It
is not working on her sense of injury, but is swallowed up by it. To speak of
penis envy or castration anxiety does not make sense when one has fallen off
the edge of the psychic universe, when the psyche itself seems on the verge of
vanishing.

When Freud writes that the business of analysis is to secure the best possible
psychological conditions for the functions of the ego (1937, p. 250), a *well-enough
functioning primary process must be included among these conditions*. Deborah slipped
through her own primary process foundations, and they became deadening. We
can only guess how this happened. Obviously, the Other failed to help her, but
she also was unable to use what help might have been offered. How did this
happen? What makes this work? Again, we are back to square zero.

REFERENCES

Bion, W. R. (1970). *Attention and Interpretation*. Northvale, NJ: Jason Aronson, 1983.
Ehrenzweig, A. (1971). *The Hidden Order of Art*. Berkeley, CA: University of California
     Press.
Eigen, M. (1986). *The Psychotic Core*. Northvale, NJ: Jason Aronson.
────── (1992a). The fire that never goes out. *Psychoanalytic Review* 79: 271–287.
────── (1992b). *Coming through the Whirlwind*. Wilmette, IL: Chiron.
────── (1993). *The Electrified Tightrope*. Northvale, NJ: Jason Aronson.
────── (1995). *Reshaping the Self*. New York: Psychosocial Press.
Freud, S. (1900). The interpretation of dreams. *Standard Edition* 4/5:1–361.
────── (1913). The theme of the three caskets. *Standard Edition* 12.

———— (1920). Beyond the pleasure principle. *Standard Edition* 18.

———— (1923). The ego and the id. *Standard Edition* 19.

———— (1937). Analysis terminable and interminable. *Standard Edition* 23.

———— (1940). The outline of psycho-analysis. *Standard Edition* 23.

Jung, C. G. (1943, 1945). Two essays on analytical psychology. In *The Collected Works of C. G. Jung.* Bollinger series, vol. 7. Princeton: Princeton University Press, 1956.

Masson, J. M., ed. (1985). *The Complete Letters of Sigmund Freud to Wilhelm Fliess 1887–1904.* Cambridge, MA: Harvard University Press.

Matte-Blanco, I. (1975). *The Unconscious as Infinite Sets.* London: Duckworth.

———— (1988). *Thinking, Feeling, and Being.* London: Routledge.

Milner, M. (1957). *On Not Being Able to Paint.* New York: International Universities Press, 1973.

———— (1987). *The Suppressed Madness of Sane Men.* London: Tavistock.

Noy, P. (1968). The development of musical ability. *Psychoanalytic Study of the Child,* vol. 68. New Haven, CT: Yale University Press.

Rodman, R. (1987). *The Spontaneous Gesture: Selected Letters of D. W. Winnicott.* Cambridge, MA: Harvard University Press.

Rycroft, C. (1968). *Imagination and Reality.* New York: International Universities Press.

Winnicott, D. W. (1986). *Holding and Interpretation.* New York: Grove.

2

The Destructive Force

It is difficult to overestimate Melanie Klein's impact on psychoanalytic thinking. So many of her locutions and concerns are part of psychoanalytic daily life. She shares with nineteenth-century psychiatry, poets, and gothic literature an obsession with splitting. In Klein's writings, splits in personality become splits in ego, object, and affect. She embarks on what may well be one of the most detailed portrayals of psychological splitting in the history of ideas. She shares this preoccupation with Freud and Jung, but gives it her own turn, takes it to places the founders of depth psychology did not quite get to. If the idea of splitting is popular today, Melanie Klein is a background influence.

Klein shares with existentialism a preoccupation with death. Our sense of self, other, and time is stained by death on the horizon. For Freud and Klein, death is not only a definitive event approaching us but also something working in every psychic pore now. Klein spins variants of Freud's death drive throughout her work. She takes seriously Freud's insistence that Eros and the death instinct permeate every fiber of psychic life. How death work and life work contribute to every psychic event involves "problems whose elucidation would be the most rewarding achievement of psychological research" (Freud 1937, p. 243). By immersing herself in death and life processes, Klein contributes toward the elucidation that Freud invites.

Klein makes psychoanalysis more honest by making explicit its implicit concern with psychosis. In an earlier contribution (Eigen 1986, pp. 5–31), I show how an underlying concern with madness contributes to Freud's structural concepts and descriptions of psychic processes. He applies notions drawn from psychotic phenomenology to the treatment of neurotics. Klein tears the veil away and focuses on psychotic anxieties, mechanisms, and defenses that make their way through infancy and remain active all life long. She gives credence to the intuition that madness runs through human affairs and plays a role in everyone's life.

The Kleinian analyst expects to work with psychotic processes and is not surprised by psychotic transferences. On the contrary, analysts touched by Klein are suspicious if psychotic depths are bypassed in analytic work. Winnicott (1971, p. 87) muses with black humor on the value of analytic work that goes on at neurotic levels for years, never touching issues of madness or a deeper malaise. Fairbairn (1954) describes neuroses as ways of binding deeper fragmentation. The titles of two recent books by authors touched by Klein (via Winnicott and Bion) bear witness to the notion that behind a neurosis lies a hidden psychosis: Green's *On Private Madness* (1986) and Milner's *The Suppressed Madness of Sane Men* (1987). My own book, *The Psychotic Core* (1986), deals with aspects of madness that characterize the human condition.

Melanie Klein does not believe infants are psychotic just because there are psychotic processes in infancy. However, she does link madness with very early processes and is obsessed with the quest for origins. Madness is not simply an aberration, something extrinsic to the human. Rather, something approximating madness is intrinsic to the way the human psyche works, although it would be brash to define man as mad. If it is brash to define man as mad, it would also be mad to exclude madness from one's sense of the human. We leave open what to make of this knot, as it is beyond our powers to untangle now.

This chapter connects Melanie Klein's interest in psychotic processes with psychic deadness. Klein's portrayals of psychotic anxieties form a nexus out of which her views of psychic deadness unfold. To feel the full force of Klein's views on deadness, it is necessary to tease apart multiple currents of her work. My points of entree are the many times she repeats the locution, "from the beginning of life." It is a phrase she repeats with different meanings. One might conclude she holds contradictory views of psychic origins or that all the originary processes she speaks of go together in fertile, complex ways. I espouse the latter view. It is important to give full development to Klein's multiple perspectives in order to see how far her picture of deadness takes us and where it leaves off.

FROM THE BEGINNING OF LIFE

Melanie Klein's essay, "Notes on Some Schizoid Mechanisms" (1946) is a richly condensed summary of her picture of psychic life, yet one cannot get the full flavor of Klein from this essay. Her book, *Narrative of a Child Analysis* (1961), shocks one into awareness of Mother's body as war zone. The drive to get control of Mother's insides, meeting up with rivals in her body, psychic dramas played out with body materials: all this receives more graphic treatment in her account of moment-to-moment analytic interactions. But the bare bones of her vision shine with special brightness in "Notes on Some Schizoid Mechanisms" (1946). It is a high point in her writings and is my focus here.

Klein uses the phrase "from the beginning" eight times in pp. 293–298; the variant, "at the beginning", appears once (p. 296). There are other references to the beginning of life in this essay as well. Apparently reference to origins is part of Klein's style. It is interesting that she does not say "from the beginning of psychic life," but "from the beginning of life." I would imagine she meant from the beginning of psychic life, but her repeated references to the beginning of life take on a certain power. One begins to think she really means the beginning of life itself or at least the infant's life.

Does she really intend us to think that the infant's mental activity begins concurrently with bodily activity, that the two grow up at the same time and are inseparable? That she asserts the first object is the breast suggests that the beginning of life she means is life from birth. Are there objects in the womb? The fact that in her writings the womb becomes an object to seek, control, and possess leaves the question open.

Melanie Klein is very Freudian in her emphasis on active mental processes. She is perhaps more Freudian than Freud himself in her emphasis on active ego processes everywhere. The fantasy of passive union with the womb is less important than the ego's womb-oriented activity. For her the womb is not merely a safe harbor, a place to withdraw and hide but also a place of creativity, power, appropriation, a status symbol. The Kleinian womb is a busy place filled with weapons, struggles, battles; it is a site of hyperactivity. It certainly does not provide the rest and respite that regression seeks. In the Kleinian world, there is no safety anywhere, not for long.

What is it like to undergo the changes an embryo or fetus does? Ocean waves and roller coasters seem tame by comparison. I can well imagine not moving much with so much going on. A regressed person in a fetal position may be trying to ride out the storm. Melanie Klein also may be true to the mother's experience, who must somehow come through a lifetime of changes in nine months and perhaps still greater changes in being with a live infant and child.

Nevertheless, it is not helplessness in the face of immense change that Klein emphasizes. The ego is part of growth processes, and ego activity adds to the dramatic alterations in progress. The ego helps shape the processes by which it is shaped. Still the ego is driven. Its fierce activity is tied to momentous changes it does not control. Like the embryo or fetus, it develops along a timetable, with characteristic structural and dynamic shifts. Is Klein's ego, like Freud's, partly a mastery ego, dedicated to making the passive active, emphasizing integration and synthesis? Does passivity exist in Klein's world? What sorts of relationships are possible between ego and the greater psychic field?

There are different sorts of deadness. Deadness can result from turning off in the face of overstimulation or an overwhelming situation. In extreme instances, one may passively die out. In contrast, Kleinian deadness seems more linked with active mastery attempts gone wrong. The ego stifles emotion in order to stay on top, a sort of rising above oneself. Klein emphasizes the ego's manic defenses and self-hardening processes, attempts to stay above or fortify oneself against painful realities. These attempts result in emotional depletion or the loss of contact with emotional reality. One of Klein's specialties is her delineation of ego defenses—splitting, idealization, manic denial, projection, and introjection—in the face of psychotic anxieties. One wonders whether part of psychic deadness is tied to the ego's attempts to do too much. Doesn't the Kleinian ego ever simply tire itself out or get tired of itself?

In this chapter, we will turn the Kleinian "beginning of life" kaleidoscope and superimpose some of the configurations that appear. We move between the ego's relations to objects, affects, and drives and their intertwining. Our starting point is Klein's famous emphasis on the death drive as a nucleus of ego activity.

FROM THE BEGINNING: THE DEATH INSTINCT

More than most analysts, Klein places Freud's death drive at the center of psychic life. Not only does she share Freud's conviction that the death drive plays a constitutive role in psychic phenomena but she also contributes original variations on the theme. She nourishes, extends, and amplifies the ways in which death currents spread through and mold psychic activities.

Klein makes the strong assertion that "anxiety arises from the operation of the death instinct within the organism" (1946, p. 296). We do not know exactly what she means by "operation" or "death instinct," but we have hints. She speaks of "the primary anxiety of being annihilated by a destructive force within" (1946, p. 297). Whatever the death instinct and its operations may be, it issues in annihilation anxiety, which is linked to *a destructive force within*.

This linkage marks a radical amplification or shift of emphasis in psychoanalysis. Primary anxiety is not tied to libido, but to a destructive force within. We are less anxious about sexuality than about destruction. In his personal life, Freud seemed more obsessed with the fear of death than castration (see Chapter 1). As he moved toward old age, death finally got its due in his formal theory (libido in youth, death in old age). Standing on Freud's shoulders in his old age, Melanie Klein looks squarely in the face of death.

What makes Klein's emphasis on death psychoanalytic, in part, is the way death spreads through the personality and works indirectly. The destructive force within, like libido, undergoes a series of displacements or deflections. It is (1) "felt as fear of annihilation (death)"; (2) "takes the form of fear of persecution"; and is (3) "from the beginning felt as being caused by objects" (1946, p. 296). This is death drive's centrifugal movement (in–out). At the same time, there is a centripetal movement (out–in), whereby outer persecuting objects are introjected and become internal persecutors. They then draw on and reinforce "fear of the destructive impulse within" (1946, p. 196). Projection–introjection function as filters or funnels for the death drive. They provide shapes, forms, arenas of objects: pathways for the death drive.

Melanie Klein maintains that *a destructive force within is* felt as the primary source of danger at the same time that one encounters it through deflections (projective–introjective funnels). The primal destructive force within is more global and formless than its projective–introjective manifestations. Melanie Klein has more to say about the latter than the former. Her specialty is to delineate ways in which the ego channels and binds the death drive—via projection–introjection and such associated mechanisms as splitting, idealization, and denial. Bion (1965, 1970, see Chapter 4) focuses on the raw, formless destructive force and its radical unbinding of what ego builds.

For Melanie Klein, the formless, originary death drive and its projective–introjective shapes work from the beginning. There is an originary simultaneity of multidirectional movements toward more or less form and more or less stability. The ego is always under pressure to deal with death drive's twists and turns. Can it possibly be up to this task?

FROM THE BEGINNING: EGO AND OBJECTS

To understand Melanie Klein's depiction of early ego-object relations, we can start from four of her assertions about the beginning of life: (1) "that object-relations exist from the beginning of life" (1946, p. 293); (2) that "from the beginning object-relations are molded by an interaction between introjection and projection" (1946, p. 293); (3) that "from the beginning the destructive impulse is turned against the object" (1946, p. 293); and (4) "that the introjected good breast forms a vital part of the ego, [and] exerts from the beginning a fundamental influence on the processes of ego-development and affects both ego-structure and object-relations" (1946, p. 295).

For Melanie Klein the first object is the breast, which is split into a good (gratifying) and bad (frustrating) breast. Affects (love and hate) associated with good and bad experiences also are split from each other. One might imagine too that there is a good ego and bad ego severed from each other. The destructive impulse is turned against the object (in–out) while goodness is taken in (out–in). This scheme has many threads to pull on.

Melanie Klein's *Genesis* reads, "In the beginning was splitting, and splitting divides good from bad: good and bad objects, good and bad instincts, good and bad affects, good and bad egos." Other readers of Genesis wonder if she missed earlier elements of creation—the formlessness, chaos, nothing, breath, emergent life and world—and perhaps missed Eden before the apple is eaten.

She begins not simply by dividing light from dark, but with the Tree of Knowledge (good and bad).

Is the first object the breast (the apple rather than God)? Is there a first object? Is there life before splitting? What is the breast that gets split into good and bad? Is there a primal swim of experience in which well-being and distress variously alternate, fuse, commingle? Do we begin with variable mixtures of agony, bliss, and ordinary just-so states? Are there elements of polarization at the outset, or does polarization take time to crystallize, or both? Is the bipolar self necessarily a split self? When do divisions become splits? It is easy to question Melanie Klein, but it would be facile to discount her. Bion (1970), Winnicott (1971), and Elkin (1972) are among those to creatively imagine alternative points of departure while making use of, rather than dismissing, Klein's insights.

A region Klein guides us into involves ways that the psyche splits inner and outer worlds to handle the death force. An overall framework of Klein's work is that psychic agencies and objects function to delimit, channel, and dampen what otherwise would be an overwhelming and lethal flow of death currents. This is more than a hydraulic metaphor. The human implications are enormous and heart wrenching. In a time when the news media are saturated with reports of child abuse, explosive victimization of every sort, terror of the streets and bedroom, and terror within and between nations and when cheap, denuded violence becomes the language of entertainment and the currency of psychic exchange, the dikes against waves of death force are leaky indeed.

A parent repents after blowing up at a child: "It happened in a flash. I exploded. I lost it. It built up. I held it in. Then it happened, like a flame igniting gun powder or gas." Child explodes, and then parent explodes—orgasmic destruction. Sometimes blowing up clears the air, but often it has devastating results. As the parent continues, it sounds a bit like masturbation or other addictions: "I tell myself I'll never do it again, but it builds, and has its way." So many people blowing up, having tantrums, inflicting and sustaining serious injury: we seem obsessed by destruction.

What it means to regulate aggression is a paramount issue of our time. Klein's work is so important because it does not offer an easy way out. Explosions, attacks, rage against the other: these are deflections of a force that would otherwise consume one's self and body. They are signs of a deeper force one tries to dodge, juggle, play for time with, and make something of. Any victory is partial and is subject to loss, breakdown, starting over. One cannot get rid of the death force, but one may to some extent take it into account. Perhaps (to some extent) one rides the waves, learns body English tricks. One does (to some extent) learn to spot and live with reversals (in ↔ out, love ↔ hate, self ↔ other), instead of merely playing one side against the other. By gazing at one's predicament, one might even become more open to a deeper, fuller flow of life.

SPLITTING OF EGO-AFFECT-OBJECT

The more one looks at the splitting mechanisms Klein depicts, the denser they become. One imagines the psyche will take in goodness (introjection) and get rid of badness (projection), a digestive/respiratory model. This is a main line of her vision, but variations thicken.

Since the death force is deflected outward, it also gets introjected. Introjection ↔ projection flows both ways (in ↔ out). Similarly, the life force may be projected, resulting in experiencing objects as better than they are (idealization). A quite complex array of projected–introjected goodness–badness (life–death transforms) result, including mutual contagion, wherein good–bad spill into each other in confusing ways. The good or bad may refer to drive, affect, object, or ego.

Melanie Klein uses the term "projective identification" to indicate that an object is identified with good or bad parts of the self. Similarly, "introjective identification" suggests that good or bad parts of the object are identified with self. Throughout her major writings she takes for granted that identificatory processes are at work in the projection ↔ introjection flow. A powerful array of psychic possibilities emerges from Klein's meditations on connections between identificatory projection–introjection and splitting. Good or bad aspects of the *self* can be identified with good or bad aspects of the *object*, and good or bad aspects of the object can be identified with good or bad aspects of the self.

If one adds dislocations and amalgams of affect, the clinical possibilities become mind-boggling. Ego, object, and affect can be taken apart and put together in myriad permutations. Bad ego can hate good ego, good ego can love bad ego, bad object can hate good object loving good ego, bad object can love bad ego hating good object, bad object can hate bad ego loving good object, good ego can hate bad ego hating good object, and on and on. This enables mappings of dazzling arrays of internal–external object-ego-affect relations. Freud's vision of instincts variously distributing (attaching–detaching) themselves with regard to objects and psychic agencies is here amplified in ego-affect-object relational terms.

ROOTS OF DEADNESS

Excessive Splitting

If splitting proliferates, it leads to "impoverishment of the ego" and "dispersal of emotions" (1946, p. 316). The result is emotional deadness, lack of emotion, and unresponsiveness. Bion (1970) works over this material in spatial terms. Emotional dispersal or thinning is partly a function of the space it occupies. A space may be too big or small for the emotion occupying it, and vice versa. The problem of space—whether there is too much or too little space for an emotion—is less important to Klein than the connection between deadness and latent anxiety. She believes that emotional deadness is a measure of unconscious anxiety. Emotion is present, but is dispersed by splitting. Deadness is only apparent, a reflection of splitting processes that stifle emotional life.

Klein is committed to a conflict/anxiety model. A central difference between her theory and that of traditional Freudians is that she focuses on early splitting mechanisms as anxiety producers/regulators, antedating oedipal repression; it is unclear what she makes of primal repression. Splitting run amok becomes a cancer eating up the psyche, substituting itself for the emotions on which it acts. The patient may feel disintegrated, emotionless, in pieces, and depleted. In effect, the individual experiences something of the defense and its result (split and vacant) while losing contact with the cut-up emotion.

Part of the enormous valence that splitting has for the subject is its function as a link with the emotion it severs. The subject may become attached to feeling cut in pieces, fragmented, and severed from himself, because of the unconscious association of splitting with the emotion it disperses. *One holds on to splitting because of its unconscious connection to emotional life.* One multiplies splits in vain attempts to capture or make contact with emotions they disperse. It may be unclear whether an individual trapped in splitting is trying to recapture or annihilate contact with his emotional life. Usually both are true.

For Klein it remains possible in theory to gather and synthesize dispersed emotion. When this happens the patient feels "his inner and outer worlds have not only come more together but back to life again" (1946, p. 316). Klein seems to associate splitting–dispersal with death and synthesis with life. Anxiety is associated with life, the return of emotion. She makes a strong case for the omnipresence of anxiety, which now is more dispersed, now more focal. When the patient comes together and alive again "it appears in retrospect that when emotions were lacking, relations were vague and uncertain and parts of the personality were felt to be lost, everything seemed to be dead. All this is the equivalent of anxiety of a very serious nature. This anxiety, kept latent by dispersal, is to some extent experienced all along, but its form differs from the latent anxiety which we can recognize in other types of cases" (1946, p. 316). The therapeutic task is to bring together split aspects of self, and with cohesion comes more emotions, especially anxiety.

Note the therapeutic optimism. Splitting induces deadness. Synthesis, the healing of splits, recovers aliveness. Deadness is only apparent. Emotions of anxiety were present all along; they were only dispersed. One is not dead, only split. Assemble the dry bones and a living, anxious being appears again.

When did Kleinian anxiety—index of the death drive—slide into Freudian anxiety, the index of libido? Freud and Klein agree that psychic acts include life and death drive components. No act is without either. Yet Klein explicitly ties anxiety to death. For the schizoid personality, one who lacks the feeling of feelings, it is a sign of life. I do not think Klein was aware of this slippage, and I do not want to criticize her for it. But we can learn from it, as anxiety floats, freely or not, between death and life.

Anxiety may be enlivening for one who lacks emotion and is unresponsive, and often this is so. Yet it is also the case that many dead individuals cannot bear *any* rise of emotion, including anxiety. Melanie Klein does not take up the possibility of death work going so far that anxiety is left behind. She holds fast to the belief that anxiety underlies deadness. It is not simply that deadness dampens anxiety, but that deadness results from attacks on anxiety. Anxiety may get cut up and dispersed, but does not die out. Scratch deadness and get anxiety; the opposite possibility is not meaningful to her.

Klein notes that analysis typically wins the patient's alliance when he or she experiences the relief from anxiety that interpretations bring. Would the technical corollary for the emotionless patient be that interpretations, which increase anxiety, bring relief? Klein is not naive enough to believe this, but she does feel that interpretations that synthesize splits in the self and dispersal of emotion will lead to the experience of anxiety (emotion).

She seems to take for granted that the capacity to have feelings is intact, but is temporarily put out of play by active defenses. The consideration that attacks against emotion (or self or object) might damage (disperse) not only emotion but also the capacity for emotions is not compelling for her. Bion (1965) raises the problem of damaged or undeveloped equipment or capacity. In such a patient, emotionlessness is not simply a reversible condition—synthesize splits to obtain emotion—so much as an index of damage or the lack of development. Maximal and minimal emotional states may flip-flop, not only as substitutes for each other but also as signs of apparatus/equipment mishap and mayhem (a catastrophe the personality has undergone or is undergoing).

The idea that the lack of emotion is as much or more a sign of the death drive as anxiety is not congenial to Klein's theoretical style. Yet one could see both anxiety and emotionlessness as fluctuating arms of death work in certain contexts. One can be obliterated by anxiety or the lack of emotion, by too much or by too little. Anxiety may collude with and express death, life, or both. Anxiety is floating, colorless, at home with many masters.

There are threads in Klein's formulations we could pull on to link emotional deadness with a death force. It is worthwhile to do so, bearing in mind that Klein took another path.

A DESTRUCTIVE FORCE WITHIN

Earlier, I called attention to Klein's references to a nuclear "destructive force within" (1946, p. 297). She focuses on ego reactions to an inner destructive force. Anxiety, splitting, projective–introjective identification, denial, and dispersal are some of the ego's responses to the destructive force. The nuclear destructive force works behind the scenes silently, but its deflections can make a lot of noise.

The destructive force remains unknown (unknowable?), an hypothesis or construct, but for Klein it is very real. The ego's primary anxiety is of being annihilated, not by external danger but by a destructive force within. The ego cannot localize the danger. It cannot pin down where it comes from or what it is. It has no frame of reference for the destructive force within. There are no boundaries, limits, or place: just the raw anxiety of annihilation, the originary dread (Bion's "nameless dread").

Klein traces the biography of annihilation anxiety via ego attempts to split and disperse its dread. The results of successive acts of dispersal can be deadening, and Klein focuses on this sort of deadness. Her emphasis is on splitting—integration mechanisms, rather than on ways that the death force might permanently alter or damage the ego or paralyze, jam, warp, and damage unconscious processing ability. Yet she feels that the ego splits and disperses itself, as well as affects and objects; apparently she felt the ego could more or less pop into shape via the interpretations of splits.

Klein does not seriously consider the possibility that there are cases in which psychic damage is so extensive that splitting is ineffectual or unavailable. In such instances, the personality has not followed the path of anxiety, but has taken another route. Klein hints this when she says that emotionlessness can be *equivalent* to anxiety. By this she means that anxiety is hidden by emotionlessness or that emotionlessness is a form or signal of anxiety. But one can add that emotionlessness, like anxiety, can act as a signal of the death drive. And, to be strictly congruent, emotionlessness, like anxiety, can be an expression of death work.

It is important to note that in my reformulation, neither side of a polarity (emotionlessness ↔ anxiety) is made primary at the other's expense. The double arrow expresses the possibility that either can transform into the other, or oppose the other, or meld together in various ways. Surely Klein's vision that emotionlessness is a form of anxiety is significant. Much mileage can be gained from understanding deadness as frozen emotion, defense against emotion, emotion in disguise (attacked, denied, split, dispersed emotion). But such a view can be cruel if the capacity to support emotion is missing or damaged.

Analytic work can have a moralistic or blaming tinge if emphasis is placed on the ego's active complicity and defensiveness, when the problem is actually deeper. There are individuals who have difficulty generating emotions or sustaining and processing emotions once they are generated. It is as if emotions belong to a universe that does not exist or fall off the edge of the universe into nowhere. For such individuals it is not a matter of putting together what was split, so much as creating conditions for growth of capacity.

To use a modified Bionic (1965, 1970) formulation, emotionlessness takes the place where emotion might have been. Lack of capacity is experienced as emptiness. The opposite also occurs: emotion takes the place where emptiness might have been. There can be not only the lack of capacity to generate, sustain, and process emotions but also the lack of capacity to sustain and process gaps, empty times, nothingness moments. Ideally, one is able to move between states, now full and now empty, using all the organ stops one can. But individuals get trapped by emptiness, or addicted to fullness, or wiped out by oscillations.

An advantage to a more open-ended formulation is that one can consider the possibility of a relatively defensive or undefensive use of feeling or lack of feeling, depending on the context of the moment. Klein is committed to viewing anxiety as primary, emptiness as derivative. The possibility that anxiety could arise as a response to emptiness—both as a dread of emptiness and an attempt to fill emptiness—is not meaningful to her. Perhaps she did not know how to empty out or value blankness for its own sake as a life-giving state. Hers is an anxiety theory, and for her emptiness is a form of anxiety. That anxiety could be a form of emptiness was unimaginable: it would not make analytic sense. Yet it is precisely a radical openness to what emptiness or anxiety might mean in a given instance that is crucial in work with individuals who need to learn how to tolerate the build-up of states and of movement between states. Both emptiness and anxiety may enliven or denude existence, depending on how they function in broader psychic contexts.

Bion's depiction of a destructive force is more devastating and open than Klein's and gets more clinical mileage. He imagines "a force that continues after . . . it destroys existence, time, and space" (1965, p. 101). It is not necessary to decide which is primary, anxiety or emptiness. Either can be obliterating. Yet the destruction Bion contemplates goes farther. A force that goes on working after it destroys existence, time, and space includes the destruction of anxiety and emptiness. Obliterating states can be obliterated. There is no end to nulling.

This possibility fits many individuals who are too damaged, collapsed, or rigidified to support workable splitting processes. In such individuals both emptiness and anxiety function to wipe out personality. Both are arms of a force that gathers momentum and may become unstoppable. If collapse goes far enough, neither primary emptiness nor primary anxiety is available, nor are their transforms, displacements, or reversals of much use. If degradation (destruction) is advanced enough, any affect or lack of affect may further promote degradation and collapse. In the context of such massive destruction, even anxiety and emptiness lose their impact and die out. Anxiety and emptiness become denuded of function other than being results or parts of destruction that keeps on going. At this point individuals are too far gone to be concerned about anxiety or emptiness. They are so gripped by the fall into deadness that they scarcely notice or care about fluctuations of anxiety–emptiness.

REFERENCES

Bion, W. R. (1965). *Transformations.* London: Heinemann.

————(1970). *Attention and Interpretation.* London: Tavistock, 1983.

Eigen, M. (1986). *The Psychotic Core.* Northvale, NJ: Jason Aronson.

Elkin, H. (1972). On selfhood and the development of ego structures in infancy. *Psychoanalytic Review* 59:389–416.

Fairbairn, W. R. D. (1954). *An Object-Relations Theory of the Personality.* New York: Basic Books.

Freud, S. (1937). Analysis terminable and interminable. *Standard Edition* 23.

Green, A. (1986). *On Private Madness.* London: Hogarth.

Klein, M. (1946). Notes on some schizoid mechanisms. In *Developments in Psycho-Analysis,* ed. M. Klein, P. Heimann, S. Isaacs, and J. Riviere, pp. 292–320. London: Hogarth, 1952.

————(1961). *Narrative of a Child Analysis.* London: Hogarth.

Milner, M. (1987). *The Suppressed Madness of Sane Men.* London: Tavistock.

Winnicott, D. W. (1971). *Playing and Reality.* New York: Basic Books.

3

Goodness and Deadness

FROM THE BEGINNING, THE GOOD CORE

What gives Melanie Klein's work its special power is not simply that the ego defends itself against annihilation anxiety but that it does so with whatever sense of goodness it can muster. Is the Good up to this task? Can it survive (triumph?) in the face of endless waves of destruction? What does Melanie Klein add to this ancient theme?

> For I hold that the introjected good breast forms a vital part of the ego, exerts from the beginning a fundamental influence on the process of ego-development and affects both ego-structure and object-relations. . . .
> The gratifying breast, taken in under the dominance of the sucking libido, is felt to be complete. This first internal good object acts as a focal point in the ego. It counteracts the processes of splitting and dispersal, makes for cohesiveness and integration, and is instrumental in building up the ego. . . .
> Projection, as Freud described, originates from the deflection of the death instinct outwards and in my view it helps the ego to overcome anxiety by ridding it of danger and badness. Introjection of the good object is also used by the ego as a defense against anxiety. [Klein, 1946, pp. 295–298]

Freud early notes that the mother regulates distressful affects of the infant. The mother comforts, soothes, cares for, and feeds the infant and makes the bad feelings go away. Melanie Klein takes a gratifying or ideal feed as the privileged paradigm of making the infant feel good.

The mother contributes the gratifying object (breast), but there is an innate tendency on the infant's part to make this gratifying or good object an ideal and complete one. The good breast becomes a heavenly one. Instead of good, beatific.

Melanie Klein does not make much of what the infant or mother contributes, but takes the amalgam as a nucleus of the ego. She takes for granted that the infant associates the goodness it feels with the object (breast) and perhaps attributes causality to the object, so that it is the introjected good breast that is a pole or core of ego experience and functioning.

Melanie Klein does not spend time thinking about what good feelings the infant might experience outside of introjection, an omission that bothered Bion, Winnicott, and Milner. Her focus is the ego's use of the introjected good breast as a defense against annihilation anxiety. The experience of goodness (introjected goodness) is used to offset, diminish, and regulate bad feelings primarily associated with a destructive force within. The infant relies on use of the object to regulate the death instinct.

It is important to note that Klein's discourse slides across many levels and dimensions without overly worrying about problems her amalgam may pose. She mentions, in passing, that the mother's love and understanding are important to the infant in going through disintegration and psychotic anxieties. Klein is not oblivious to Mother as regulator, transformer, and holder. Yet she seems to regard the mother as something of a safety net or back-up system, "the infant's greatest stand-by" (1946, p. 302), as most important if the infant's introjective–projective systems fail.

In Klein's work there is a slippage and confluence between reality and fantasy, with variable shifts of emphasis. Her hallmark is her emphatic insistence on the real effects of fantasy. Introjective and projective identification are great fantasy pumps. They put bad stuff and feelings into the mother and take good things and feelings from her. Although one projectively fantasizes bad into the other and introjectively fantasizes good into the self, the consequences of these fantasies are very real. "It is in phantasy that the infant splits the object and the self, but the effect of this phantasy is a very real one, because it leads to feelings and relations (and later on thought-processes) being in fact cut off from one another" (1946, p. 298).

> As far as the ego is concerned the excessive splitting off and expelling into the outer world of parts of itself considerably weaken it. . . .
>
> The projection of good feelings and good parts of the self into the mother is essential for the infant's ability to develop good object-relations and to integrate his ego. However, if this projective process is carried out excessively, good parts of the personality are felt to be lost . . . ; this process too results in weakening and impoverishing the ego. [Klein 1946, p. 301] *

All sorts of combinations of projective-introjective fantasy involving good-bad ego/affect/object are possible. Optimally, fantasy regulates the balance of good and bad feeling: pumping out the bad pumping in the good. For Klein this is more than fantasy regulation of mood and well-being. Fantasy plays an

---

* Quotations from this source reprinted by courtesy of the Estate of Melanie Klein and The Hogarth Press.

important role in regulating the death drive. Well-being, which for Klein is associated with the good breast or introjected good object, is a tool in this fantasy regulation. The good ego-object-affect-breast combination keeps saving the personality from death. Fantasy—or failure of fantasy—has very real consequences for the life and death of the self, and possibly the organism.

It is part of Klein's genius to depict ways that this simple scenario of expelling bad and taking in good is ever imperiled. One gets rid of the good and takes in the bad, as well as the reverse. In addition, good and bad elements of self-affect-object spill into each other. Excessive splitting and contamination go together. The ego fantasy pump cannot keep up with the death drive and frequently is commandeered by it. When it is, both good and bad feelings can be part of and further death work.

Excessive Goodness and Deadness

One of psychoanalysis's most important contributions to understanding the human condition involves the various ways it explores relationships between idealization and violence (Eigen 1986,1992,1993). Melanie Klein adds variations to this theme and also links idealization to deadness.

Klein takes for granted the infant's natural tendency to idealize the good object, whether it is inner or outer. This tendency seems to be an in-built, spontaneous one. When frustration and anxiety mount, the infant takes refuge in the internal, idealized good object. The infant seeks to burrow into, hold onto, and enfold itself with its sense of well-being and goodness. The idealized good object is a buffer against death force agents, internal persecutors, bad states.

If persecutory fear becomes too great, idealization may be overused to defend against or balance it. In extreme instances, the ego becomes a shell around a split-off idealized core, which is working overtime to blot out the onset of horrific states, whether invasion by split-off anxiety, menacing presences, or persecutory affects-objects-ego bits. Ego functioning becomes vastly thinned and curtailed inasmuch as its focus gets reduced to revving up contact with the idealized core. The ego may experience its loss of functioning as a growing deadness: the ego is really dying.

The idealized, introjected good core may get projected onto external objects to such an extent that the ego feels it has no goodness of its own. It may feel utterly at the mercy of others for anything good: only the object is good. The ego may lose faith in its ability to love and create, as idealization takes the place of the capacity to love, think, and perceive. To use some of Melanie Klein's expressions, "good parts of the personality are felt to be lost" (1946, p. 301), and there is "a feeling that the ego has no life and no value of its own" (1946, p. 302). Thus excessive idealization, whether of internal or external objects, leads to "weakening and impoverishing the ego" (1946, p. 301). The ego loses spontaneity and aliveness as it clings to idealized inner or outer objects for salvation. The sense of deadness suffered correlates with the very real loss or constriction of ego functions.

Idealization and Hallucination

The correlation of deadness with the loss of ego function is heightened by Melanie Klein's linking of idealization with hallucination. "Idealization is bound up with the splitting of the object, for the good aspects of the breast are exaggerated as a safeguard against the fear of the persecuting breast. While idealization is thus the corollary of persecutory fear, it also springs from the power of the instinctual desires which aim at unlimited gratification and therefore create the picture of an inexhaustible and always bountiful breast—an ideal breast" (1946, p. 299).

Melanie Klein takes off on Freud's picture of the infant hallucinating a breast when it is hungry: hallucinated fulfillment takes the place of painful hunger and no breast. She imagines that the infant hallucinates an ideal breast (an ideally good state) while omnipotently denying frustration, pain, persecutory feelings, and bad states. For Klein, denial equals annihilation in the unconscious, and bad states are tied to an image of a bad object—the frustrating, absent, persecutory, or unfulfilling object. Thus what gets denied and annihilated is not just a state or an object, but *an object relation* and, more, the ego's capacity for an alive object relation: "Omnipotent denial of the existence of the bad object and of the painful situation is in the unconscious equal to annihilation by the destructive impulse. It is . . . not only a situation and an object that are denied and annihilated—it is *an object-relation* which suffers this fate; and therefore a part of the ego, from which the feelings towards the object emanate, is denied and annihilated as well" (1946, p. 299).

The suggestiveness of Klein's descriptions goes far beyond her actual vocabulary. Her descriptions seem to treat denial and annihilation as if differences between them were insignificant. Yet denial of psychic reality may differ in important ways from the obliteration or annihilation of psychic reality. Denial may be equivalent to annihilation in the deep unconscious, but one cannot say that annihilation is equivalent to denial. Similarly, although denial and splitting go with projection–introjection, it is not clear that they are always salient or primary factors in hallucination.

There is a suggestion in Klein that annihilation and hallucination of unlimited gratification go together. Her overreliance on splitting and denial as death drive regulators obscures other ways in which annihilation and hallucination relate to each other. Hallucinating a beatific state when, in fact, there is pain is an amazing capacity. In such a state there is no room for bad feeling. Bad feeling is obliterated or blurred by good feeling. One may cling to and become addicted to the ideal good state. In such a case, the onset of bad feeling may trigger an intensified clinging to the beatific moment. The bad feeling may not be split off and denied so much as overwhelmed, flooded, blacked or whited out by addiction to an annihilating, totally filling blast of light or other ideal state. That is, uniting with an ideal object can have an annihilating impact in its own right without the use of denial and splitting, although these mechanisms also may be present. Even denial and splitting are washed away by the annihilating beatific flood, which leaves no room for anything else.

If flooding is more primordial than splitting-denial, one can imagine seismic shifts of affect, with the ego trying to hold on to or to let go one or another state. Various mixtures and alternations of holding on–letting go may come a little closer to depicting some responses to the flow of blissful–distressful moments, prior to splitting–denial.

TOO MUCH GOODNESS

Even such terms as holding on–letting go may be too activist to convey a sense of the atmospheric problems involved. There are individuals who feel deadened by too much good feeling, and others who feel killed off by too much bad feeling. In the former, too much good feeling has a numbing effect. These individuals may complain that they cannot feel themselves. These are "nice" people who do not feel real. They ordinarily feel all right, but lack intensity. They cannot crack the shell of good feelings and get to themselves.

One such person, Mr. Y., lived a charmed life. From childhood on he was good in everything; he was a star athlete, at the top of his class academically, and everyone liked him. His charmed existence continued through adulthood; after attending the best schools, he got the best jobs, and people gravitated to him and made life easy. Yet he felt he wasn't living his life; he wasn't "in" it. It was as if his life took off without him. It was not that he was an observer or that someone else lived for him. It was more that his life took off without consulting him. It never felt bad enough, long enough, for him to call it into question. Yet as time went on he missed himself. He came to therapy for help in slowing his life down so he could get aboard. Mr. Y. felt good, but complained of deadness. The good feeling he felt numbed and deadened him.

Such notions as splitting, repression, or empty parenting did not seem to fit Y.'s world. They did violence to it. What seemed more apt were notions having to do with timing, pace, and connection. How could Y. and his life connect with each other? What would each have to do to develop a partnership? Y.'s life didn't seem to leave much room or time for him. How could Y. and his life learn to take each other into consideration? Like sex partners who missed each other, could they develop a better sense of timing? Apparently Y. and his life never had a chance to be alone together, to experiment with each other, to learn about each other's needs and tempos. They did not wait for each other or find a common pace.

The good feeling that Y. felt was his life's, not his. It sped him along, made it impossible to complain. As the years went by, the good feeling became deadening, cloying, annoying. It got in the way, like a veil around possible experience. Y. was kidnapped by his life, carried along by good feeling. He came to therapy for help in finding, claiming, and connecting with his life. As time went on, perhaps his life would also want to find and be with him.

Y. was a relatively healthy example of a process that can be lethal. I have seen people who are little more than shells of good feeling. They live in tepid pools of well-being. When questioned they say they feel fine, but do not do much with their lives. In extreme cases, it is as if blank good feeling ate their insides away. Such people can spend their lives going in and out of hospitals. The good feeling periodically wears off and violence may threaten, or the person may become incoherent and confused.

Notions like splitting or repression do not hit the mark with these individuals. They are less split or repressed than drugged. It is as if their system gives itself periodic shots of mild euphoria, which gradually dies out. Bad states are less denied and repressed than blurred, blanked, or blissed out. A cloud of well-being envelops the personality for a time and then thins and disperses. The psychophysical system produces narcotic states that act as pain killers.

To an extent, such individuals learn how to manipulate the use of good feeling as a pain killer. It is as if they find a secret set of brain implants and learn what buttons to press. When so engaged, they often have a mildly cryptic, cherubic, zomboid look. At some point they become distracted and seem to forget where the buttons are, or forget to press them. Perhaps the good feeling becomes too engaging and the stupor too extensive. In extreme cases, blank good feeling gobbles memory, thought, imagination, perception, and, finally, itself.

Obliteration by goodness periodically wears thin, and the onset of bad states may mark the onset of breakdown and the need for hospital care or merely the break-up of the marriage, relationships, or work. Bad feelings may be as blank and meaningless as good feelings: they just increase as good ones wear out. Hospital care (or a new relationship or job or child) makes the bad feelings go away, and the individual can once more coast along on good or better feelings from months to years.

I often find that such people were unable to tolerate being a disturbance to their parents, nor could their parents tolerate the disturbance a child naturally brings. In some way, these children became the facsimile of good feelings that their parents wished to experience. Parents like to see their children feel good. But these patients lost their minds in order to maintain an atmosphere of stuporous good will. Did their parents exhibit an emotional frailty that was too much for an infant to bear? Why do good feelings dissolve functioning in some people and support it in others?

Freezing and Dissolving

Some individuals are frozen in bad feeling, others in good. It is as if they are sealed in blocks of affect ice of one or another valence. One can imagine that the originary affect flow got frozen in a limited sampling of positions by inhospitable climatic conditions.

The personality contracts around affects it is used to, home-base affects that govern the tone and emotional atmosphere of one's life. Most people seem to take for granted and somehow work around or with the dominant affect nuclei that set the tone of their lives. A certain personality hardening makes life livable. Kleinian hardening involves defensive processes, such as splitting, denial, projection–introjection, and repression, that deflect and distribute affect pools in characteristic ways, e.g., in typical arrays of ego-object dramas.

There are individuals also whose lives seem reduced to a preoccupation with raw affect sensations. One or another affect blots out or becomes their entire sense of being. They seem to fall into affect states as into quicksand. The emotion may be intense and enlivening for a time, but eventually becomes monotonous or consuming. What ought to be a rich and varied stream of emotions becomes a series of monotones or holes. The sense of one feeling playing off and enriching others is missing. Each affect becomes the world for a time, and the self dies out with each one.

Such individuals do not seem able to utilize splitting, denial, or projection–introjection to funnel and rework affect. These defenses would make for a more variegated emotional terrain. They could pit feelings against each other, pit a feeling against itself, develop comparisons of feelings. The quicksand state is characterized more by sinking and dissolving than by dissociative processes. One affect sinks in or is dissolved by another: there is dissolution rather than dissociation. Perhaps, in such individuals, there is an inability to maintain dissociations (dissociations dissolve) and a correlative splitting deficit.

It is clinically important to recognize forms of disappearance other than dissociation and repression. Expressive terms like contraction, freezing, sinking, and dissolving keep the clinical atmosphere open. There are individuals who seem to sink and dissolve in fathomless affect pools that finally dissolve themselves. Many of these individuals challenge our ability to think and feel and push us over the edge of what it is possible to imagine. We ought not make believe we know too much about such null states, especially if we lack the ability to help these people.

REFERENCES

Eigen, M. (1986). *The Psychotic Core.* Northvale, NJ: Jason Aronson.
———(1992). *Coming through the Whirlwind.* Wilmette, IL: Chiron.
———(l993). *The Electrified Tightrope.* Northvale, NJ: Jason Aronson.
Klein, M. (1946). Notes on some schizoid mechanisms. In *Developments in Psycho-Analysis,* ed. M. Klein, P. Heimann, S. Isaacs, and J. Riviere, pp. 292–320. London: Hogarth, 1952.

4

Bion's No-thing

The term *no-thing* in Bion's work is embedded in a rich network of associations and moves in several directions at once. It points to a general characteristic of mental life as such—its intangibility, invisibility, immateriality, or spacelessness. It also points to "specific no-things," which may function as mental aches akin to hunger or gaps that call for accretions of meaning. Meaning itself is a no-thing, not a thing.

Bion's introduction of terms like no-thing and no-thingness into psychoanalysis indicates that the domain of psychoanalysis cannot be exhausted or even approached properly by means of a medical model (Bion 1970). Like Lacan, Bion refuses to understand psychoanalysis in exclusively naturalistic terms. To treat the psyche like a thing is to kill it. Unlike Lacan, Bion does not shy away from the ineffable as a term and reality that may promote or destroy growth.

INTOLERANCE OF NO-THING

For Bion the term *no-thing* functions as a guardian of psychic life. It protects the psyche from overconcretization, literalization, or objectivization. Once no-thing becomes central in awareness, one cannot in good conscience make believe that the psyche can be reduced to the status of a thing.

To say that no-thing is seems to be a contradiction in terms. Yet the "is not" of no-thing that keeps space open for development or for undoing development is, for Bion, a crucial psychological reality. How one relates to what is not plays an important role in how one relates to what is.

The temptation to fill in, to thingify, or otherwise to nullify no-thing is ubiquitous. The natural pull of perception ties us to objects, and when our gaze turns inward we are attracted to or frightened by fantasy objects. Mental sets or habits become part of a gravitational pull with chronic ways of thingifying no-thing. Bion also notes that a certain rigidity, tied to a defective or embryonic mental apparatus, can prevent no-thingness from playing a fuller role in our development.

To escape the difficulty of interacting with no-thing, we not only fill no-thing with things but also relate to no-thing as a thing. Representations and thoughts are no-things that lend themselves to thingification inasmuch as they are easily confused with and reduced to their objects. Such confusion not only characterizes psychosis but also common sense—it is natural for the common-sense attitude to take the object world for granted and not inquire into how objects are psychically given. In the following quotation Bion, typically, keeps his vision on the cutting edge of extremes:

> Intolerance of a no-thing, taken together with the conviction that any object capable of a representative function is, by virtue of what the sane personality regards as its representative function, not a representation at all but a no-thing itself, precludes the possibility of words, circles, points and lines being used in the furtherance of learning from experience. They become a provocation to substitute the thing for the no-thing, and the thing itself as an instrument to take the place of representations when representations are a necessity as they are in the realm of thinking. [1965, p. 82]

Bion emphasizes *intolerance* and *conviction* as ways of preventing no-thing from having a basic say in personality. Intolerance and conviction are facets of rigidity. Conviction alone need not reflect rigidity, but may arise out of a concern for experience. However, this passage couples conviction with intolerance to show that filling in no-thing is not necessarily a neutral action.

For Bion sanity includes respect for polar terms of experience. If an object has a signifying function, one can credit the object *and* its meanings. One touches a tree but not its meanings, yet relates to both dimensions.

In madness, respect for the tension between dimensions slips, steps are skipped, end terms are fused, and mediating terms exaggerated. An object that can function as a representation is taken as a no-thing itself, and a no-thing (e.g., a system of meanings) is taken as an object. By making objects into no-things and vice versa, the mind practices a decisive evasion. No-thing as a term of experience is nulled by being converted into objects of common sense or nightmare. One soothes or scares oneself into oblivion and tries to soothe–scare others as well.

For Bion the tolerance of no-thing is linked with modulated openness and learning from experience. Conversely, the eradication of no-thing, by treating objects as no-things and no-things as objects, makes it impossible to use symbols as vehicles for experiential learning. He associates this state with murder. The above quotation continues: "Thus actual murder is to be sought instead of the thought represented by the word 'murder,' an actual breast or penis rather than the thought represented by those words, and so on until quite complex actions and real objects are elaborated as part of acting-out" (1965, p. 82).

If action is substituted for thinking, murder may take the place of a murderous thought. This can and does happen in a literal way, just as promiscuity or addiction can fill the space where erotic and nourishing reverie might have been. However, Bion means something more than literal murder and sexual enactment as results of short-circuited thinking. Murder is not confined to or perhaps even primarily concerned with bodies.

Short-circuited thinking is already a kind of murder, a murdering of the mind. When words are used to evacuate rather than to build meaning, meaning is murdered. No-thing is murdered insofar as it is treated as an object. The realm of experiencing as such is lost or aborted: physical things or thoughts as things are substituted for the evolution of experience. Actual murder is substituted for thoughts of murder. That is, the capacity to think about murderous feelings is killed off. Instead of learning from experience, one kills experience or rather kills the capacity to support experiencing. Actual psychic murder is substituted for meeting oneself and others.

A playwright may use scenes of rape or murder to express violation and death of the self or personality. His portrayal may achieve greater or lesser success depending on his ability to sustain the build-up and unfolding of emotional intensity and the dramatic representational world with which he is working. Possibly he may slip so that his scenes become part of and even further the death process he wished to illuminate. A play may kill or heighten experiences with which it grapples. Similarly, an analytic interpretation may kill or support the growth of experience, including the experience of violation and dying out of self. Much depends on the analyst's ability to sustain the build-up of the patient's impact until the realities at hand find voice. Inability to achieve this build-up may murder the experience of the patient's psychic death and perhaps the possibility of life as well.

That the murder at stake includes the killing of mind, psyche, self, and personality is underlined by Bion's emphasis on stupor. The passage continues: "Such procedures do not produce the results ordinarily achieved by thought, but contribute to states approximating to stupor, fear of stupor, hallucinosis, fear of hallucinosis, megalomania, and fear of megalomania" (1965, p. 82).

Hallucinosis and megalomania do not always play a negative role in Bion's thought and perhaps at times stupor has a positive function as well. Stupor can be a going blank, into a state of emptiness. Hallucinosis can be trancelike intuition. Megalomania may be giddiness or dizziness upon seeing too much at once, a godlike moment of revelation. Fear of such stupor-hallucinosis-megalomania can be inhibiting. One sides with common sense at the expense of alternate states of consciousness. One refuses the risk of becoming too unfamiliar.

In contrast, stupor associated with the killing off of mind-psyche-self-personality is not patient blankness or mute gestation, but an attempt to rid oneself of no-thing, to blank no-thing out, or to fill it with numbness. Instead of waiting on the living moment, one throws oneself away. In this context, hallucinosis is not a gateway for intuition, but a dump for the debris of what might have been mental activity. Megalomania is not a "high" linked with traversing the immeasurable awesomeness of the psychic universe, but an empty pretension closing door after door.

One cannot rest in a dead mind. One finds no repose in stupor-hallucinosis-megalomania. One is afraid of one's mental death, even if one is very far along the death process. One is trapped between stupor-hallucinosis-megalomania and the fear of it and oscillates between them. One is unable to use or relate to either fear or stupor, but is arrested in a kind of narcotic electrocution.

To an extent, the conviction that no-thing does not exist or that an object is no-thing itself rationalizes the inability to tolerate no-thing. This is akin to behaving badly in school because one is ashamed that one cannot read. One masks deficits with bravado when the simple admission of inability might lead to learning.

An individual's difficulty is compounded by the inability to admit inability. There seems to be a tendency to blur the painful experience of inability and to fill this space with stupor-hallucinosis-megalomania and fear. This is akin to Freud's fantasy of the infant hallucinating a breast when it is painfully hungry. Eventually proper skills, motivations, and maps develop, but the tendency to blot out painful emotional realities remains.

The ability to play down emotional pain is necessary for the healthy enjoyment of life. The difficulty Bion writes about arises when the need to dull pain hardens into an anti-representational attitude, a conviction that representing painful emotional realities is useless. This conviction is tyrannical. It does more than rationalize and mask deficit or inability. It immobilizes the psyche in face of its task to increase the capacity to connect with experience in fruitful ways.

REFERENCES

Bion, W. R. (1965). *Transformations*. London: Heinemann.
———. (1970). *Attention and Interpretation*. London: Tavistock.

5

Moral Violence

Bion characterizes psychic murder as *moral* violence. The conviction that the object is no-thing itself acts as a coercive demand that the object be more and less than what is possible. The psyche becomes entangled in the reductionistic misuse of basic categories and functions, e.g., space, time, causality, and definition.

SPACE AND TIME

The crime against the object or no-thing or personality is also a crime against space and time. In one clinical example Bion shows how space and time can be used in a shell game of identities: "*His* presence shows that he knows that I am present. This fact is used . . . to deny my *absence*. He reacts in the session as if I were absent. This behavior . . . is intended to deny my *presence*" (1965, p. 53).

The patient's presence indicates that he knows the analyst is present and that he is present as an I, a person. The fact of presence is turned into a denial of absence, which annihilates the analyst's person, since no person can be fully and only present. That is, the analyst's presence is taken as a sign that he ought not be absent. He must be there totally for the patient. This means that he cannot have his own mind or history or unconscious (which can never be total presence).

It is as if the presence the analyst can give whets the patient's appetite for what cannot be given. In this context what is missing fuels the hatred of emotional reality rather than inspires the urge to grow. The analyst is then angrily reacted to as if he were wholly absent, so that the kind of presence he might provide is wasted. The slipperiness or fluidity of psychic space and time is used to trap and pin the object. The object can be accused of being somewhere else, in the wrong place, and unable to fulfill impossible demands.

"The state of mind I have described is represented for me by a model—that of an adult who *violently* maintains an exclusively primitive, omnipotent, help-less state. The model by which I represent *his* 'vision' of *me* is that of an absent breast, the place or position, that I, the breast, *ought* to occupy but do not. The 'ought' expresses *moral* violence and omnipotence" (Bion 1965, p. 53).

In this tyrannical state of mind there is no room for a place or position where the object is not. The no-thing is filled, deformed, or killed off by the demand or conviction that an object *ought* to be there. There *must* be no place where an object used to be or might be, only total presence. With this affective ideol-ogy of absolute control, there can be no spontaneity. The personality cannot endure the tension of openness.

Space and time mean there is always elsewhere, another place, another time—the space and time for thinking, feeling, imagining, and acting. In prin-ciple, space and time are developmental concepts: something more *can* hap-pen. Processes are at work; experience builds on itself. There is an unfolding, gaps, leaps, something new, something old, multidirectional pulls and move-ments, tensions between continuity–discontinuity. The closing off of no-thing places severe restrictions on developmental or multirelational processes. For example, time must be reduced to "now" or "never" (in this instance, now = never):

"The factors that reduce the breast to a point reduce time to 'now.' Time is denuded of past and future. The 'now' is subjected to attacks similar to those delivered against space, or more precisely, the point. It is both exhausted and split. This leads to expression which can mislead for such a patient will say 'at the moment' when he means 'never' and 'yesterday' or 'tomorrow' when he means a split-off fragment of 'now'" (Bion 1965, p. 55).

Someone may seem to be communicating when in fact he is signaling that his world is extremely reduced and that he lacks the tools that make commu-nication possible. He swings between omnipotence–helplessness in a black hole now, using words and behavior to signal his conviction that no development is possible. The flow of time and history is stultified by an impossible demand: to have or be everything without being capable of tolerating anything. Evacua-tive activity, especially getting rid of self, becomes an obsession and psychic murder a way of life.

CAUSATION

At a higher level a person may be able to "have" and "use" thoughts and even use them to think about emotional reality. However, his thinking process may aim more at tying up emotional reality than contributing toward its evolution. Causal thinking readily lends itself to hardening psychic arteries. An individual may develop a version of his life that acts as a barrier against further discovery.

He "knows" what happened and why. If the analyst enters the knowledge game, a fight for superior omniscience may take the place of the quest to deepen and enrich experience. (See my book, *The Psychotic Core*, 1986, chapter 8, for a systematic distinction between omniscience and omnipotence.)

Thinking through emotional problems is hard work involving swings between depression, anxiety, and excitement. To learn from experience requires the tolerance of gaps that exert force on the field of meaning. Fertile meaning grows out of experience and gaps in experience and is not imposed in a disconnected way. One stays open to further nuances, shifts, corrections. More upheaval is always possible.

The difficulties inherent in sustaining affectively relevant thinking and communicating may, at times, not only seem oppressive but also persecutory. One may feel attacked by natural limitations and barriers, such as deficiencies in one's mental equipment. The challenge of sustaining thought processes may itself be felt as a persecution: one is persecuted by the persistence of unsolved, possibly unsolvable problems.

Often one cannot solve difficulties head on, but must regroup, try various approaches, wait, and rest. The same problem may re-emerge in a new light, or new ways of relating to a problem may develop. In such instances the sense of persecution may act as a spur. A problem grips one, will not let go, and forces further movement. Meaning grows organically from the press and tug of experience.

However, the sense of persecution may escalate so that one "is persecuted by the feelings of persecution" (1965, p. 57). One becomes too impatient and intolerant of working with difficulties and the concomitant waiting, resting, and resetting. Experience itself becomes too persecutory to bother with, and one develops the conviction that respect for experience is futile The sense of persecution becomes too depressing, and depression becomes too persecutory. The rhythmic pattern of breaking down and building up inherent in mental life is aborted or runs amok, and the individual tries to rid himself of his psyche as much as possible.

Causal thinking can facilitate psychic evacuation or play a role in short-circuiting psychic processes. It binds the sense of persecution with rationalizations, "reasons" that explain away pain. One flies over difficulties with a kind of scanning that does not allow a closer look. One substitutes pseudo-coherence for the hard-won coherence that grows in the struggle to give experience a voice.

The source of anxiety in the patient is his fear of depression and an associated PS ↔ D interchange, the mechanism of the selected fact. I categorize the idea of cause, in this context, as D_2, that is, a relatively primitive pre-conception used to prevent the emergence of something else. The patient's communication in so far as it is to be described as logical, is a circular argument, supposedly based on a theory of causation, employed to destroy contact with reality, not to fur-

ther it. In this respect it qualifies for one of Freud's criteria for psychosis—
hatred of reality. But the reality that is hated is the reality of an aspect of the
patient's personality. [Bion 1965, p. 59]

It is not necessary to give a detailed explanation of Bion's "grid" and such
terms as "D_2" to understand the gist of what he means here. In the present
context "pre-conception" functions as a barrier against the evolution of
psychic life. The pretense or conviction of "knowing the reasons" stops discovery. Instead of using maps to explore, one substitutes maps for wrestling
with oneself.

Bion contrasts causal thinking with learning via the selected fact. In the latter process some aspect of a situation triggers the growth of meaning. One
experiences differences in ways that terms of a situation are interrelated. There
is a spontaneous redistribution of processes, a series of transformations. One
develops through shifting relational networks.

The growth of meaning triggered by the selected fact is linked with a relatively free PS ↔ D_2 interchange. Groupings of phenomena form, break apart,
and re-form. One gradually builds more tolerance for various tensions, including affective states, which are associated with splitting and creative bringing
together. In this context paranoid-schizoid and depressive mechanisms contribute to the overall growth of experience, meaning, and personal being (Eigen
1985).

Bion stresses the moral component of causal thinking as especially destructive of experience and imaginative reflection on experience. A moralizing
attitude may pervade causal thinking and act as the link between objects or
between parts of the patient's or analyst's constructions. The shift of emphasis
will be away from letting experience build to making it fit a moralistic bias.

The observation of the constant conjunction of phenomena whose conjunction or coherence has not been previously observed, and therefore the whole
process of PS ↔ D interaction, definition, and the search for meaning that is
to be attached to the conjunction, can be destroyed by the strength of a sense
of causation and its moral implications. Patients show that the resolution of a
problem seems to present less difficulty if it can be regarded as belonging to a
moral domain; causation, responsibility, and therefore a controlling force, as
opposed to helplessness, provide a framework within which omnipotence reigns
(1965, pp. 64–65).

---

[1] Bion's symbol PS ↔ D represents a spontaneous oscillation between nulling and
creating meaning. This bipolar capacity is part of our equipment, and we evolve as we
enter new relationships with it. Perhaps it too evolves as we use it. PS, D, and PS ↔ D
represent different ways of relating to no-things and different ways that no-things are
constituted. They signify particular attitudinal contexts, psychic capacities, and operations or ways that psychical objects (specific sets of no-things) are given and used.

Moralistic, causal thinking substitutes for the open growth of meaning. For example, assigning blame ("You are the cause of my problems"; "It is all my fault") may be an attempt to control rather than suffer an experience. Hidden in this attitude is the demand that absolute control *ought to be* possible, that this whole mess is *caused by someone.* It is easier to pin the tail on the donkey than to experience difficulties requiring solution. The individual's demand for omnipotent causality organizes life, instead of building capacities needed to work with experience and its evolving PS ↔ D interactions.

DEFINITION

Definition, like causal thinking, may be used to bind or organize experience in overly restrictive ways. Bion contrasts definition with notation as ways of marking a constant conjunction or newly perceived relationship. Noting and attending to a newly observed grouping of phenomena leaves the question of definition open.

It may be argued that even notation requires a certain amount of implicit definitional activity. To mark x off from y implies the observation of different groupings of characteristics. To understand or perhaps even observe a fact, one must have a hypothesis about it. However, the urge to define is not the same as the practice of opening oneself up to the spontaneous arrangement of phenomena. Definition may close as well as open observation. Too often, definition is substituted for exploration. Definitions give one the illusion of knowing more than one actually does, especially with regard to emotional life. One may become trapped by definitional biases and lose contact with the domain that gave rise to the observations upon which explicit definitions are based. One can define phenomena out of existence.

Bion especially notes problems associated with the negative aspect of definitions. Definitory hypotheses work by marking a constant conjunction and excluding others. A field marked off by definition may gain meaning through constant conjunctions outside the defined area. A too-rigid dedication to the definitory field may mitigate against the perception of deeper and broader sets of relations.

Freud notes that thinking is work. Bion focuses on the work aspect of thinking and on problems in building a psyche capable of sustaining the tension of such work. In many instances the psyche may not have evolved enough to support healthy primary process thinking. Often precocious secondary thinking masks deficits in the ability to do adequate primary process work. In such an instance "definition can be used to inhibit thought" (1965, p. 99).

Definition may be substituted for the task of building primary process thinking that is capable of working with affective states in fruitful ways. Bion calls attention to transformations involved in constituting the kind of primary process that can do viable work, such as turning raw or cataclysmic affective states into usable dream images. Emphasis on thinking as inhibiting action draws attention away from the problem of constituting productive primary process work. Higher-level thinking may work overtime to cover defects in affective processing. The individual, for example, may use naming and definition to bind or contain persecutory feelings rather than to explore them. In Bion's words, "If persecutory feelings are strong the constant conjunction of elements can lead to a naming of the conjunction with intent to contain it, rather than mark it for investigation" (1965, p. 99).

In such an instance the individual has all he can do to keep up with his self-attacks or nameless dreads and intimations of catastrophe. He has all he can do to try to cauterize his sense of fragmentation or to put a verbal tourniquet around disintegration. Here the aim of naming is to stop horrible movement. The result is the proliferation of elements meant to tie the psyche up rather than to enable it to evolve.

A less extreme but still serious use of thinking to exclude growth capitalizes on one's ability to take nothing for granted. One can use "cat" not only to exclude "dog" but as a letter grouping that also excludes animal characteristics. The "smart" subject can perform a series of reductions in order to be left with as little meaning as possible. What remains of the word "cat" with its sensuous reverberations is simply a visual sign indicating the place where the full word used to be, a "no-cat." The mind bent on destroying meaning can denude a term "to the point which is merely a position without any trace of what used to occupy that position" (1965, p. 99).

Such a mind, although filled with a hatred of emotional reality, is very active. The subject may take perverse enjoyment in twisting meaning inside out, in reversing and reducing the significance of things. He is adept at beating meaning at its own game. He sees meaning at every turn and is ready to knock it down, to keep as closely as possible to a baseline of pure meaninglessness. The subject thrives on meaning in a backward way. He can define the therapist and himself out of existence by emphasizing what they are not. The therapist who sees this happening may be terribly frustrated. Nevertheless, with patience and painstaking work, one may see the day when this mental "live wire" takes himself seriously.

REFERENCES

Bion, W. R. (1965). *Transformations*. London: Heinemann.
Eigen, M. (1985). Towards Bion's starting point: between catastrophe and faith. *International Journal of Psycho-Analysis* 66: 321–330.
——— (1986). *The Psychotic Core*. Northvale, NJ: Jason Aronson.

6

Two Kinds of No-thing

One can use symbols to represent or get rid of emotional reality. Symbols usable in a process of discovery express gaps susceptible to investigation. Fertile symbols mix the known and unknown in productive ways. They hold the unknown (no-thing) open so that growth is possible. The same image, sound, movement, or letter grouping can be part of an attempt to evacuate and null emotional reality. Perhaps one cannot take the build-up of tension involved in the growth of a thought or feeling. Perhaps life has taught one to hate emotional reality: one may have learned from bitter experience that emotional reality is worthless or impossible.

An individual, for example, may experience a sense of rebirth for which he is willing and able to struggle. However, the sense of rebirth may also be used to evaporate emotional reality. An individual may not go through what is necessary in order to make his vision more real. One must evaluate a rebirth symbol with regard to its function in a particular context. At times it is not a symbol at all, but rather a sign that the individual is in trouble beyond his capacity and control. The same rebirth symbol may help open or close emotional reality, depending on such factors as attitude and capacity.

A mixture of deficit and hate may make it exceedingly difficult to bear the rise of complex emotional realities. An individual may collapse to the point of least resistance and fill the deficit with hateful actions. Hateful actions often involve hateful definitions and the assignment of blame, as in the case of racial prejudice. Bion's references to violence and murder evoke a sense of unbearable intensity that is escaped by short-circuiting psychic life. A reduced psyche incapable of supporting affective growth takes the place of an individual reaching through and beyond difficulties. A truncated time and space, moralistic causality (blaming), and definitions that cancel rather than open life are rigid remains of what might have been a rich and open psyche.

Bion uses various sets of signs and symbols to evoke a sense of the two main no-things at stake. The aim of his notations is to facilitate the growth of experience. He traces a hair-breadth line between creative and destructive attitudes. The life and death of the psyche are at stake. If we develop ways of experiencing and representing life-and-death processes, we may stand a chance of acting less destructively and find ways of making the most of ourselves.

THE POSITION AN OBJECT DOES NOT OCCUPY: POINT (·) AND LINE (———)

Bion used the point (·) and line (———) to represent the breast and phallus. A (·) may stand for what is left of the breast after attacks and denudation, or it may function as a sign for what is unknown about the breast, to be amplified by experience. In the first instance one cannot tolerate the growth of meaning and relationship. A deficient mental apparatus or too much hate reduces the breast or object to its bare minimum, to what might be manipulated or controlled or made to fit into the subject's megalomanic–helpless position. In the second instance the unknown elicits curiosity and learning.

For Bion the breast and phallus are highly significant subsets of what the (·) and (———) may be used to represent. The signs have a more general function than the terms "breast" and "phallus," since they can be used to represent transformations typical of many kinds of objects. They can be used to signal that processes of denudation or growth of meaning are at work and to mark creative or destructive phenomena for exploration.

Thus (·) and (———) are signs with a genetic history or direction. They indicate that meaning is being built up or torn down. If meaning is built up, it may enable the further growth of experience or act as a rigid organizer that reduces experience to its mold. Similarly, tearing down meaning may clear the way for new meaning or be an attempt to undercut the possibility of meaning altogether.

A value of using signs like (·) and (———) is to emphasize the unknown in every situation. We do not know a priori what is functioning and how. Bion is concerned that psychoanalysts prematurely leap into the *why* when the *what* and *how* are also inexhaustible; · and ——— are unknowns to be approached by observation. Bion writes, "The point (·) or the line (———) and all substantival terms may . . . be regarded as unknowns having two values: one, a sign for a constant conjunction and the other, a sign for the position, unoccupied, of the object" (1965, p. 100).

An implication of Bion's formulation is that the unknown is a permanent part of experience. All the somethings in the world cannot fill in the no-thing. The point and line will always resist meaning and meaninglessness. They can always signal something more or something less. They cannot be reduced to meaning—they cannot be made totally meaningful. Nor can they be placed, try as one might, totally outside the domain of meaning.

In some sense Bion's work might be criticized as being surprisingly sopho-moric. He takes a commonplace, the unknown, seriously. The sense of the unknown plays an important role in mental health. How we relate to the un-known is crucial. Bion's apparently complicated work is embarrassingly simple: it guards the unknown in human experience. Intellectual imagination probes the limits of intellect in order to keep experience alive and open. Upheaval, horror, and deadness are met along the way. They are challenges that human sensitivity faces.

In the example above, a point is a sign for a constant conjunction, and a sign for the position that an object does not occupy. An object may be regarded as a constant conjunction or as open sets of relations. In this regard, Heidegger (1957, pp. 25–42) writes that "identity is a relation." An object is a relational field that grows in meaning. It is known and unknown. It gains in meaning in many ways, including by being part of larger constant conjunctions or relational fields. The known about an object emerges as a figure out of a larger unknown. More limited and specific unknowns are carved out of gaps in knowledge.

The position an object does not occupy may be understood in common-sense terms as the place where an object was or will be. The object's absence is felt against its past or future presence. It is in this domain of common sense that one becomes trapped by longing. One imagines the object was there in a way that may be duplicated. What is missing is attributed to the missing object, and one believes that the object's presence will make all the difference (or undo the difference). Often enough, the object's actual presence becomes sorely disappointing, and one's longing becomes a source of confusion.

For Bion the position an object *does not occupy* includes but goes beyond common-sense terms. To view the object in terms of constant conjunctions that grow in meaning means that one never sees exactly the same object twice, that the object is experienced in terms of what it is not yet or is no longer, and that the very is-ness of the object includes references to movement, lacu-nae, incompletion, possibilities. To see the object solely in terms of what it is—or what one imagines it to be—is a tyranny. One is boxed in by the concrete demand for absolute presence or immutability. The position that an object does not occupy leaves room for movement and requires giving up an ideology of control or mastery.

If the object may be treated as a constant conjunction, so may the position it does not occupy. That position is inherently linked with the object as the background of felt meanings against which it stands out as figure. One's rela-tionship to silences that riddle and sustain an object grows. The position that an object does not occupy clings to the object and is not a simple fact of absence that can be undone. Only by going through the object to what it is not can one appreciate what it is.

The relationship between an object and the position it does not occupy is akin to the structure of metaphor. No presence can fill in the position an object does not occupy, not any more than literal meaning can satisfy the demands of metaphor. Metaphor creates new realities by bringing together terms that make a difference. Bion points out that it is precisely the difference between terms that is generative. If the terms were identical or too similar, nothing creative would occur in their interaction. The fact that one term does not take the place of another is crucial: a new place of interaction is created.

For Bion a central task of humankind is to grow a psyche capable of sustaining the evolution of new places of interaction of diverse terms of experience. All too often one or another term collapses or bullies others so that each fails to make its contribution to the growth of metaphor, psyche, individual, group, or society. It is difficult to sustain the tension of interaction of viewpoints and the contribution each makes to the growth of experience. Learning from experience involves learning not to take oneself or others literally. We make our contributions like terms of a metaphor and become parts of new unities that make life more meaningful. By building a tolerance for what we and others are not, we make room for positions we do not occupy, so that there can always be more interactions that make a difference.

Bion's use of a point to represent an object, the object's directional thrust, and the position that an object does not occupy warns us against taking subjective processes literally. A literal mark does not tell us what it may mean in a given situation, since the same sign can point in many directions. The point is a condensation packed with possibilities. It gains meaning as experience of it grows.

Bion notes that a point is indestructible (1965, p. 95). There is no end to the fragmentation it can endure. A point is a representation, a construction, not simply a literal mark. This product of mind may be used by mind for a variety of purposes, including portrayals of agonizing clinical realities.

For example, an individual may be bent on doing away with psychic life as much as possible, yet be unable to do away with it altogether. He seeks a point of absolute pointlessness. He cuts himself ad infinitum, yet the pieces act like so many subjective points that turn against him. He undergoes massive numbing or blanking out, yet his mind works at top speed in the interstices of the blankness and numbness. Even as he jumps out the window he fails to rid himself of his tormenting mind. In his fall a heightened point of consciousness mocks him (Eigen 1973). A point may represent a no-thing, yet an individual can neither reduce himself to a point nor a no-thing. He can no more convert no-thing to a point than he can make the point vanish forever.

Strictly speaking, a point is a no-thing insofar as it functions as a representation or construction. In the psychic domain, the subject works with different kinds of no-things, such as a point, a line, fantasy objects, and intuitions. Any representation may be multidirectional and polyvalent. For example, a point may fade or grow larger. Only by living with a particular point can one tell whether it expresses a movement toward zero, toward one, or toward multi-plicity. A point may also be used to represent a static no-thing, a dead rather than fertile void.

MINUS SIGNS

Bion refines his formulation by using minus signs to signify the position that an object does not occupy (1965, p. 100). He does this for convenience, so that we have a shorthand for distinguishing the object (+ ·) from the position it does not occupy (— ·). This is a transitional formulation that he later replaces with arrows in reverse (←↑). It serves the purpose of visually representing the idea/experience that every object has a position that it does not occupy. For Bion, the position that an object does not occupy is a generic part of the con-cept of object, a condition for the growth of object experience, an invariant structure or principle that makes experience of the psychoanalytical world of objects possible.

Each (psychological/psychoanalytical) object (a no-thing) represented by a point (another kind of no-thing) has plus and minus aspects. The plus and minus aspects may have various meanings depending on what sort of processes they represent or are part of. For example, the growth of meaning can be used dogmatically and rigidly to close off further growth or as a bridge leading to bridges. Undoing meaning may open doors. In certain instances an individual may misuse the capacity to undo meaning, in which case the nulling capacity snowballs and the creating–nulling rhythm gets lost.

Ideally, an individual entertains what Bion calls a "binocular" perspective. He experiences an object in terms of what it is and is not. Bion relates the fail-ure to distinguish positive and negative aspects of a · or ——— to the personality's relationship to the · and ——— aspects of itself. One fails to live with a particular · or ——— in ways that disclose its direction, meaning, or function in a given situation. Insofar as one can relate to · or ——— aspects of self, a more global · or ——— will transform into further positive and nega-tive facets as possible meanings develop.

At a near common-sense level — · or — ——— "retain meaning, as does the no-thing (because at least there is a trace of whatever it is that does not occupy the position) so long as time itself is not reduced to the moment with-out a past or a future" (1965, p. 100). The place that an object does not occupy may be rich in reverie, longing, hope, expectation, irritation, desire, or openness. + · and — · go together and qualify each other as experience evolves, with varying emphasis on one or the other in a particular instance. (I will continue to focus on + and — · rather than ——— for ease of exposition).

If the psyche is not capable of supporting a coherent temporal flow, · may

represent "a position without duration" and so be meaningless. In such a case
— · (positions unoccupied by ·)would also be meaningless and indistinguish-
able from · . As suggested above, such a position represents a developmental
failure. In some way the psyche collapsed or failed to constitute itself as viable.
For Bion it is important to explore the nature of the collapse or deficiency and
its consequences.

In earlier work (1985, 1986), I brought out ways that Bion approached a
less accessible dimension of psychosis than Melanie Klein. He explored realms
masked by projective identification and by its relatively structured and rigid
use of space. For some individuals the hatred of emotional reality is so intense
or their mental apparatus is so defective that they cannot use projection to
organize experience. Even when projective identification is achieved, it may
be used to bind a more formless horror or nameless dread.

Throughout his writings Bion explores the sense of catastrophic formlessness and its role in creativeness and psychosis. He cannot rest with any of his
formulations and keeps trying to strip the skin away from a catastrophic dread
that can undergo transformation into personal development or contribute to
the personality's living death. The notion of a · that represents position without duration is one such attempt to describe the reduction of life to utter
meaninglessness.

To the degree that a patient has come close to achieving the position represented by the meaningless · , he may try to "manipulate the analyst to give
interpretations so that the session is used to deny complete meaninglessness
and thus to provide reassurance against the dread that all meaning, all source
of meaning, has been annihilated. This dread is associated with belief in the
breast as the source of meaning as, physically, it is felt to be the source of milk"
(1965, p. 101).

Thus a patient who has more or less managed to achieve a meaningless
existence may develop a parasitic relationship with the analyst's meaning-
creating function. Hope is not lost if one is still frightened by the approach of
total meaninglessness and the analyst is used as a source of reassurance that
life is not as bleak as the patient fears it is.

To the extent that the analyst falls victim to his good will and soothes meaninglessness away, he may be hated for joining a lie. He becomes a thief who
steals the patient's meaningless self. Hope boomerangs and becomes too great
a burden: it adds to meaninglessness if it leads to dishonesty. Patient and analyst dread the vista of utter meaninglessness. It does not seem possible to maintain integrity and humanness in such a situation.

Bion offers no way out of this problem, but he does offer more ways into it.
He calls attention to the patient's delusional confusion of the source of meaning with the breast as the source of nourishment. One comes to confuse a
meaningful experience—intense satisfaction at the breast—with the source of
meaning itself. Meaning, which is not simply physical, is understood in terms

of a physical model—the breast as the source of milk. A physical object can be treated like a thing and destroyed. However, neither meaning nor meaning-lessness can be destroyed. They are immaterial, invisible, unlocalizable and, in principle, infinite.

If · is used to represent a meaningless position (e.g., position without dura-tion),— · may express directionality within a one-dimensional world on the way toward zero dimensions, a movement of meaninglessness toward more meaninglessness. — · represents meaningless positions that are not yet occu-pied or the principle that there is always a further meaningless point to which one has not yet come. If this is so, suicide may not be an effective way to end the course of meaning and meaninglessness, since there does not appear to be a one-to-one correspondence between physical and mental domains. A patient who knows this may stay alive in order to force the analyst into mean-ingless positions that remain beyond him. The therapy duo may become col-lectors of meaning-less points, but continue to search beyond the points collected.

If patient and analyst succeed in using the analyst's ability to interpret as reassurance against the loss of meaning, a stalemate results. The patient is protected against the challenge of building the capacity to tolerate the inter-play of meaning and meaninglessness. Fear of meaninglessness has the last word. Meaning is used to ward off experiencing the loss of meaning and loses value as a vehicle for expression and exploration. Meaning itself becomes meaningless, an evacuative technique or cosmetic. Dread is blunted or lost as skill in cynically treating meaning like a thing increases. A triumphant use of one's own or the other's cognition is substituted for experiencing one's con-dition. One kind of cipher is superimposed upon another.

In contrast, if spurious mastery is avoided, patient and analyst may explore hitherto unsuspected realms of no-thing. They begin to tolerate glimpses of a fierce nulling will and a tendency that continues after will fades. Different tones and functions of no-thing can be discriminated and partly linked to attitudi-nal contexts.[1]

Bion's focus on no-thing led through a series of signs that represent the growth of awareness of what no-thing can mean, (e.g., · and ———). The use-fulness of these signs as tools for exploring transformations of no-thing is far from exhausted. Nonetheless, Bion reaches a point in his discussion where he

---

[1] Bion's symbol, PS ↔ D, represents a spontaneous oscillation between nulling and creating meaning. PS, D, and PS ↔ D represent different ways of relating to no-things and different ways that no-things are constituted. They signify particular attitudinal contexts, psychic capacities, and operations or ways that psychical objects (specific sets of no-things) are given and used. Since I discussed these symbols more fully elsewhere (1985), my present emphasis is on · , — · , and ←↑. In this I am tracking a specific line that runs through Bion's portrayals of no-thing.

feels the need for signs that represent more purely the directionality, dynamism, and movement of no-thing. He uses reversed arrows (←↑) to indicate that the movement toward, into, or through no-thingness is infinite. This is true not only in the realm of meaning but also in the realm of meaninglessness.

ARROWS IN REVERSE (←↑)

Bion's two backward arrows (←↑) must be understood with reference to his grid, which can be found on the inside covers of *Transformations* (1965) and related works. The grid's vertical axis (from top to bottom: ↓) marks the growth of a raw affective impact into elements usable for dreams and myths, and from there to progressively more differentiated and abstract levels of thought. The horizontal axis (left to right:→) discriminates ways in which the mind works on affects, images, and thoughts at successive phases of their development (or maldevelopment). My simple summary needs qualification and refinement, but serves the purpose of indicating that Bion's backward arrows (←↑) represent the grid working in reverse. (↑) represents the undoing of meaning, its movement backward toward a mute affective impact and beyond that toward zero. (←) represents the undoing of psychic work or mental capacities, so that what we ordinarily mean by mental activity—the mind's use of meaningful objects— becomes null and void.

Bion conveys the character of the nulling movement in the following quotation: "If we use the grid we may replace — · and — —— by ←↑ and ←↑. Such signs represent objects that are devoid of characteristics and lack duration, or position—and, therefore, existence. But the sign ←↑ indicates that the object is not static. ←↑ represents a force that continues after · has been annihilated and it destroys existence, time, and space" (1965, p. 101).

A few pages earlier Bion writes that the point is indestructible (1965, p. 95). Now he conceives of its destruction and of an annihilating force continuing after point, existence, time, and space have vanished. He adds in a footnote, "I do not wish to commit myself to the theory that there is a realization approximating to this force" (1965, p. 101). Bion is not saying that there is a psychic state in which there is nothing but pure destruction. However, conceiving of such a possibility can help one observe vast nulling processes in certain clinical realities; this is a little like postulating a pure vacuum to help one understand falling bodies.

Bion's depiction of a destructive force that is not limited by existence, time, and space may be theoretical, but it is not an arbitrary fancy. It grows out of clinical and personal experience and is rooted in the conviction that it is our evolutionary task to develop a psyche capable of working better with its capacities, including destructive tendencies. One ought not to assume one knows more about destructiveness than one does, nor explain it away too easily. Bion sets a barrier against precocious and facile attempts to "explain" destructiveness by noting how illimitable and inexhaustible it may be.

That ←↑ represents a force that continues after annihilating ·, existence, time, and space indicates that it continues its work off the grid after the grid has been annihilated, bypassed, reversed, or otherwise put out of play. The arrows point past the grid's origin, through zero, into a sub zero dimension. They lead through no-thing after no-thing after no-thing, one kind of nonexistence after another.

There are many different kinds of no-things, some leading into existence and some out of it. Bion makes sure that the realms of no-thing associated with ←↑ are not mistaken for more usual no-things associated with thinking about objects in their absence. He writes, "The state represented by ←↑ is different from that represented by · or ———. If these signs merely represent the place where the object was or could be there is nothing inherently difficult in supposing that they could be used for thinking about objects *in their absence*" (1965, p. 101).

Thinking about objects in their absence characterizes normal representational thought. The place-that-an-object-is-not invites reverie, science, writing, or art. Such actions follow or discover rules that enable no-things to be communicated. Emotional, spatial, or musical realities may be expressed, discovered, created, or elaborated by points and lines arranged in telling patterns. To an extent, the author exerts control over the points and lines he uses and combines and rearranges them until he is reasonably satisfied with the results or feels it unlikely or too difficult to do better.

Where ←↑ replaces the manipulation of point and line, such esthetic, scientific, or common-sense control slides away and veers toward zero rules and limits. What remains is a force outside existence, an inexistent force that continues gathering momentum after it has annihilated existence. I would say that it is a force that clears out all resistance (and thus differentiation), but Bion means it to represent resistance as such, an active force that stops and undoes growth in psychoanalysis, a force within and between personalities that prevents their unfolding. For Bion it is a force that continues after human personality is totally eradicated.

Bion makes it clear that he is trying to investigate an inexistent force or inexistent dimensions populated by inexistent objects. He writes:

The problem posed by ←↑ can be stated by analogy with *existing* objects. ←↑ is violent, greedy and envious, ruthless, murderous and predatory, without respect for the truth, persons, or things. It is, as it were, what Pirandello might have called a Character in Search of an Author. In so far as it has found a "character" it appears to be a completely immoral conscience. This force is dominated by an envious determination to possess everything that objects that exist possess including existence itself. [Bion 1965, p. 102]

Existing no-things may be used to point to inexistent no-things, but the two realms or categories are distinguishable. As with Freud, Bion uses analogy as a tool for psychic exploration. A language has grown up to give expression to murderous, greedy, envious, ruthless, and predatory no-things that lack respect for truth, persons, or things. We experience these no-things as real and existing, although they are attitudes and systems of psychic propensities that cannot be touched like a chair or dissected like a brain. We speak of a bad attitude and link it to destructive actions in daily life, although the bad attitude is not a thing that can be located in spatial terms.

For Bion an existing no-thing, such as an evil attitude, may be the outcome of work done by a no-thing outside existence. An existent no-thing may function as a home for a nonexistent no-thing. Bion gives "immoral conscience" as an example of an existing no-thing that may house a nonexistent no-thing or systems of no-things. In this case what we call character is the result of and/or a place of residence of a force beyond existence. The nonexistent force infiltrates existence in order to proliferate and annex all of it and turn it into nonexistence. In such a case of "possession" the aim of character is to annihilate existence. This happens as a matter of course when character formation is too rigid and stops aliveness.

The old saying that a psychopath (sociopath) has no conscience is grossly misleading in light of Bion's insights. The problem is that he has too much of the wrong kind of conscience: an *immoral conscience.* A malignant kind of superego (de)formation replaces ego development. The psychopath is driven by immoral imperatives and autistic righteousness. He feels wronged and aims to set things right. The world owes him better, his just deserts. He recoils against life's injustice and takes life into his own hands to supply the necessary corrective: his triumph. So-called id and mastery demands become rights of character: "I *must* take/have/be what I (think I) want or else." To whatever crimes or sins he commits, his superego whispers or, more likely, shrieks or cackles, "It is only just." Ego analysis is futile without addressing the nonexistent force that underwrites the persistent self-congratulatory, mocking superego.

On one level, wronged existence demands more existence, often in the key of vengeance and greed. Immoral no-things make use of things for their own purposes, pleasure, or power. Space, time, truth, things, and people become occasions for manipulation, scheming, amoral triumph. Bion penetrates further to the sense of nonexistent no-things that act parasitically and swallow existent no-things and things. It is as if nonexistent no-things are not satisfied not to exist. They cannot bear that anything should be what they are not—that any thing or no-thing should be at all. They can tolerate neither the one-sided fanaticism of immoral conscience nor the complexity of flexibility. They use existence to feed nonexistence rather than the reverse.

If nonexistence envies existence, it cannot be satisfied by existence. Existence remains a tantalizing, if alien, Other. The term "possession" is a buzzword for Bion. Throughout his work he sees it as part of a controlling attitude that blocks the flow of life. Here it is associated with envious determination—the immoral conscience, character stifled by relentless will. As an analogy for the nonexistent force that swallows existence, Bion depicts a personality reduced to will or determination. The "I have a right to/I must get" of psychopathy is character reduced to inflexible determination, a will intolerant of resistance or limits. Yet this will is a barrier par excellence, an enemy of maturation. Nothing outside it qualifies or balances its determination to reduce life to a single purpose, to food for itself. Everything exists to feed its nonexistence.

The patient caught between existence and nonexistence often uses what existence he has to signal that he does not exist. The force of nonexistence acts as a kind of undertow that existence can scarcely resist. Yet there may still be enough alive negativity to compel helpful attention before the personality goes under. The case is far worse when existence is something the patient made up in order to have a take-off point for feeling that he does not exist.

SPACELESS SPACE

An individual may identify more with nonexistence than with existence, impulsively oscillate between them, or experience paralyzing conflict. He may exist enough to feel nonexistence as genuinely painful or be so mired in nonexistence that almost any kind of aliveness is excruciating. A person may go so far out of existence that existence appears as an hallucination or as something conjured up. Each of these cases is characterized by some ratio of nonexistence to existence.

What sense does it make to postulate a nonexistent force or no-thing that swallows up psychic reality or existent no-things and things? Bion notes that he is extending use of Freud's discovery of "the other space," a space not governed by common-sense perception and the law of contradiction.

The rule that a thing cannot both be and not be is inadequate. [1965, p. 102]

The problem is simplified by a rule that "a thing can never be unless it both is and is not." [1965, p. 103]

Bion gives Falstaff as an example of a no-thing that is an existing thing. Falstaff may be more real than some people we meet in daily life. In what sort of place does he have his reality and make his impact? No-things do not exist like actual people, but people cannot truly exist without no-things. Rules that apply to things do not apply to no-things.

When Bion writes that "the invariant under psycho-analysis is the ratio of no-thing to thing" (1965, p. 103), he does not merely point to relationships between abstractions and physical reality. He is attempting to describe the variable realness of no-things. Some no-things are more real than others. Not all characters embodying Falstaff's traits are as real as Falstaff. Falstaff is closer to "the thing itself."

Falstaff is a nonexistent no-thing that achieves existence and a certain kind of thing status as a convivial representation of immoral conscience. He gives pleasure, entertains, instructs, illuminates, makes life more real. Bion expresses this by indicating that $+ \cdot$ and $- \cdot$ can coincide. In Shakespeare's play the no-thing is enriching, the nonexistent force or element or object makes a positive contribution to our lives.

Another favorite of Bion's was Milton's *Paradise Lost*. In *Transformations* (1965) he quotes this work only once and in a different context, but in conversations he often quoted whole sections of this poem. Milton's Satan represents the negative no-thing's agony at its failure either to achieve or swallow up existence. It portrays the envious determination, self-pity, and sense of injustice that drives immoral conscience toward triumph at any cost. Satan's woe and hate fuel a character that is a rigid distillation of something more formless.

Bion's reversed double arrows ($\leftarrow\uparrow$) represent the purely negative operation of the formless force—a dynamic state denuded of character, beyond the ruthless operation of immoral conscience. It achieves different sorts of existence in Falstaff and Satan, who simultaneously represent stages in the breakdown of existence. As noted earlier, the force represented by $\leftarrow\uparrow$ continues to work even after it destroys point, existence, time, and space. It is pure, formless destructiveness, where the term "destructiveness" is a rigid and limiting naming of a domain for which we lack a language.

Bion variously describes $\leftarrow\uparrow$ as a force, "the ultimate non-existent 'object',", "the 'space' and 'time' annihilated object," and an all-consuming "space," a space that annihilates anything that attempts to appear in it (1965, p. 104). Fears of such a space are often seen in psychotic and claustrophobic patients. Bion also cites the Mad Hatter's tea party in *Alice in Wonderland* as a portrayal of aspects of timeless and spaceless space.

Individuals in the grip of such a space feel they have no right to their own space, no rights of self—everything must or ought to belong to space. They feel pressured to give themselves up. Anywhere the individual turns he feels himself "occupying property that belongs to 'space'" (1965, p. 104). He feels forced to misuse, disregard, or abandon the development of personality and psychic functions. "'Space' and the psyche are not felt to be capable of coexistence" (1965, p. 104). Evolution of psyche is stifled, swallowed up. Psychic life disappears or is never born. So much of Bion's writings show ways we substitute a make-believe psyche (an hallucinated psyche or delusional belief in a psyche that is not there) for psychic gaps and deficits.

Bion notes that the term "space" is too positive to cover the full scope of what he has in mind. In its positive aspect it is analogous to "pure, violent emotion, dominated by greed" (1965, p. 104). It empties itself of all objects as fast as they appear, yet is itself, so to speak, filled with infinitely nulling emotion. He thus adds the term "no-space" as the place where space or emotion was, the no-place of no-emotion. "Space" and "no-space" (emotion and no-emotion) may be approximated by anxiety and repose of psychotic intensity (1965, p. 105).

A certain doubleness pervades all of Bion's formulations, even of the force that tends to reduce everything to nothing, the force that continues working after the psyche disappears. A kind of maximal tension characterizes the attempt to achieve maximal tensionlessness. Another way of stating the relationship between space and no-space, an analogical approximation of what is expressed by ←↑, is that low-pressure no-space (no-emotion) devours high-pressure space (infinitely greedy, violent emotion), whereas space continues to occupy no-space.

Bion further trims his reversed double arrow notation from ←↑ to ←↑ (1965, p. 107), but we must save discussion of this transformation for another study. Now it is enough to note that he places a + and — in front of ←↑. Doing so, in part, indicates the tension and oneness of whatever sets of polarities are used to approximate the work that ± ←↑ represents, e.g., the psychospiritual equivalence of stupor and greedy ambition, the stuporous drive to kill life rather than let it escape one's clutches. ←↑ is Bion's most simplified and elegant arrow notation for the force that takes us off the grid and continues working after undoing psychic life. It is off the map and perhaps unmappable. Yet, oddly, it seems to throw up representations of itself and its own undoing activity, sorts of bleeps that need to be interpreted or explored in some way. Bion refuses to assign a too restrictive or definitive meaning to these notations (e.g., ←↑), but uses them as flares that provide glimpses of dark work before they fade from view.

REFERENCES

Bion, W. R. (1965). *Transformations*. London: Heinemann.
——— (1970). *Attention and Interpretation*. London: Tavistock.
Eigen, M. (1973). Abstinence and the schizoid ego. *International Journal of Psycho-Analysis* 54: 493-497.
——— (1985). Toward Bion's starting point: between catastrophe and faith. *International Journal of Psycho-Analysis* 66: 321–330.
——— (1986). *The Psychotic Core*. Northvale, NJ: Jason Aronson.
——— (1993). *The Electrified Tightrope*. Northvale, NJ: Jason Aronson.
Heidegger, M. (1957). *Identity and Difference*. New York: Harper & Row, 1969.

7

The Area of Freedom:
The Point of
No Compromise

Why did Winnicott's paper, "Transitional Objects and Transitional Phenomena" (1953), become his most popular work? "Mind and Its Relation to the Psyche-Soma" (1954), read two years earlier at the British Psychoanalytic Society, was at least as important, and Winnicott expressed even more satisfaction with some later papers.

One reason is that the transitional object paper gave practitioners some thing to hold on to. Discussion of processes could be anchored to observation of behavior, e.g., attachment to a doll or blanket. For many practitioners, Winnicott's paper became a kind of transitional object itself, a me–yet–not–me possession, a vehicle to aid expression and orientation. It offered something more or less concrete to dig into and rally around.

Papers on the transitional object proliferated. They were part of the new "Age of the Mother" in psychoanalysis. Early mother–infant interactions came to center stage. Winnicott's speculations were refreshing because they were not couched in dogmatic language. Practitioners from any school could use them. They were especially welcome to those who felt inhibited by Melanie Klein's and Margaret Mahler's concepts, yet were receptive to a depth psychological approach to intersubjectivity.

Winnicott's work is a breath of fresh air. He makes his way through the claustrophobia of psychoanalytic minefields and gives voice to his sense of freedom as a psychoanalytical person. I do not think Winnicott's work can be understood without reference to the importance he placed on "feeling free." Even practitioners who view the transitional object in a most reduced sense, merely as "mother substitute," understand that it represents a growth of freedom for the self.

OBJECTS, PHENOMENA, AND AREA

Winnicott's formulations allow themselves to be taken in many directions. Transitional objects may be soothing insofar as they stand for the breast or mother. They may be used to deny separation. However, in certain instances they emphasize separation and stand for an endless gap they forever try to fill. Transitional objects may carry forward the richness of experience or be a place marker for an experience never had. They may stand for rich or unreal mothering and mediate a rich or unreal self.

Transitional objects are important for what they are not, as well as for what they are. They are not mother or self, although feelings of mother and self are invested in them. They are something else—something other than Mother and me, although filled with the latter two. They are something less than Mother and me and something more. They are objects that can be handled, cared for, abused, lost, and rediscovered. They can be controlled.

Above all, they are *mine*. Winnicott describes them as first not-me "possessions." Not the first object of object relationships, but "the first possession." The importance of possession is already a sign, a premonition, of all that cannot be possessed, of the vast claims I will have to abandon, of the vast claims I will have to discover, of new unknown worlds ahead in which possession and freedom clash and play.

Winnicott introduces his concept with the term "objects," but quickly enlarges it to "transitional phenomena" and "transitional area." He speaks first about concrete objects because it is easier to see an object than to grasp an area of experience. People know what he means when he calls attention to an infant's addiction to a blanket or doll. Winnicott uses this object as a lever to open up an area of experience that is neither quite inner nor outer. The first bit of not-me possession is neither wholly other nor simply part of the self. It is not a hallucination, but an actual object filled with meaning, with meaning for me: it is my *own* with bits of me and Mother and itself blended in a way that does not fit any single category.

Transitional phenomena may include an infant's babbling or a child's repeated songs while preparing for sleep. The transitional expands into art, science, religion, and culture in general or contracts into addictions and fetishes. Winnicott's concept covers a lot of ground. It is no wonder he has been criticized for being vague. Vague but usable. It is no wonder that many practitioners have tried to tie him down.

THE INTERMEDIATE AREA

Winnicott pointed to the area that "felt free" by noting that it was neither Klein's internal object world nor Freud's reality object world. Winnicott did not want to be trapped by subjectivity nor by the claims of objective perception. The terms "inner" and "outer" were buzzwords for Winnicott. In psychoanalysis they were tied to dogmas related to "internal fantasy," "reality resting," and the like. He did not find enough room in Klein and Freud for the sort of *experiencing* that felt free.

Inner and outer also had broader connotations both clinically and culturally. In informal clinical terms, "internal fantasy" called up the specter of being stuck in one's own world, entombed in a fantasy bubble. Idealism seemed to be mired in various (often productive) solipsisms. The attitude embodied in Hobbes's saying, "The mind knows nothing but what the mind creates," was mathematically fruitful. The various German egologies drilled wells of subjectivity. Nevertheless, there were casualties (eg., the premature deaths of youthful explorers of subjectivity, as well as madness). The subject entrapped by his own webs began to feel unreal to himself. The split between the internal subject, on the one hand, and his body as object linked with the material universe, on the other, became too much to bear. Human personality collapsed under the strain. Everything inside and outside began to feel alien.

With Freud, the last bastion of personal unity—the ego—was undercut. Freud succeeded only too well in his will to celebrate the mortification of the Western ego, no longer master in its own house. Germanic egology recoiled on itself, and the backlash set in. For Jung, subjectivity was an archipelago of centers orchestrated by a grand Self synchronous with the World Spirit, which included materiality in its unfolding project. Winnicott's touch was lighter. He did not want to be boxed in even by Jung's open-ended schemes. No psychoanalytic language that he knew of enabled him to feel free or did justice to the freedom feeling. At the end of his life, Winnicott was still shedding language skins.

The problem pressing on him was how to develop an account of experience that was not boxed in by inner and outer. One gambit was to develop the category of "between" or the "intermediate." Existentialism and phenomenology were well on their way by the time Winnicott began searching for a voice. Martin Buber had developed his own "between" in *I and Thou* (1958). His saying, "All real living is meeting," catches something of the tone Winnicott was searching for.

Nevertheless, Buber was not a pediatrician who became a psychoanalyst. He was not obsessed with the birth and growth of the infant self or the hair-breadth twists and turns of psychosomatic tonalities in sessions. For Winnicott, the "between" was a developmental concept. He was concerned not only with the moment of meeting but also with the meeting's biography and evolution. He was concerned with an area of experience that felt free. But the freedom feeling too has its developmental movement, its unfolding. Winnicott described a succession of homes for it. The "transitional area" was one of his attempts to let freedom ring, but not his last. Winnicott's attempts to offer a developmental account of personal freedom also underwent development, as he became freer.

THE SUBJECTIVE POOL AND LINKING WITH EXPERIENCE

Winnicott associates transitional objects and phenomena with *illusion*, which he describes as "at the basis of initiation of experience" (1953, p. 14). Transitional objects are also signs of "progress towards experiencing" (p. 6) and of an "area of experience." The emphasis here is on *experience* and *experiencing*. What is crucial for Winnicott is linking up with one's own experiencing, that which makes one feel true and real.

When one is most alive and real, can one locate experiencing as simply inside or outside? Inside and outside contribute to aliveness, but is this most precious x localizable? I think of St. Paul not knowing where he or mind or body was during a moment of grace. At such a moment, inner and outer did not seem to be relevant categories. Either and both would be too confining.

Winnicott uses the term "illusion" in a positive sense to signify the continuity or lack of rupture in the me-yet-not-me moment, in which self and object are not located in opposition to each other. The infant is not asked to decide whether he has created or discovered the object. The need to objectify or locate self and object would rupture or put the brakes on linking and would dispel illusion.

Winnicott was concerned about avoiding promiscuous use of the term "symbol." X as a symbol of Y(or of W, Y, Z, A, B, C) is a form of thought overused in psychoanalysis. Actual experiencing is swallowed up by symbol hunting. Thus although the transitional object may have symbolic meanings, Winnicott insists that "the point of it is not its symbolic value so much as its actuality" (1953, p. 6). Whatever it may stand for, it simply is. The *being* of the transitional object is what counts most. In its being, it stands beneath distinctions that support use of the symbol.

In an important sense, "being" is a developmental concept for Winnicott. Whatever being is, it is involved in a process of becoming. A clearer sense of distinction between inner–outer grows in the process of development. For Winnicott, "the term transitional object . . . gives room for the process of becoming able to accept difference and similarity" (1953, p. 6). What is important here is the process of becoming, of developing a sense of division rooted in the unity of being. He speaks of "giving room," of making space for what is not overly restrictive, of room to breathe and move, an area of freedom. One *comes through* union, distinction, distinction-in-union in order to link up with the experiencing that is fed by, yet transcends, dualistic categories.

Winnicott uses organic growth terms, like root and core. "I think there is use for a term for the root of symbolism in time" (1953, p. 6). He is concerned with an area that underlies and gives rise to the growth of symbolism. His focus is not the symbolic end products themselves, but on processes that give birth to symbols.

He finds it important to point out that the term "symbolism" changes meaning, that our understanding of symbolic processes is limited and open, and that use of symbols is not uniform. For one group, the wafer in communion is the body of Christ, for another it is "a substitute, a reminder. . . . Yet in both cases it is a symbol" (1953, p. 6). And in both cases there may be a heightening of experiencing, an intense sense of the meaningfulness of life, a healing of divisions. Whatever the ratio of symbol:real may be, the *experience itself* contributes to the sense of life's holiness.

We may enter into various relationships with illusory experience as it branches into art, religion, or madness. "We can share a respect for *illusory experience*" (1953, p. 3) or form groupings on the basis of such shared experiences. Winnicott calls the similarity of illusory experience "a natural root of grouping among human beings." Again, *root*, a growth term, is used. Winnicott tries to feel his way toward the roots of personality or self and social groupings. He rides experience like a gentle surf board, as far as he can. He wants to live his way toward where we come from, to a growing place or places out of which personality branches. Roots grow throughout the life of a plant and remain vehicles of nourishment for upper areas.

Winnicott does not like being tied down to his own terms. He means to use them flexibly, although there is a gentle fierceness in his writing, something rigorously uncompromising. He is concerned that the experiencing he so values may be compromised or swallowed up by terms. It is the growth of experiencing, especially freedom, that concerns him. Terms are pointers and expressive vehicles that may further experiencing, but they are dangerous helpers, easy to solidify or pervert.

It is thus important for him that entrance to the transitional area may take many forms. The vast area between subjectivity and objectivity teems with possibilities. One may link up with transitional experience even from a split-off sliver of self, a self lost in unreality. As an example, Winnicott describes a case in which the only thing that was real for a woman was the unreality of her life (1953, pp. 20–25). Her transitional area of experience masked and gave voice to a sense of something missing at core and roots. *She* was missing. *Real* parenting was missing. Yet she and her mother could appear marvelous. They had so much to offer around the blank core, including real goodness and good intellect.

Her transitional objects in childhood supported her sense of the basic goodness of life and tried to convince her that things were going well, that life was as it should be. In this case, transitional objects supported a lie. They maintained her, but threw her off the scent. To the degree that they functioned symbolically, they symbolized something that was not real. They themselves were a reality manqué. What was most real about them was their maintenance of a false self. They blotted out what was missing. The very goodness of her parents made repeated loss of them devastating, until what became most real was the loss that could not be represented and lived. The sense of loss became buried in an image of goodness. It had to be discovered in the patient's inability to live, in her loss of real experiencing.

The patient sank into a "pool of subjectivity" and discovered how she tried to maintain herself over the underlying sense of no-life or nothing. She hoped the analyst would join up with the inner mother who buoyed her up and protected her from the null dimension. She hoped the analyst would be there as she wished her parents were, so that the missing reality would stay out of reach. If this tendency won out, the analyst would sink into "the general pool of subjectivity" (p. 25) and join up with her mother to protect her from the gap or absence.

Instead she was able to make use of the analyst's silence and his destruction of silence to recognize the silence at her core, the no-parents and no-self. She could experience her need to use the analyst's life to stay above the deadness. She could taste the freedom that recognition of lack provides. She began to treasure the space made possible by real absence, a gap not stuffed by falseness. She could do this because of the real support the analyst gave her to experiencing what was not there. At last the missing real, the no-thing or thing that was not there, became part of real existence. In what was missing, she found room to link up with herself, stretch, and begin to grow.

FROM OBJECT TO MISSING FUNCTION

What a distance was traversed in Winnicott's paper on transitional experiencing! From the discussion of concrete objects clung to by infants to a missing sense of realness in an adult patient. In pathology, objects are used as substitutes for missing functions. In a healthy infant, use of objects carries the real self forward. Winnicott focuses attention on both health and pathology in transitional experiencing.

His example of an adult woman's missing sense of realness announces the central theme of his mature clinical writings: the search for a real or True Self. What he is most vexed with in his adult patients is their missing sense of realness, their failure to link up with, sustain, and live from True Self feeling. Some live in a fantasy world, some in a world that is too realistic. The link between attitudes or functions is missing. The experience of the between, the intermediate area, the wonder of illusion, is deficient. *The first possession* with which Winnicott was concerned was the patient's own, most real and True Self.

His earlier clinical studies tended to emphasize the patient lost in his or her own world, the pool of subjectivity, a fantasy bubble. His later writings tended to emphasize individuals trapped in an overly sane, realistic, objective attitude. In both instances, he laid increasing stress on the developmental function of rage in clearing away obstructions and restrictions. In this effort, "The Use of an Object and Relating through Identifications" (1969) was a high point (see also Eigen 1981a, 1986).

USE OF OBJECT

The apparent simplicity of Winnicott's formulations masked a burgeoning complexity. The simple presence or absence of an object tells little about how the object is used. What is missing in an object may be used to reject what is available. What is present can be used to hide what is missing. One can build a case for or against self or object with whatever is or is not there. Complexity itself can become maddening, a source of rage. How good it is to clear the air of all the directions in which our complicated unrealness can take us. How good it is to explode and clear the air of our oversimplified one-sidedness. Both complexity and one-sidedness can be stultifying.

In his "use of object" paper, Winnicott (1969) emphasizes the use of rage or fury or destruction in feeling and becoming free. The personality explodes in reaction to its sense of unreality. The self tries to break out of its fantasy bubble, its one-sidedness or aimless complexity. Rage, fury, and destruction burst forth. Everything hinges on the response of the object. If the object survives the attack well enough, the patient gains a new sense of realness and tastes the joy of making use of others for real growth purposes. Genuine appreciation grows. A new dimension of object relating opens.

"From now on the subject says 'Hullo object! I destroyed you. I love you. You have value for me because of your survival of my destruction of you. While I am loving you I am all the time destroying you in unconscious *fantasy*'" (Winnicott 1969, p. 90).

A real sense of contact emerges. The impossible happens. I can really use another for my own true growth. I do not have to falsify myself in order to be with another person. All the destruction in me did not destroy what counts most, but actually made relating more possible. I do not have to develop along the line of false appreciation. I do not have to feel like an ungrateful monster for biting the hand that feeds. We survive each other. We grow with and through each other.

Winnicott emphasizes the importance of the object not retaliating or otherwise collapsing under the onslaught. In the face of a bombing, the other acts naturally, remains himself, sees what is happening, and is responsively supportive without the loss of integrity. The result is subject-to-subject contact and the freedom of using true properties of another for personal growth. In this context, fantasy elaborations of what we take from others are productive, since we keep returning to the place of meeting, clear our minds, and start again.

We live between aloneness and intersubjective aliveness. "Between" is not killed by "making use of." These dimensions extend each other. They carry the real self to more and more worlds, more openings, more experience, from light to light.

Winnicott's message certainly sounds like an idealization, a wish. Can such interactions really happen? Is communication without compromise possible? Is such flexible benevolence on the part of another under attack possible? I answer a qualified yes by making use of Winnicott's concept of "unintegration."

UNINTEGRATION

There is gentle light in Winnicott's writings but also soft darkness and what cannot be called simply light or dark, the intermediate area beyond clear-cut categories. What supports the emergence of the transitional area and objects that shine in transitional experiencing, and what supports the emergence of self facing a usable other, is the hidden capacity of the personality to give itself up and drift.

Freud spoke of "free association" for the patient and "free-floating attention" for the analyst. In his letters to Fliess, the capacity to drift is an essential element of his method and language of creativity. In spite of many differences, Winnicott and Freud both feel that creativity makes life worth living: "life is worth living or not, according to whether creativity is or is not a part of an individual person's living experience" (Winnicott 1970a, p. 39, see also Eigen 1983a). Freud speaks of riding on the unconscious and letting the horse go where it will. Winnicott emphasizes drifting with experiencing or the lack of experiencing, the importance of just being: "Be before Do. Be has to develop behind Do" (1970a, p. 42), and "Creativity is then the doing that arises out of being" (1970a, p. 39).

Winnicott shares Freud's belief in the critical importance of unconscious feelings. His emphasis, however, is not on the "repressed unconscious" but on the fact and feeling of existing "as a basic place to operate from" (1970a, p. 39). He means existing in a highly personal way, as one's own self. The fierce personalism that stamps Winnicott's work is deeper than and provides relief from one's official personality.

At the end of his life Winnicott was more concerned than ever with new beginnings, with working and living from scratch. Experiencing for him meant *creative experiencing*, newness, freshness, aliveness, coming into life for the first time, finding, allowing, stretching, turning oneself over. He dreaded becoming addicted to some official version of himself, let alone to someone else's version of selfhood.

> Evidently I must be always fighting *to feel creative*, and this has the disadvantage that if I am describing a simple word like love, I must start from scratch. . . . By creative living I meant not getting killed or annihilated all the time by compliance or by reacting to the world that impinges; I mean seeing everything afresh all the time. I refer to apperception as opposed to perception. [Winnicott 1970a, p. 41]

To see everything afresh all the time, to incessantly start from scratch, means letting built-up versions of self go so that one can drift. Winnicott likens this to a time in infancy before there were built-up versions of self. He pictures a time of "primary unintegration" when the baby drifted through a variety of states without organizing them in line with specific ego scripts (Eigen 1986, chapters 4 and 8, 1989; Phillips 1988, pp. 78–81; Winnicott 1945, pp. 149–155). At times the baby "came together" in more unified ways. Integrated units of experience come and go. The baby did not yet feel pressured to harden itself into one or another integrated mold. He did not yet develop the need to rigidly cling to and use integrated moments in chronically defensive ways.

The mother's job is to support responsively the infant's being, so that it could follow its own impulsive doing and its own interests and rhythms, as it passes through unintegration to integration and back again. "In order to be and to have the feeling that one *is*, one must have a predominance of impulse-doing over reactive-doing" (Winnicott 1970a, p. 39). This "impulse-doing" meant acting out of unintegration, forming oneself anew out of the drift, coming together freshly, seeing things with new intensity, throwing oneself into the fullness of experiencing, being gripped by doing that will make life meaningful because it grows out of "a basic place."

We can see how thoroughly Winnicott's commitment to freshness has undergone distillation in his final positive emphasis on unintegration. Much earlier he referred to unintegration as resulting from the "failure of technique of child care" (Winnicott 1952, pp. 98–99). At the end of his life, he writes, "It is only here, in this unintegrated state of personality, that that which we describe as creative can appear" (Winnicott 1971a, p. 64). Even earlier Winnicott distinguished unintegration from disintegration, a radically terrifying, catastrophic state. In his later paper, he also warns that the creative use of unintegration hinges on sensed environmental support; otherwise, it may go on too long and pass into disintegration.

Unintegration and Madness

In a sense, unintegration refers to an innate capacity to unhinge oneself, to let links that become chains drop away. When Winnicott introduces the notion of primary unintegration, he mentions in passing how sanity can be imprisoning: "There is . . . much sanity that has a symptomatic quality, being charged with fear or denial of madness, fear or denial of the innate capacity of every human being to become unintegrated" (1945, p. 150).

A posthumously published paper, "Fear of Breakdown" (1974), represents the most definitive and beautiful crystallization of Winnicott's mature views on madness. Adult fear of breakdown refers to breakdown that already happened. The infant undergoes agonies that its equipment cannot process. Experiencing is life for Winnicott, but it also may present too much, too soon; recall that for Freud, the primal trauma was flooding. Sensitivity is taxed with more than it can bear and manage. We have to grow equipment to process what is too much for us. We have to become the kind of beings that catch up with our breakdowns, not so much to master them as to enable experiencing to develop.

Early parenting tries to compensate, as much as possible, for the infant's insufficient equipment. The mother does a great deal of processing of what the infant is going through for the infant. She holds the situation open until the infant has the time and ability to accommodate its own experiencing capacity. She helps the infant over periods of breakdown. She helps her child develop a certain flexibility, not simply compliance, in the face of incapacity and gives her child time to recover and grow.

The situation is complicated by the fact that the parent inevitably adds to the infant's burden and vice versa. At any time, too much of the wrong thing or too little of the right thing may be present. The mother may inadvertently tax the equipment she means to ease and cause breakdowns that she then tries to repair; her own equipment may be sorely taxed as well. What is crucial is that personal care survives the breakdown: the mother's devotion comes through her own and the infant's incapacity, for she is the kind of being one can forgive and link up with after the storm or blackout. The thread of personal being survives and may be strengthened by disruptions, as new areas of experiencing continue to open up.

Typical Winnicottian therapy addresses "the schizoid spot" that develops to compensate for the persistent failure in personal care (Winnicott 1971b, p. 67). When the link with one's most basic self and mother cannot survive disruption and breakdown, the individual "cures" himself not simply by the use of repression or splitting but also by means of serious dissociations from himself and others. Depersonalization/derealization not only signals breakdown but also results from it. As Freud indicated, the building up of delusional compensations is an attempt to maintain or regain a sense of continuity, an attempt to continue or start again: self–other connectedness survives horrific devastation, especially devastations tied to vicissitudes of self–other connectedness/ disconnectedness.

The sense of unreality acts not only as a protective cocoon or distancing operation. In the case of Winnicott's patients, it is also a goad, an irritant. They are appalled as their life passes by unlived. Whether they are withdrawn or are very active and keep up the appearance of living, they are compelled to bear witness that something crucial is missing in their sense of self. They are bothered by being dissociated from themselves and others. They are basically sensitive beings who are bothered by their success or failure in attempts to immunize themselves from their sensitivity (Eigen 1992).

Winnicott's therapy created an atmosphere in which two people could be alone together without all the time trying to make sense of what was or was not happening. Developing a capacity for play (transitional experiencing) went along with tolerating unintegration and madness:

> The person we are trying to help needs a new experience in a specialized setting. The experience is one of a nonpurposive state, as one might say a sort of ticking over of the unintegrated personality. I referred to this as formlessness in the case description. . . . In the relaxation that belongs to trust and to acceptance of the professional reliability of the therapeutic setting . . . there is room for the idea of unrelated thought sequences which the analyst will do well to accept as such, not assuming the existence of a significant thread. [1971a, p. 55]

One does not have to irritably reach after facts or meaning or anything at all. One can just be and grow into and out of just being. One can be missing. The great secret of being missing, which is so taboo, can be experienced. One can relax into not being there and stop pretending. One can stop forcing oneself this way or that. The possibility of being truly alive—free—in the presence of another person emerges.

Winnicott always emphasizes the importance of nonintrusiveness on the part of the analyst. He is all too conscious of the way analysts impose their dogmas on patients, substituting one sort of straitjacket for another. Patients are prone to be compliant/rebellious, and too often, therapy provides an ample opportunity to continue a reactive style in more subtle ways. In Winnicott's writings, nonintrusiveness is often linked with the analyst's silence and capacity to wait. He wants to give individuals every chance to get beneath reactive styles, to unintegrate, to grow out of chaos or no-thing. He wants to give them every chance to be free.

He wrote that when he was younger he was more prone to say clever things, but in time he learned the wisdom of silence so that the patient can find himself. Nevertheless, it is also clear that Winnicott talked, could talk a lot, could be directive, presumably as part of "holding" or "provision." Winnicott indicated that he did not remain silent long if he felt the patient would be injured by too much silence. He might say something to let the person know he was there or to become aware of limitations of Winnicott's understanding. Silence can foster a sense of omniscience that speaking dispels (Eigen 1986, 1989).

Winnicott also indicated that a patient may benefit from displays of the analyst's hate and madness. There are instances when what is missing is the realness of hate (Winnicott 1949). Nothing may seem real or believable until hate is real and believable. At times what is missing is the realness of madness. Some of the best, most surprising, and usable things an analyst can say may at first seem crazy to the patient (and possibly the analyst), yet ultimately make the patient (and possibly the analyst) feel more real (Winnicott 1971b, pp. 73–74).

Winnicott writes a lot about the craziness of secretly being the opposite sex (1971b, pp. 72–85; 1971c, pp. 119–137). We all have unconscious cross-sexual identifications that can lead to fear and confusion and feel like a kind of madness. But there are more unbearable and nameless agonies, more formless dreads (Winnicott 1974). The analyst who can live at the cutting edge of his own madness may enter into a creative and redeeming relationship with madness (Green 1975). He may provide immunizing doses of madness in such a way that the patient begins to link up with the unnamably unbearable and develop a relationship with the horrifying holes that scare experiencing away.

The analyst's use of madness, if placed in the service of growth processes and not simply or mainly narcissistic masturbation, enables the patient to link up with what he supposed could not be tolerated. Experiencing can link up with itself across periods of breakdown to the extent that one *owns* madness (Winnicott's transitional *owning*) and learns the art of enabling it to contribute to overall movement. As Milner emphasizes, what seems mad and perhaps is mad can prove saving (1987; see also Eigen 1973, 1986). Without madness one cannot be free, although literal insanity is terrifyingly enslaving (Eigen 1984, 1986, 1992).

Writing about transitional experiencing was one step in Winnicott's growth toward being able to admit and use madness, to the point of feeling freer through it and becoming more radically helpful. To the overly operational or objective attitude, transitional experience must seem a bit mad. Similarly, the subjectively enclosed individual might idealize transitional experiencing, but actually find it threatening and disorganizing. Both must let go of one-sided madness to tolerate the sort of paradoxical madness that Winnicott treasured, the madness associated with creative living and the birth of culture. The letting go Winnicott describes in object usage and unintegration is part of the mad growth that makes life worthwhile. Through it, our sense of the mystery of freedom deepens.

It is no accident that two of Winnicott's most mature sympathizers recently published books with madness in the title (Green 1986, Milner 1987). My own book, *The Psychotic Core* (1986), must be considered in this category. Late in life Winnicott wrote, "I was sane and through analysis and self-analysis I achieved some measure of insanity" (1964a, p. 450; quoted by Phillips 1988, p. 152). In the closing sentence of *Winnicott* (1988), Phillips remarks that "his measure of insanity is, I think, an inspiration."

THE INCOMMUNICADO SELF

Winnicott's most well-known and apparently valued contributions revolve around his emphasis on the infant–mother dyad: there is no such thing as an infant, but an infant–mother psychosomatic field. The quality of the surrounding and supporting milieu is the crucial medium for development of the psychosomatic life of the child. Throughout his career, Winnicott stressed the contribution of the ordinary good-enough mother and what can happen should the environmental provision be lacking. Elements of child care that foster personal growth were his persistent concern. It is natural for practitioners to pick up Winnicott's emphasis on the "holding environment" in clinical situations.

It is also natural for practitioners to do a double take when, in the midst of his interactive emphasis, they come upon passages that claim that the most precious core of self is noninteractive—permanently incommunicado. These are Winnicott's most passionate passages, almost pleas or prayers. They contain his most religious language:

> Each individual is an isolate, permanently non-communicating, permanently unknown, in fact unfound. . . . At the centre of each person is an incommunicado element, and this is sacred and most worthy of preservation. . . . Rape, and being eaten by cannibals, these are mere bagatelles as compared with the violation of the self's core, the alteration of the self's central elements by communication seeping through the defences. For me this would be the sin against the self. [1963, p. 187]

The sin against self is communication with the core of cores, the self beyond reach, the self that is essentially private, one's psychic heartbeat. This is Winnicott's moral imperative: do not reach what must be unreachable. Do not seep into the core of another person so as to steal him from himself.

Not many practitioners have taken this teaching of Winnicott to heart. Someone as close to Winnicott as Guntrip tried to brush it aside. Guntrip never accepts Winnicott's positive valuation of aggression (Guntrip 1975, Eigen 1981b, 1986), but he also rejects Winnicott's emphasis on the essential incommunicado self, a permanently noncommunicating core of cores (Guntrip 1969, Eigen 1973). A self that depends on an interpersonal matrix for its development—how can what is most precious about it be outside the range of human communication? A self that must not be found, that requires hiddenness—this does not sit well with the "neediness" Guntrip feels to be most basic. For Guntrip, Winnicott is not Winnicottian enough.

However, the problem is that Winnicott is all too Winnicottian. He fought everything else. He made use of everything else. It is hard to think of Winnicott as a fierce fighter because he was a gentle soul, so light of touch. His writing melts in one's mouth like butter. Yet he gave voice to his own brand of biblical reality in developmental terms, as uncompromising as a prophet.

The incommunicado self is the center of his work, the still, quiet center. Everything else revolves around it, grows out of it, guards it, extends it. Transitional experiencing, object usage, and unintegration link up with the unlinkable. They open a path of experience and expression for what is most true and real and free about oneself, a kind of vector of freedom, a thread of personal creativeness. Winnicott's language expresses, opens, and discovers waves of what is most precious and personal, the core that must not be betrayed. He finds a way to make people feel pulsations of the core in everyday life, in analytic sessions, in cultural work.

Guntrip is dismayed by Winnicott's insistence on an incommunicado core, in part because it reminds him of Freud's id, which is basically out of contact with the outside world. Indeed, Winnicott knowingly uses Freudian locutions to paint a picture of a state of being before the awareness of externality. Winnicott's insistence on a sacred, silent core is his version of the primordial beyond contact.

Freud has a passionately personal relationship to his concepts. But for the sake of formal presentation and scientific respectability, he followed acceptable epistemological guidelines. We never know the id and the rest of the repressed unconscious directly, only by inference and hypothesis. If it is a reality, the id is as out of reach as are external things in themselves. By contrast, Winnicott's assertion of a core out-of-contact self is meant as more than a bow to Kantian considerations and is certainly not meant to appease canons of scientific respectability. It is an expression of personal faith, an attempt to preserve room for the most precious point of existence.

Winnicott describes freedom partly as flexibility of defensive organization, and he recognizes the usefulness of an adaptive false self. But he also writes that for each person there must be a place of no compromise: "I suppose that it would be true in a general way to say that although a compromise is usually possible in everyday life, there is no compromise for each individual in some area that is chosen for a special treatment. It may be science or religion or poetry or games. In the chosen area there is no room for compromise" (Winnicott 1964b, p. 70).

Winnicott—spontaneously, through creative struggle over years, his "secret" continuity across chasms—built an expressive fence around the core of cores with his concepts of transitional area, true self/false self, use of object, unintegration, and use of madness. For Winnicott these were not concepts cut off from experiencing but expressed what for him made life feel most real. May we not say that here is his chosen area where there is no room for compromise?

MORE THAN THE HEART CAN BEAR

Winnicott does not underestimate the complexity of the situation in which we find ourselves. In order to use objects or madness and live creatively, we must have the equipment to do so. Psychophysical equipment may be damaged from birth or from something lacking in the environmental provision. It may suffer from immaturity that in some way remains chronic. Depth psychology tries to enable the growth of psychic equipment as much as possible and develop better compensations to the extent that the equipment is irreparable.

One does not help another individual find or grow equipment for creative living without sacrifice. Winnicott repeatedly speaks about the importance of the analyst growing the capacity to wait (responsive waiting, waiting-in-aliveness). The analyst must outgrow cleverness for his own satisfaction and cultivate the silence that lets the core of core do its work. At the same time, the analyst must act naturally, like the ordinary good-enough mother who, for a time, spontaneously molds herself along the infant's developmental lines. Such paradoxical demands permeate analytic work. The analyst must bear and enjoy the tension of paradoxical living, as paradoxical truths shift from stage to stage.

The ordinary good-enough parent bears a lot. Analyst and parent alike suppress themselves in order to help children and patients find their paths. To a very significant extent, the helper dampens himself and becomes compliant and uncreative in order to be a good-enough helper. Winnicott notes that this is partly offset by the satisfaction gotten for a job well done. Our identifications with the helped one and the helping process partly compensate for the temporary or long-term loss of self: "Where we are bringing up children or starting babies off as creative individuals in a world of actual facts, we do have to be uncreative and compliant and adaptive; but, on the whole, we get round this and find it does not kill us because of our identification with these new people who need us if they too are to achieve creative living" (Winnicott 1970a, p. 54).

People who have undergone grave, deadening processes in order to survive cannot take too much life in the analyst. The analyst learns to keep stimulating aspects of the session within semi-tolerable bounds. If necessary, he becomes dead enough for the patient to feel safe enough to come alive more. As the patient is able to tolerate more aliveness, the analyst may allow his own personality more play. In therapy, analyst and patient must grow the equipment to bear and ultimately enrich each other.

Yet even if the analyst must sit on himself and make it look easy, muted aliveness remains. In some way the analyst finds ways of surviving the impact of deadening processes, even those self-imposed for therapeutic reasons. The core of cores remains unaltered, hallowed, and hallowing. It resurfaces and continues being, quietly glowing beyond the necessary darkness. The inherent creativeness that makes life worth living for the analyst, suitably modulated, finds ways to let the patient discover and reach for his own openings.

Winnicott firmly believes that we need to attack goodness (1970b, pp. 262–268). He also believes that we deeply wish for the survival of the goodness we attack. We need to attack falseness, compliance, and hypocrisy, and we hope there is enough to us and our lives that something really good and true wins out. Yet that goodness too must be tested. Can it truly endure? Is goodness indeed more basic than evil, or is it one more phony layer aching for exposure? Can the good take our hatred of it as well as our love?

The pressure the analyst is under is immense. An ultimate aim of the analysis is the real survival of goodness. This requires the sacrifice of personality and natural inclinations. It also requires the maintenance of basic aliveness and spontaneity. The analyst must rein himself in, yet survive his own discipline. The analyst must survive being an analyst. Paradox is all!

The fact that mutual adaptiveness, recognition, and appreciation characterize mother–infant relationships from earlier on than previously believed does not mitigate the fact that the mother modulates use of her equipment to work with the infant's capabilities. Devotion enables the mother to find ways of being spontaneously that are usable by the infant. The fact of the matter is that the mother cannot do with the infant what she can do with other adults. Yet there is something she can get from being with a baby that slips away from adult living. A loss, a gain.

The mother grows equipment she did not know she had by playing down well-used equipment. As her child grows, old equipment comes back ready for use in new ways. Every analysis that goes deep, long, and far combines these processes. The analyst must grow the equipment usable for the particular analysis at hand. Who knows what twists and turns of self this might take? Let us say it—who knows how he will have to twist himself out of shape for a particular person who could not bear to be with him otherwise? Still the analyst's ruthlessness and madness also will contribute to the patient's growth, if real creativeness is to survive destruction, if aliveness is to come through—if goodness is to stand the test of the analysis and survive the destructiveness of patient and analyst alike.

Similar considerations may operate in our relations with colleagues. Will our professional milieu survive us and we it if we make our fullest and truest offerings? To what extent do professional interchanges support transitional experiencing and object usage and contribute to the real growth of personality and culture? We need each other to bounce off, fight with, communicate and noncommunicate with, interact with, gain real confirmation/disconfirmation. But how much exposure can we bear? How much do we dare or have the right to dare?

Winnicott's first major heart attack came shortly after his father died, and this was followed by a long-needed divorce. Apparently Winnicott's psyche–soma was unable to hold and process the affective impact at hand without explosive collapse. The timing of his coronary, linked as it was to a revolution in his life, seems to establish a somatic vulnerability tied in with Winnicott's exquisite sensitivity.

As a result of the crises, he resumed his life on better footing and made enormous strides on both personal and professional fronts. *True Self* activity increased. It is no accident that he associated the True Self with heart and breathing: "The True Self comes from the aliveness of the body tissues and the working of body functions, including the heart's action and breathing" (Winnicott 1960, p. 148). In this quotation one might substitute the word "especially" for "including."

Near the end of his life, Winnicott was even more vulnerable somatically, partly because of a fragile, aging body but also because of his need to be alive in experiencing, which at times left him too open. His sensitivity could be too much for his psyche–soma to bear.

When I saw him in the middle 1960s he told me he was considering speaking in New York. He repeatedly asked how he would be received. Clearly he was worried about the New York psychoanalytic climate. It was as if he was afraid to believe that they could really receive what he had to say, that equipment to make use of his work grew there. He had hopes, but he was aware of his vulnerability, although he had had practice being odd man out in his own world. I was flattered by his anxious questions, but I was only a graduate student. He treated me like an equal, like *someone.*

I would be receptive. I would love to hear him talk. I knew that others in my situation who would too. But what did I know about the particular world he addressed with his fears and hopes? At that moment, my own oddness in graduate school vanished. I saw his awkward intensity and thought, "He's like me. It's all right to be the kind of person I am." He moved around the room, found an edge of the couch, and doubled over, reaching for a way of conveying something about the kind of work he did. He wanted it to be alive. He did not seem to care much if he looked foolish—he was digging into something, being true to an experience, a life work, an area of discovery. He was giving me permission to be myself, so much as I dared. Now I am tempted to write that in his anxious state he was expressing a foreboding, a premonition.

He came to New York and gave his "use of object" paper in 1968. I am told he was attacked and did not defend himself; true to the mother-analyst's position in this paper, he did not counterattack or retaliate. He went to his hotel room and had a heart attack. The tension between hope and fear, between ruthlessness and waiting, must have mounted to a breaking point once again. He was lionized posthumously.

Winnicott continued working creatively three more years until his death. His prayer, "May I be alive when I die" (C. Winnicott 1978), pertains to more than physical death. It refers to his need for sensitive aliveness in the midst of nothingness, attack, catastrophe, madness, and a variety of agonies. Winnicott sometimes paid a high price for his need for aliveness, but it gave as well as perhaps took everything. Winnicott's title for his autobiography was *Not Less than Everything* (C. Winnicott 1978).

We do not know to what extent or in what ways his vision of the self's *attempt* to burst shells and find real experiencing was fulfilled within his lifetime or after his passing. Clearly, he did not always survive the destruction that greetcd him, his own or others. But his vision of survival is a legacy. In one of his last pieces, while speaking of the monarchy, Winnicott writes:

> The survival of the thing (here monarchy) makes it valuable, and enables people of all kinds and ages to see that the will to destruction had nothing to do with anger—it had to do with love of a primitive kind, and the destruction occurs in the unconscious fantasy, or in the personal dream that belongs to being asleep. It is in the personal inner psychic reality that the thing is destroyed. In waking life, survival of the object, whatever it is, brings a sense of relief and a new sense of confidence. It is now clear that *because of their own properties things can survive, in spite of our dream. In spite of the backcloth of destruction in our unconscious fantasy. The world now begins to exist as a place in its own* right; a place to live in, not as a place to fear or to be complied with or to be lost in, or to be dealt with only in day-dream or fantasy indulgence. [1970b, pp. 263–264]

Here is the voice of a master, the ring of simple nobility. It comes from and touches the heart. The living of this vision—finding, creating *its* realness—involves risks that require equipment to support them. The achievement Winnicott depicts is made possible by evolution of psychosomatic equipment sufficient to support it, at least for moments and then across moments. One's equipment may fail and leave one stranded in aliveness too much for the heart to bear. What is alive in one's work may be passed on to others. Surely something of Winnicott's "area of no compromise" is growing for us today.

REFERENCES

Buber, M. (1958). *I and Thou.* New York: Charles Scribner's Sons.

Eigen, M. (1973). Abstinence and the schizoid ego. *International Journal of Psycho-Analysis* 54:493–497.

———— (1981a). The area of faith in Winnicott, Lacan and Bion. *International Journal of Psycho-Analysis* 62:413–433.

———— (1981b). Guntrip's analysis with Winnicott. *Contemporary Psychoanalysis* 17: 103–117.

———— (1983a). A note on the structure of Freud's theory of creativity. *Psychoanalytic Review* 70:41–45.

———— (1983b). Dual union or undifferentiation? A critique of Marion Milner's view of the sense of psychic creativeness. *International Review of Psycho-Analysis* 10:415–428.

———— (1984). On demonized aspects of the self. In *Evil: Self and Culture,* ed. M. C. Nelson and M. Eigen. New York: Human Sciences.

———— (1986). *The Psychotic Core.* Northvale, NJ: Jason Aronson.

———— (1989). Aspects of omniscience. In *The Facilitating Environment: Clinical Application of Winnicott's Theory,* ed. M. G. Fromm and B. L. Smith. Madison, CT: International Universities Press.

——— (1992). *Coming through the Whirlwind.* Wilmette, IL: Chiron.
Green, A. (1975). The analyst, symbolization and absence in the analytic setting (On changes in analytic practice and analytic experience). *International Journal of Psycho-Analysis* 56: 1–22.
——— (1986). *On Private Madness.* London: Hogarth.
Guntrip, H. (1969). *Schizoid Phenomena, Object-Relation, and the Self.* New York: International Universities Press.
——— (1975). My experience of analysis with Fairbairn and Winnicott. *International Review of Psycho-Analysis* 2:145–156.
Milner, M. (1987). *The Suppressed Madness of Sane Men.* London: Tavistock.
Phillips, A. (1988). *Winnicott.* Cambridge, MA: Harvard University Press.
Winnicott, C. (1978). D. W. Winnicott: a reflection. In *Between Reality and Fantasy*, ed. S. Grolnick et al. New York: Jason Aronson.
Winnicott, D. W. (1945). Primitive emotional development. *International Journal of Psycho-Analysis* 26.
——— (1949). Hate in the countertransference. *International Journal of Psycho-Analysis* 30.
——— (1952). Anxiety associated with insecurity. In *D. W. Winnicott: Collected Papers.* New York: Basic Books, 1958.
——— (1953). Transitional objects and transitional phenomena. *International Journal of Psycho-Analysis* 34:89–97.
——— (1954). Mind and its relation to the psyche-soma. *British Journal of Medical Psychology* 27:201–209.
——— (1960). Ego distortion in terms of True and False Self. In *The Maturational Processes and the Facilitating Environment.* New York: International Universities Press, 1965.
——— (1963). Communicating and not communicating leading to a study of certain opposites. In *The Maturational Processes and the Facilitating Environment.* New York: International Universities Press, 1965.
——— (1964a). Book review: *Memories, Dreams, Reflection* by C. G. Jung. *International Journal of Psycho-Analysis* 45:450–455.
——— (1964b). The concept of the false self. In *Home Is Where We Start From.* New York: Norton, 1986.
——— (1969). The use of an object and relating through identifications. *International Journal of Psycho-Analysis* 50:711–716.
——— (1970a). Living creatively. In *Home Is Where We Start From.* New York: Norton, 1986.
——— (1970b). The place of the monarchy. In *Home Is Where We Start From.* New York: Norton, 1986.
——— (1971a). Playing: creative activity and the search for self. In *Playing and Reality.* New York: Basic Books.
——— (1971b). Creativity and its origins. In *Playing and Reality.* New York: Basic Books.
——— (1971c). Interrelating apart from instinctual drives and in terms of cross-identifications. In *Playing and Reality.* New York: Basic Books.
——— (1974). Fear of breakdown. *International Review of Psycho-Analysis* 1: 103–107.

PART II

CLINICAL PROBES

8

The Immoral Conscience

Self-righteousness often masks an immoral conscience. It may sound odd to call conscience immoral—isn't conscience the home of our sense of morality?—but the sense of rightness that conscience carries may work for good or ill.

Milton's Satan in *Paradise Lost* is filled with self-pity, agonizing and majestic loneliness, and ruthless envy and revenge pervaded by a sense of being justified. His course is set by a sense of being wronged, getting his own back, setting things right. All real tenderness or caring for another's good is annihilated. What is left is maligned consciousness that is convinced that whatever it does is justified by its sense of injury.

The child abuser often justifies his or her actions with self-righteous accusations against the victim: the child is evil and needs correction. The child abuser often declares that he or she was just trying to set things right. The abuser may have been an abused child, which adds to his sense of justice.

The old saw that psychopaths or sociopaths lack a conscience is wrong. The problem is they have too much of the wrong kind of conscience, an immoral conscience. A voice tells them that they are right to steal, kill, maim, injure, whatever their heart desires—it is only just. They are balancing the scales. Hitler was driven by such an immoral conscience with his sense of national self-righteousness, and it did not take much to enlist the immoral conscience of multitudes. But one does not have to be Hitler to be a Hitler.

THE NEED TO BE RIGHT AND FEEL GOOD

Ben

Ben was a therapist dedicated to living the good life.[1] He did things that made him feel good and helped others do the same. Ben was also a truthful person.

---

[1] I have written about Ben's therapy at length in my 1992 book, *Coming through the Whirlwind*.

He loved psychological truth. In public demonstrations he was adept at getting people in touch with sadness, fear, or rage—all in the service of discovering joy. Truth meant working at what stopped good feelings, so that one could, as Joseph Campbell suggested, "follow one's bliss."

In his personal life, Ben had a short temper that he did not think he needed to control. On the contrary, he was proud of his outbursts. His fury was part of his realness. Ben felt doubly justified if the target of his anger could not show anger like he could. In such a case Ben was being real not only by showing his rage but also by helping another person do the same.

Ben's dedication to feeling good, true, and real masked intolerance, rigidity, and the need to control. Those who were inhibited or slow in self-expression were judged as phony. They were not real like he was. At best they were not in contact with themselves. More likely they were superficial or lying to themselves. His rage would help them be more real.

The results were disastrous in Ben's intimate relationships. Similarly, his economic situation was precarious. Whatever he built fell apart. His dedication to feeling good worked well enough in the 1960s, but he did not know what hit him when inflation soared. He reached middle age with little to show for it, except a certain talent in the therapy situation and an image of himself as a fine performer.

He had always assumed that some day he would become a father and build a family. However, he could not see that he drove away those closest to him. He placed others in an impossible predicament. He demanded that they be as free as he, yet serve him and cater to his whims. They should be his clones and servants—mirror selves. Ben's bouts of anxiety and depression increased as his failure to control others and life began to matter more. Time was passing. He was getting older. His life failed to take hold and build on itself. With all his "realness" he was left only with an image of himself as a performer—and this image, that had so long offered him warmth and solace, now chilled him.

Ben found his way into my office when his latest relationship was faltering. He was deeply involved with a serious woman. He could not fault her for being superficial, but he raged at her for being more depressed and contained than he. Ben experienced her sense of inferiority as withholding. She needed time to process experience and she balked at his push for quick emotional fixes. She was not easily rushed or bullied. Ben's insistence that she be instantly available threatened to ruin their chances of staying together, and they were considering marriage.

The long uphill climb of our therapy is beyond the scope of this chapter. Ben stayed with me for many years, and the course of his life was reversed. He has made something substantial of himself and has built a professional, family, and personal life that matters. My emphasis here is on his almost total blindness to the immoral aspect of his attitude toward others and himself. He felt right in what he did, no matter how wrong things turned out. His training and expertise as a mental health practitioner fed, rather than balanced, an underlying self-righteousness. He hunted truths like a headhunter might hunt heads—yet his use of truth always seemed to bolster his position.

I could empathize with the traumatic background that fostered dissociations in his personality, but it was more important that Ben develop the capacity to *see* himself. He was good at accusing others or himself and weeping and raging in reaction to his accusations, but he was not very good at staying with an experience and letting it build. His dedication to truth seemed to get rid of experience.

The immoral conscience kills experience. Its sole aim is to be right and feel good. Such an attitude does not care if it twists self or other out of shape. Ben had chronically twisted his sweetheart's words and actions in ways that made her seem ugly to herself. What mattered was *his* will or ego or needs. He spoke rapidly and he turned whatever she said against her, so that she was driven to silence. He won, she lost. But he had been on the verge of losing the possibility of living a satisfactory life.

THE FORCE

The immoral conscience works like a blind force. It impels one to act as one does. One apparently cannot help oneself. Yet it has its own radar that can be devastatingly accurate. There is cunning precision to its explosiveness. It can be destructive in uncannily fitting ways. Greek tragedy attests to an esthetic, if terrifying, order that links unconscious intentions with punishing events. Perhaps this aspect of Greek tragedy was what most attracted Freud, whose work was a detailed working out of "fate neurosis," the ways that fate follows lines of character.

Perhaps the Jewish Bible is not far off in linking the fate of a nation with its (in)ability to follow God's good laws. Humankind is now at a place where the work of immoral conscience is poisoning the planet, and the goodness of law is made poisonous or vacuous by cynical manipulation, disregard, or fundamentalist rigidity.

Bion (1965) writes of a force that continues "after . . . it destroys existence, time and space" (p. 101)—after it destroys personality or selfhood. Such a force is like a Pac Man that feeds on existence. It envies aliveness and does not want any life to escape it. Yet wherever it does its work, existence or aliveness disappears.

We cannot say that such a force truly exists—since by definition it destroys existence, including its own. But Bion makes a terribly strong and dramatic statement by picturing the rolling on of destructiveness ad infinitum, a rolling on through subzero dimensions after all that can be destroyed has been destroyed.

Such a grim depiction of pure destructiveness may exist only as an idea, but it stands as a warning not to explain destructiveness away, not to pretend that we can control or master destructiveness in any simple way. We can try to do the best we can in working with immoral conscience, our *fatal flaw*.

Our fatal (fate-full) flaw tends to hit us through blind spots—it is our blind spot par excellence. Must we wait to see the results of the whole of our lives before we learn about it? Must humankind wait to see the results of the whole of history before learning? And what kind of *seeing* is possible or fruitful? What can we *do* with our *seeing* (or see and do with our doing)? Are we capable of the kind of learning that can make a difference?

Walker

Walker was more than depressed. He felt drawn out of life by a lethal mixture of inertia and poisonous thoughts. He seemed to come to therapy in order to be able to say that at least he tried it before going under. He could use his time in therapy to say that nothing works—an excuse to give himself up totally to the force.

Walker felt too weak to do anything about the force. It sapped his strength, sucked him from within. Most terrifying of all was the way he justified the force. He marshaled intellectual arguments on its behalf and sided with the mocking, cynical voice that cackled, "Everyone is phony. Life is a sham. It is all a big lie. Nothing is worth it." Most chilling of all was the self-righteous edge of his tone and demeanor as he justified the devil's call (see Eigen 1984 for portrayals of the devil in psychotherapy).

Events in Walker's life made his submission to the force understandable. His father had been blown up on a ship while trying to help others. His older brother had been accidentally shot to death by a friend in high school. His intelligent mother had tried to shape him according to what she said rather than what she did. She got remarried to someone—a Harvard graduate—who drank himself into oblivion and, finally, death. And she drank herself blotto daily.

For years Walker had tried to help her but failed. He never quite gave up because he so wanted and needed to save her. Yet he hated her for lying to him as he was growing up. She foisted her snobbish, self-righteous better-than-thou ideology on Walker, who was enjoined to act and to be better than she. She groomed him to be what she pretended to be. The falsity of it stuck in his gut without his realizing what was happening. He kept trying to repair the damage by making her better, by making her live up to her own expectations, by making her come alive.

There was a time when Walker tried and life carried him along. He married and built a house himself—he was very handy. He drew, built furniture, and played music. He studied healing and for a time was a healer. He was a photographer and something of a computer expert. He never went to college. Instead he joined the army and afterward raced cars.

In time his wife went off with his best friend and a good portion of his inheritance. He never recovered from the blow—his wife was proof of life's futility. To try was conceit. The undertow began to steal him from himself.

Walker missed many of his sessions. When he showed up he reported the latest string of futilities. There were momentary flareups of aliveness—a walking trip in the wilderness, a few moments with a new girlfriend, some success as a computer expert. But his eyes were riveted on the darkness. Life drained away. Moments of aliveness mocked him and merely reinforced how dead he felt the rest of the time.

He was absolutely righteous about his conviction that deadness was the truth about his life, that everything else was phony or futile. Feeling bad had won out over feeling good as the baseline of experience, but the need to be right was as intense as ever—to be right about life's uselessness. The proof was the lying Walker saw everywhere. The proof was the way human beings poisoned the world. The proof was in the seemingly irreversible collapse of his own mind and body, more like air slowly leaking from a balloon than an explosion. Walker saw the truth and was convinced he was right and that what he saw was not worth seeing. For Walker only the force was real.

Although Walker gave up on life, life did not give up on him. People liked him and his beautiful, if dark, way of speaking. He tried to be helpful to others in his own way, at least at times. He was a bit like the son of Kong, the white ape who was as helpful as his father, the dark King Kong, was destructive. As the son of Kong drowned he saved others by keeping them in the hand he raised above the flood.

There were openings and countermessages in his dreams from the very depths of his being (or nonbeing). They produced images of cataclysms, especially floods, in keeping with his official presentation of himself. They portrayed helplessness, upheaval, the loss of self. But good women figures and creative men also appeared. These reflected tendencies that Walker insisted were dying or gone or useless. His dream life did not seem to believe him, nor he it.

Life did not die out in Walker's dreams. The dreams went their way, tending to their business, sometimes producing images that went along with Walker's attitude, but at other times rubbing him wrong. They refused to be bullied or encompassed by his despair. His dream life remained, at least in part, beyond the force. It continued to produce bits of potentially usable creativeness that came through the faithfully expressed cataclysms.

One of these good dream figures was a teacher whom Walter never saw before. The teacher was kindly, firm, and inspiring and used whatever materials were at hand. Walker's damaged state did not stop him. The teacher was partly an idealized version of myself, but also the guide within. I, like his dreams, kept coming back for more, a male authority dedicated to new possibilities.

He would have to run away from me before I totally succumbed to him. Would he have to run away from his own psyche as well? Could he truly and permanently escape his inner guide?

Walker tried to kill therapy off and, to a significant extent, succeeded. But body breathed, mind thought, soul felt—even if the force nulled their work as fast as it started. Walker's psyche produced the teacher who transcends death. If such an image was possible, Walker could not have given up completely. The wish for creativity was somewhere alive and challenging. It was easy for Walker to connect with destructiveness, but not with creativeness, and it was this living link that, above all, was missing.

IMMORAL CONSCIENCE AND OMNISCIENCE

Freud made much of the "omnipotence of thought," but did not systematically distinguish between omnipotence and omniscience. Following Freud, the mental health field has neglected the distinction between omnipotence and omniscience, although much is to be gained by reflecting on their difference.[2] Omnipotence tends to refer to the exercise of limitless power in physical terms, of mind over matter. Omniscience refers to more purely mental power, mind over mind. Both can be exceedingly dangerous, but unbridled omniscience represents the greater danger for humankind as a whole.

The imaginary omnipotence of the bully sooner or later comes up against some chastening physical limit. A stronger bully will knock him down, and he will be forced to find his place in the scheme of things. This applies to individuals and social groups alike. One runs up against undeniable limits in the struggle for physical power.

The situation is not so clear in the realm of mental power. Mind is invisible and intangible. The belief in secret mental powers is not easily subject to disconfirmation because it transcends the play of bodies. The terror that one's very mind or self may be taken over by alien mental powers is greater than the brutal ordeals of physical slavery. Religions instinctively express this terror by representing the greatest bliss and torment in immaterial terms (i.e., God and Satan as pure spirits).

In today's world the know-it-all is more lethal than the bully. If one thinks one knows more than one does and acts on this overestimated "knowledge," the consequences can be grave indeed, given the deadly scope and art of current weaponry. What one thinks one knows or fears one doesn't, imaginary rather than actual knowledge is likely to determine the outcome of an uncer-

---

[2] Exceptions may be found in the work of D. Meltzer (1973), W. Bion (1970), and especially H. Elkin (1972). I discuss omniscience at length in *The Psychotic Core* (1986), Chapter 8.

tain chain of events. It is difficult to bear the tension of uncertain outcomes. Omniscience forecloses uncertainty. Miscalculation from the standpoint of omniscience can be disastrous; the Bible was right in associating the seduction of omniscience with disaster.

In clinical terms omniscience murders experience and is very prevalent. The conviction that one knows what one doesn't and is right in one's stance molds experience along very narrow channels. One uses truths one discovers to blind oneself to other truths. A kind of psychic rigor mortis sets in. One truncates experience to fit one's preconceptions rather than suffer the upheaval of bathing in living waters. One gladly glosses over the sense of pretending to know more than one does for the ease of manageability of untidy subjectivity.

Ben flew above his experience, whereas Walker was stuck below it. Each felt he was right about his world view. For years Ben *knew* he was on the side of inner truth and was helping others to get there. His anger was justified. He was trying to open others up. He was trying to get them to be as honest as he so that they could live their own lives. He was adept at turning everything around to fit his viewpoint. He could not see that over the course of many years his life was at a standstill or going downhill. It took time, loss, the threat of further loss, and desperation to make an opening possible. Even then Ben fought for his rightness, his truth—against the clang of years. He would have to stay with what he knew was right and oppose time and existence, or learn to work with the flow of life.

Walker too was addicted to a rigid, murderous truth. He could see life's lies at a glance and was determined not to give into the seduction. Life made promises it could not keep. Phoniness was everywhere. People did not know how to get along with one another, and it was no longer worth learning and probably not possible. Walker felt right about the nothingness of things and his "why bother" conclusion. The rightness of his truth annihilated possibility.

Ben could not drop down to life, and Walker could not rise up to it. Ben could not give up his manic high—he was an emotional turn-on addict—and Walker could not escape inertia and lethargy. One could not stop flying; the other could barely crawl. For Ben and Walker existence recoiled against itself, yet each held onto his rightness for dear life or, more precisely, held onto rightness against life.

The sense of being right substituted for real living. It provided some compensation for what one didn't or couldn't have or be. It filled gaps and stopped movement to unoccupied positions. It killed off the possibility of there being unoccupied positions to move to.

Both Ben and Walker followed conscience, their sense of rightness, their truths. But something was off with their conscience. Each outsmarted life's defeats and openings. It was as if *rightness* occupied the place where *living* might have been. Ben not only revved things up but he also had a morality of superaliveness. Walker not only pulled the plug but he also had a morality of futility. The rightness of each was intense. Ben's rightness added intensity to rigidity, and Walker's rightness added intensity to slackness. The intensity of rightness tied Ben and Walker to oblivion.

In the course of a long therapy Ben raged against seeing himself, but seeing himself also led to heartfelt weeping. He cried his heart out over the kind of person he was—what life had made of him and he of himself—and struggled for a more appreciative and serviceable vision of virtue, deformation, and lack. To this day Walker has not yet wept these bitter tears, at least not with me, and the outcome is in jeopardy.

RIGHTNESS, DEFICIT, AND HATE: A NOTE ON EVOLUTION

It may be that our minds originally grew up to fit the needs of survival. At some point in our history mind became aware of itself, and we grew into creatures who possessed a sense of emotional truth. For some portion of humanity issues of *how* we survive became as (and sometimes more) important than survival itself. The possibility of conflict between integrity and survival arose.

Bion (1962, 1970, Eigen 1986, 1992) notes that a mental apparatus that grew up to meet survival issues may be ill equipped for issues of emotional truth. The *intrinsic quality* of life, the lies we live, the collective and individual self-poisoning processes, the search for fuller, truer living—our equipment to handle such concerns may be in infancy or perhaps just being born. It may be only in the last 5 to 20,000 years that our interest in these kinds of problems has begun. This may be part of what the Bible means by dating Creation about 5,000 years ago.

Our equipment gives birth to problems it cannot handle. It is hoped that this will stimulate the further development of equipment. In this process a sense of deficit—acute at times—must be lived with. At times we are like the child who covers up his inability to read with bravado or even delinquency. It is doubtful we will ever catch up with ourselves or learn to read ourselves satisfactorily. But we can keep on learning. We can become partners in the business of developing the equipment (capacities) to better work with ourselves.

Hate often molds itself along lines of deficit. We have a sense of injury. We compare ourselves with others and note injustices. Hate and envy may propel equalizing activity. We may try to get ahead of others and ourselves and outflank our sense of deficit. However, materialistic success may not compensate for deficiencies in our equipment to utilize such success.

Our productions—emotional, economic, and technological—outstrip our ability to process them. Hatred as a chronic response to deficit may increase productivity for a time, but may narrow or diminish or harden the growth of ability to process it. I do not think we can live without hate, and hate certainly has its uses—we hate lies and injustice as well as truth—but hate does not solve the problem of the growth of equipment.

The need to feel right can be exploited to cover deficits and is often linked with hate. Together they are elements of an immoral conscience that makes believe it knows more than it does—misuse of unconscious omniscience—to gain some spurious advantage over others, self, life, or deficit. A danger is uncontrolled inflation succeeded by unprofitable collapse, a destructive sequence—victory of the force that wipes everything out.

Life's equipment is blessed with normal tranquilizing mechanisms. Babies blank out when they are too stressed. To an extent it is normal to soothe away bad feelings with good ones, to substitute pleasantness (imaginary or real) for difficulty. Feeling right is one such natural narcotic. Like hate, it blurs emotional complexity and uses intensity to narrow the psychic field. To be right about everything is promiscuous, but can we settle for less? To be right about anything can be dangerous depending upon dosage and its use (misuse). To be right about something—our lives, our truths—to finally get it right—what can be more gratifying? What else is it all about? Yet we ought to label our sense of rightness: "High Voltage—Handle With Care."

REFERENCES

Bion, W. (1962). *Learning from Experience*. London: Heinemann.
———— (1965). *Transformation*. London: Heinemann.
———— (1970). *Attention and Interpretation*. London: Tavistock.
Eigen, M. (1984). On demonized aspects of self. In *Evil: Self and Culture*, ed. M. C. Nelson and M. Eigen, pp. 91–123. New York: Human Sciences.
———— (1986). *The Psychotic Core*. Northvale, NJ: Jason Aronson.
———— (1992). *Coming through the Whirlwind*. Wilmette, IL: Chiron.
Elkin, H. (1972). On selfhood and the development of ego structures in infancy. *Psychoanalytic Review* 59:389–416.
Meltzer, D. (1973). *Sexual States of Mind*. Perthshire, Scotland: Clunie.

9

The Counterpart

OVERVIEW

What a burgeoning literature there is on the *counterpart*. From its inception, depth psychology has been fascinated with the multiplicity of the self. Freud informally wrote of the unconscious as another kind of consciousness. His structural theory charts the interweaving of systems of otherness within the personality. Jung amplifies this vision by describing an archipelago of encounters with the otherness of self, linked by growth of a true self thread. For Lacan, the unconscious is Other, made up of multiple Others, another place or scene, another language.

Winnicott's false self is a counterpart of the true self. It may protect the true self or act as a substitute, a counterfeit. The false self is a reactive defensive system. The true self is the active center of personality. It is allied with undefensive being, out of which creative doing grows. True self impulses grow out of open being. Pulsations of the true self often seem mad, tyrannical, or fearful, as well as inspiring, whereas a healthy false self may make life more fun, effective, and sane. Some people, like Van Gogh, live solely from true self feeling (see Winnicott on Van Gogh in Rodman 1987, p. 124). Too great an intolerance of the false self or false self deficiency can be disastrous. Sometimes it is hard to tell the difference between the true and false self, and sometimes the distance between them is unbridgeable.

French authors have used the terms "crypt" or "vault" to describe a sealed-off aspect of personality. More recently, Bollas (1989) uses the term "ghostline personality." Such attempts portray dead counterparts.

This discussion of the otherness of the self is organized around three main themes: the taint, the split, and the force or nullity.

THE TAINT

Smith frequently described himself as tainted.[1] The taint ran through his personality, his being. He felt this from his earliest days. He was a very alive and energetic man and lived a full life. He did a lot of true self living. Yet he felt the fabric of his life was warped: his true self was warped. He was a gay psychoanalyst who had affairs with young men. At the same time, he remained married to one woman throughout his adult life and had grown children, one of whom was a homeless schizophrenic.

When I saw Smith, he was a nearly broken man suffering from advanced heart disease. He sought help because one of his affairs threatened to ruin his professional career. It seemed as if the skew in his self had taken a cumulative toll.

What was the true self, what false? Smith kept up a front with his family, yet had true affectional ties with his wife and children. He loved music. He was at once controlling, assertive, manipulative, and seductive, a charming man. At professional meetings, his remarks were discerning, probing, and open. He was sensitive to the most alive currents in the field. In his homosexual affairs, he lived out dramas around what Khan (1979, pp. 12–16) describes as "the idolized self," a kind of manic, megalomanic bingeing on ideal feelings. At such moments, he felt most alive, but out of the corner of an eye he stared at the warp. The warp never left him.

Poets write of a worm that spoils the rose of experiencing. Religions depict a tendency to spoil integrity or goodness. The Jewish Bible erects a bulwark against the spoiling tendency, a system to manage the evil inclination, but difficulties proliferate. What violence the love of Jesus has unleashed upon the world! Psychoanalysis explores links between ideal and violent feelings and joins the sensitive thread in history of those who unmask lies we live.

Weil's (1958) "repressed bad self," a "garbage" or "shit self"; Balint's (1968) "basic fault," especially the abysses of the "malignant regression"; and Bion's (1970) evocation of a poisoned self, a self not simply poisoned by a bad breast but by the lie one lives—these are among many ways to circle in on the "off point," the skew, the warp, the wound that never heals.

THE SPLIT

The taint is often organized and expressed by splitting processes. In Smith's case, splitting was highly complex and dangerous. An observing mental ego

---

[1] Smith is also described in my earlier writings: "On Demonized Aspects of the Self" (1984) and *The Psychotic Core* (1986).

never stopped working and oscillated among several attitudes. At times it was a befuddled onlooker, as if stupefied by events. Consciousness ticked like a clock, but did not make sense of anything. Smith's life might have been lived by someone else except that, by an accident of fate, it happened to be happening to him.

By degrees a bemused smile would appear on the face of consciousness, a dapper devil, a sickly transcendence, the mockery of the victim victor, the eternal "heh-heh." Below the smile was the mute explosive body, really a body self: a screaming self, an exploding heart, or perhaps a heart that failed to explode but withered.

Ideal feelings blew in and out, lighting the whole system and then leaving it in darkness. At times, the ideal filled Smith's eyes: a young man appeared who looked like perfection. At times, an eye-heart connection was made, and Smith courted his beloved as in a dream. More rarely still, a blessed moment of eye-heart-genital connection arose, which, as likely as not, would be spoiled by something. At times, the spoiler was an acute pang of hate, or doubt, or too zealous possessiveness. At times, painful differences obtruded as fusion mounted, or revulsion and unsatiated demand soiled the aftermath.

Smith might try to rev up the ideal feeling: if only it would last long enough to see an experience through. He could coast on it for a time, but effort was needed to keep it going. His realistic eye never stopped seeing. No fault escaped him, not his own, nor his lover's, but as long as the ideal feeling lasted, faults were irrelevant, even funny and endearing.

When "normal" ego functioning returned, Smith's efforts went into repairing the damage. He picked youths he could nurse. They fell apart, and he took care of them. His mental or transcendental ego became parental, while his body ego fragility and fragmentation were experienced through his lovers. He sometimes devoted years to efforts of rehabilitation and tended to be successful. Launching someone's life gave him great satisfaction. Smith bulled past intimations of his own weakness and felt strong and good as the helper. His life was encompassed by a sense of goodness. An inner factory incessantly turned bad feelings into good ones. Yet success was cloying. The warp never left. The taste of the warp pervaded the goodness. His body could not support the life his psyche fabricated, and eventually it collapsed beneath him.

In my books and papers I explore aspects of a split between an occultly transcendent mental self and a fusional–explosive body self. This split is the core pathological structure of our time. The mental self may use knowledge of the world to navigate portions of life relevant to it. It may rely on cognitive maps, instrumental learning (means–end or causal relationships), and interpersonal observation. However, the mental self is more or other than scientist, philosopher, and political strategist. It is plugged into the ideal as well as real.

Psychic systems carve themselves out of an ocean of ideal feeling. Megalomania is more than inflation. It is a reminder of the more from which we come.

Deflation is as much a disease as inflation. The operational personality overly relies on means–end know-how, and denudes life of fantasy. The smaller self fears losing territory to the larger self, and the larger self fears squeezing into restrictions and boundaries that the smaller self takes for granted. Which is more afraid of which? (My book, *Coming through the Whirlwind* [1992], includes dialogues between smaller and larger aspects of self as an attempt to heal the split between them.)

Ideal feeling may take the form of omniscience in the mental self, omnipotence in the body self (Eigen 1986). Omniscience-omnipotence often fills gaps where one might sense deficit. Coming up against deficit opens glimpses of underlying streams of ideal feeling held at bay by acts of knowing. The complexity of relationships between terms of experience may prompt us to side with one term against another (splitting), rather than stay alive to the play of similarity–difference. We are engaged in a long-term learning process, thousands of years old, in which we dimly apprehend workings of the diverse capacities that make us up and carry us along. Our destiny is to become partners with our capacities.

At times, it seems that ideal feeling becomes tainted and distributes itself along mental self–body self axes in poisonous ways. To an extent, splitting activities try to contain the taint. Klein (1946) and Fairbairn (1954) describe ways that selective dissociations save pockets of health from destructive absorption. We know only too keenly how containing structures become tainted and become part of the problem. We are always part of the problem, since we are figures in larger structures.

THE FORCE: ADVENTURES IN NULLITY

Bion writes of "a force that continues after . . . it destroys existence, time and space" (1965, p. 101). After everything is destroyed, the force continues destroying. Destruction goes on in subzero dimensions. The existence of such a force is perhaps impossible, since it cancels existence, but that is precisely its power. Dante's Hell is amateurish next to regions of nullity evoked here.

The false self slows the force down. It variably absorbs, deflects, or binds fringes of the force. The false self can also further the work of the force. At such times it appears to be an offshoot, a ray of the force, driving the self deeper into nullity. More often the false self is on the side of life. It expresses a refusal to die out or give up. It may protect the true self like a bad big brother. True self elements are usually mixed up in it.

The mix-up of true self–false self may hopelessly confuse a person. The force feeds on and takes advantage of this confusion to infiltrate the personality, so as to annihilate not only the true self but the false self as well. Usually we worry about desecration of the true self, the holy spark within. We battle with compromises and lies that poison as they save us. Yet the false self has its own brand of holiness, as it tricks and wheedles and perseveres, like Jacob and Rebecca, to carve out a place where the best in us comes out. It refuses to forfeit the Blessing.

The force's conquest of the true self seems to be easier than conquest of the false self. The force turns the energy of personality against itself (aggression against libido transforms into destructions of libido as a companion to the destruction of personality by libidinal flooding) and uses evidence of corruptibility to solidify despair—the conviction, hypnotic suggestion, or hallucination that integrity is lost forever and life is not worth living. At this point, it seems that the force is content with turning the false self into a devil or systems of devils that persecute, rather than protect, true self elements. These elements collapse under pressure as morale is undermined by bullying, cajoling, and propagandizing. The force promises the false self that it will lose nothing and gain everything: it will get more of what it wants and grow stronger, both opportunistically and through long-range planning.

Taking advantage of enticements or opportunities can now be used as evidence of underlying weakness, a succumbing of true self elements. What is noble in the self hates itself. The false self capitalizes on the true self's grief by converting its hatred of its corruptibility to hatred of weakness as such. The false self feeds on true self weakness and traduces and recruits true self elements; it uses those elements to justify itself, if shame still exists in the scheme of things. The false self gloats at the true self's shame, provoking the true self to hide or disappear (go to another world) or seek the false self's protection. The force uses the false self to block or spoil the true self's connection with God (destruction of dependence as opening). True self hopes against hope that false self will save it, converting dependence to parasitic addiction (idolatry), as it plunges toward idiocy.

The bloated false self exploits the true self's crises of faith. As long as there are crises there is agony, the personality's fever. What a relief to give in to false self and feel peace for a time. The true self "learns" that its connection with God is too weak to save it: for all things that count in life, its connection with God is simply irrelevant. The false self does so much more for it, so much more quickly. So the true self buries itself in the false self's energy, and for a time life may go on better than ever.

The true self's fearful clinging gives false self the illusion of indispensability. At the height of its power, the false self ignores its sense that the force is using it. It is too caught up in its own momentum to care. Yet once the true self has shifted its center of gravity from God to the false self, the false self's work is over. The force dismantles and destroys it.

That the force goes on working after it destroys existence, time, and space means that it destroys the various counterparts of existence, time, and space (Bion 1965, pp. 110–112). The false self is a privileged system of counterparts or substitutes. It does not realize that victory weakens it. By absorbing the true self, it cuts itself off from the larger destiny of existence. By weakening or nullifying the true self's connection with God, the false self loses support of its own ground. Head and gut split off, and the heart spins into oblivion or sentimentality.

Bion partly represents this state of affairs by putting existence and related terms in quotes. The force may be represented and personified by a nonexistent "person" whose hatred and envy is such that "it" is determined to remove and destroy every scrap of "existence" from any object that might be considered to "have" any existence to remove. Such a nonexistent object can be so terrifying that its "existence" is denied, leaving only the "place where it was." This does not solve the problem because the place where it was, the no-thing, is even more terrifying because it has, as it were, been further denied existence instead of being allowed to glut itself with any existence it has been able enviously to find. Denial of the existence of the "place where it was" only makes matters worse because now the "point," marking the position of the no-thing, cannot be located (Bion 1965, pp. 111–112).

Bion's conclusion (probably his starting point as well) is that the force may be anywhere. We reach a world of horrific boundlessness in relation to which the term "nameless dread" seems strangely small. If God is a circle whose center is everywhere and circumference nowhere, the force is the counterpart whose center is a vortex or black hole (anywhere and everywhere) and that is determined that no part of God or God's creation will escape it.

Bion gives figurative form to this horrific formlessness by personifying it as a *nonexistent "person."* It is hard not to think of Milton's Satan with his yawning abysses, formless infinite, and darkness both visible and palpable. But it is far too easy to transform Satan into a dashing adventurer, swashbuckling and appealing (romantic vitality), a sophisticated and debonair gentleman (ironic) or entertainer (cynical), an efficient engineer, businessman, or entrepreneur. None of these images is derealized or depersonalized enough. They are bits of wish fulfillments, promises. Such devils are too lively to circumscribe the realms at stake here. A therapist might be quite happy if a patient who is a nonexistent "person" should be lucky enough to fall into the hands of such a devil and risk a breakthrough into life.

It is clinically important to see shades of unreality. In Bion's description, "person" is in quotes; nonexistent is not in quotes. Here, nonexistence is real: the force is real. Yet "person" has become a cipher, a "place" where a person was, a person manqué, an as if personality. Let us assume that the force has already devoured the person or the realness of the person. Now it devours the unperson or unrealness of the nonperson. It devours the shell that is left, the counterpart of the person, the empty phony version, the dead false self. The dead false self is an impostor or proxy of the lively false self. Our Bionic Virgil leads us through worlds of counterpart systems, region after region of nullity.

If the therapist directs his remarks to the person, when the person has va-cated to region after region of nonperson, his efforts are likely to be appropri-ated by fringes of the dead false self system and shuttled toward the vortex to disappear. Elements of the therapist's communication and true self elements of the patient may sometimes find each other, whether in the vortex, dead false self, live false self, or in God. Such finding is always possible: it is never too late. But life calling to life does not nullify the helpless paralysis in which life is stuck: it may seem too late when living is more horrible than dying.

Much depends on the therapist's range finder. If, by a stroke of luck, ge-nius, or hard work, he hits the right shade at the right time, something may happen. Usually the shade will shake it off: disturbance is taboo. Freud's depiction of a system that aims to reduce stimulation to zero is an example of a range finder that scores a hit. We observe shades zeroing the struggle to com-municate. The person does not seem to have a chance. Nevertheless, a shade occasionally shakes off the mist, and instead of only an agonized groan and the fall back to zomboid oblivion, a creaky, pained smile of recogni-tion reaches out with bony fingers, remnants of a bashful ecstasy. Dry bones, indeed! So much of the problem is that ecstasy has no place to go, and the force channels it.

SMITH'S DISSOLUTION: PEACE AT LAST

Throughout most of his life, Smith maintained or lived off a live false self. However, enough true self elements found recognition through the live false self to make live worth living. His sexual and reparative activity, musical inter-ests, psychoanalytic work, and involvement with his family all enhanced his sense of aliveness. Yet he felt a thread of falseness running through the activities he valued most. Even his most intense sexual moments felt "tainted" (Smith's term). He *knew* he was a superior psychoanalyst, but he did not let intimations of his autocratic and manipulative use of patients slow him down. He *knew* he was a good father and husband and glossed over his part in his wife's and children's difficulties.

Smith had a hardened and impenetrable view of the objectivity of life's events, including characterological makeup. He did not accept responsibility for his children's madness. They had their own lives to live, as did he. We all march to our own drummers, have our own timetables. His wife chose him, and he chose her: they were responsible for their choices. Their lives would have been shallower and poorer without each other. In his own way, he was devoted to his family: he *stayed* with them. He was proud of his steadiness, his staying power. He lasted the course. He stayed with his profession as well. He saw it through. He played down his awareness of how controlling and emotion-ally detached he had been. If he had regrets or self-recriminations, they were consigned to oblivion. He pointed to the good he had done, and he had done much good. He used his analytic training to maintain a balanced view of things, tipped in his favor.

Smith could not let down. Even when he finally wept, he did not let down so much as let things out. Rage toward the mother with whom he identified poured out. She was the strong, mad boss who teased him with the chickens she decapitated. His father caved in and killed himself when Smith was 5 years old. Letting down was more than dangerous: it was deadly. He was aware of becoming a version of his mother, not only to survive but also to be empowered. He feared and hated her, but sympathized with her too. She saw the family through. Without her crazy strength, life would have crushed them. Her power that was part of him enabled Smith to lift himself out of poor, deprived surroundings and make something of himself.

Smith remained plugged into her mad strength all his life. He lost contact with his fear and weakness. He was rightfully proud of how far he had come. He scarcely believed it. Who would have believed his rise from southern rural poverty to big city success? In his estimation, he had made it. He had done it by himself, but could not have done it without the vitality he felt from her. He was trapped by her strength.

Why did Smith come to see me? He was nearly twenty years my senior and more highly positioned. I seemed frightened and weak next to him. Perhaps he thought he could rehabilitate me like the youths he took over. Yet come he did, and he persisted until his death.

We had seen each other at professional meetings and had been in a peer study together. I was surprised to learn that he had listened carefully to my remarks. He felt he could count on me to speak truth and hear him out. I thought I had been quiet in the peer group, although I did get into arguments. Smith felt I honestly tuned into things. He felt he could be free with me. I gradually learned that he also saw in me a strength that came through suffering. Nevertheless, next to Smith I could not help but feel I was to hold the place where fear and weakness might have been, and often I was fear itself.

I do not think I ever quite exuded the self-confidence and ease that Smith did. My self-esteem seemed low next to his. Perhaps he hoped to play the phallic idol to my admiring self, but the transference did not quite take this turn. He was so identified with the saving maternal aggressor that it seemed my job to speak truth for the child that got left behind: the child that became a no-thing.

His personality seemed eaten by a secret battle to be something rather than nothing. His life was marked by fierce struggle, and his pleasure in professional competence, love of music, and sexual ecstasies provided some relief. Without work and music, life would have been hell. Sexuality led him into tormenting, dangerous situations. He tried to make family life a haven, but it was filled with pain and failure. His wife and children accused him of trying to fob them off with a shell of himself, although he had given them whatever he could. Worst of all, Smith related to his secret pain as something to handle, as if expertise could deal with it and somehow nullify it.

He did not expect *me* to nullify it, but *he* chronically did so. Smith was the psychoanalyst who understood the origins of his difficulties. He knew all the why's. He rode above his feelings as fast as he bared them. He could not simply suffer and cry and say how awful it all was. He always had to be doing something to it, to understand it, turn it this way and that, to stay on top of it.

For a time, I suspected Smith of using me to keep his job. I wrote all the needed letters confirming that he was working on his problems, that the workplace need not fear him. As usual, the threat of disaster abated. The young man who had accused him visited Smith in the hospital after a heart attack and dropped the charges. Smith said the young man's family was grateful to him for guidance he gave. Smith always managed to get out of bad situations.

But he could not stop his body clock. I felt more at ease after the crises with work passed, and Smith continued working. It did not occur to me that he had come to therapy to die. He seemed to be battling for life. To me, Smith seemed to push past himself, not getting low enough to connect with himself. To me, it seemed that a chronic false self style had become his real self. But Smith kept saying that he was getting closer to himself, that he had never come this close. He said that, at last, he was getting to his center. He felt a peace that had eluded him. Only in retrospect do I see that Smith linked up with himself before he died. It was a praiseworthy feat, because he did it through layers of ego coverings that never left.

Now I wonder if Smith did not choose me precisely because I was offbeat, not in the mainstream. His maverick qualities hid under a far more conventional bearing. He tied things up more than I did. I was more at loose ends. It was precisely my quirkiness he valued. I must have reminded him of himself, an alternate self, a counterpart. We shared an ironic sincerity, a sense of devotion. We both had a cynical, mocking side, but mine was tempered by faith, his by ego control. Faith is the center. l wonder if this aspect of the devotion to which he resonated was what attracted him.

Perhaps I was not only a proxy for the outsider he left behind but also a caring, mischievous child. In some ways, my lack of development worked for me. Smith's stronger, more sophisticated ego placed too much strain on his body. I could not hold onto myself as long as he seemed to be able to hold onto himself. He was able to maintain a sort of psychoanalytic consciousness far more rigorously, incessantly than I could. I dropped into dumb being more readily and completely than he and had to rouse myself to think something, whereas he was always thinking. He was always controlling trauma by psychoanalytic thinking. Sometimes he made my head spin in sessions, and I had to shut off.

I never scored a hit when I referred to diffusion or fragmentation, but I cannot help feeling that the wholeness Smith felt listening to music, especially the works of Gustav Mahler, was partly a measure of absent dispersal. In addition, his liking me in my awkward intensity, his acceptance of me when I was ill at ease, surely this must have been some kind of mirror. I well understand how he helped people. Yet he was not only smooth, nor I only awkward. There was an earthy aspect to his sophistication, and I was far from naive.

What I now see, through our defensive layerings and differing styles, is soul smiling at soul, soul recognizing soul. This is what we felt when we exchanged glances at meetings or felt warmly toward each other across a room. I would not say we were soul brothers or partners, but there was some kind of kinship. It is not enough to say we both knew hell: not all hells get along together. Perhaps it was where our souls open to heaven that most attracted Smith. Our therapy was not only about missing fear and weakness. Together we created/discovered a place where ecstatic longing could not be x'd out by psychoanalytic consciousness or by a narrow form of it.

The path led not through diffusion but through emptiness. Smith did not let down, but began to speak of emptiness. It is hard to convey how miraculous this felt. What an emptiness ran through the fullness of his personality! What emptiness he gave vent to! He spoke of a bottomless, inexhaustible emptiness, a painful, agonizing emptiness. The fullness of living did not stop because of this emptiness. The fullness of living kept right on going; it had its own power and momentum. But emptiness was everywhere, in the fullness too. This was the closest Smith came to losing ego control, with the exception of the first panicky moments of therapy when he feared the loss of his university position. In those first visits, I felt that Smith's personality was disintegrating, but he pulled out of it like a skilled pilot. l suspect that finding a place to deposit himself (psychoanalysis) enabled the nose dive to stop and the controls to return. It was only through the emptiness of his controls that Smith could contact himself. The gradient of the psychoanalysis was toward this emptiness, although neither he nor I could know this. To me, it seemed that Smith's contact with himself was several times removed, but it felt otherwise to him. Emptiness wiped out distance: he felt the pain directly.

The painful emptiness stayed with Smith, and he with it, for nearly half a year. Through it he began to feel ecstasy. The ecstasy did not nullify the emptiness, not any more than the emptiness nullified the fullness of living. These currents went on together, sometimes more and sometimes less distinguishable. It seems accurate to say that when the intensity of emptiness peaked, another dimension or world of experiencing opened.

Smith's ecstasy was not what one might call a cosmic ecstasy, but rather a psychoanalytic ecstasy. His smaller psychoanalytic "why" consciousness, addicted to causal visions and explanations, continued ticking. But now the illusion of control this gave him seemed less important than the moment of experiencing. He began to dip into his emotional currents a bit more like the way he listened to music. The emphasis was less on the power of understanding than on emotional impact and appreciation. His love for psychoanalysis reached a new place.

During most of his adult life Smith used psychoanalysis to maintain his equilibrium and enhance his self-esteem. It functioned as a kind of psychic cooling system. Now it became a tool to heat things up. Smith now clung to psychoanalysis as a vehicle for heightening experiencing, rather than as a weapon of pseudomastery.

Psychoanalytic thinking was the thread that knit his life together. What would have become of him without it? It was not just his formal analyses that were important but also the whole psychoanalytic milieu: the readings, meetings, colleagues, a total way of life. The psychoanalytic insights that popped into his head were supported by an entire community from which he drew nourishment. Friends, enemies, critics, admired and despised protagonists: through psychoanalysis he found a *world*, a place.

Now he found much more. Psychoanalysis was becoming what he always hoped it might be: a way to face himself, to open himself. It was in relationship to psychoanalysis that Smith came closest to an act of repentance and atonement. He felt grateful for psychoanalysis because it had given him a life. For the first time he not only *saw* but *faced* the misuse of his lover (psychoanalysis was his true love). He had used psychoanalysis to close wounds, not to open his heart. At last, psychoanalysis shined as an opening of self. What peace this lacerating moment brought!

"I don't want to lie now," said Smith. "It's important not to. I can't stand lying anymore. This is the first time I'm not bullshitting myself. I must get to things as they are. I've got to." Smith called to himself through his shells with an urgency that shattered lies. Can anyone stop lying? Wouldn't the total lack of self-deception be inhuman? Perhaps only the devil, the father of lies, is totally honest. Yet Smith *had* to break through to himself.

Apparently Smith knew something I didn't know. I now see that he sensed that death was imminent, that he was in a now-or-never situation. He kept up a good front to the end; after hospital stays, he continued his psychoanalytic practice. I know he valued his work with me. He repeatedly said, with tears in his voice, that at last he found a place where he could get to himself. But I suspect his most important work went on outside sessions, out of view.

He linked getting to himself with my honesty. He felt lucky beyond belief to be with someone he experienced as honest. In thinking about this now, I feel honored by Smith. I suppose the cynical me can note how lucky I was to be honored by the sublime Dr. Smith: how flattering to be the only honest man in the world! I needn't tell you I'm no more lily white than you are, my reader. But I do feel honored to have played a role in helping someone die better than he otherwise might have. I suspect many therapists have discovered that our work blossoms at the moment of death. Smith needed me as his *true self counterpart,* and through this protective identification or bit of mirroring, he located a missing area of self.

If Smith was able to use something in me to find a new face, a more honest face, thank God. I feel grateful to reciprocate his gratitude. I can picture Smith staring inward with the worn semi-leer he never fully shook off. As he stares, he sees the face of true self stare back at him, with a smile and wink, gazing through him to the horizon, the eternal opening.

In the last months I saw him, Smith spoke of a peace he never knew before. He was still alive and tortured and striving. But he also felt a deep peace, a reconciliation. He made the link that needed to be made. His insides found features he could recognize in a way that could not be wasted or twisted by words. I suspect what he found could not be communicated, except to say that he found it.

In the last dream that Smith reported, a black cat vanished through a basement window into the darkness below. We didn't interpret the dream. The session flew by. I looked forward to seeing Smith again after the weekend. He died walking to the subway after a full day's work.

WHERE THE FORCE GOES

Where did the force go? Guilty me says it caused my failure to interpret Smith's final dream. Perhaps if I had said the right thing, Smith would have lived a little longer. The dream obviously was about death. Did the cat get my tongue?

Fie on you, guilty me! Thank God Smith's cat went through the basement, rather than Smith going through the roof.

Yet I believe the force was active to the end and beyond the end. As Bion suggests, it goes on acting after it destroys time, space, and existence. The force does not stop in the face of reconciliation, peace, or atonement. If anything, these barriers increase its fervor. Goethe made things too easy for Faust by depicting the inevitable last-minute salvation. New beginnings need new sets of problems. Goethe was right to end with an image of working the earth, the work that never ends.

The force and salvation stay mixed up to the end. Smith died happy, but was never free from misery. As he got closer to death, his ability to live paradoxically increased. He became less able to tilt paradox to one side or the other. To close paradox meant to close his heart. He had a lifetime of practice in closing his heart. Smith's bit of opening and peace opposed a lifetime of bad habits.

At the moment of death, new battlegrounds open. New possibilities mean new conflicts, new tensions, new twists. We do not go from conflict to a conflict-free world. Growth in enlightenment is better than that. The force is not wished away by death.

One can invent interpretations of Smith's death, especially its timing. Let us say straightaway that it might all be physical: his biological clock ran out. But it is difficult not to entertain more possibilities. During most of Smith's life, the force was happy with Smith's false self, his character, the sets of bad habits we call personality. There was enough life and true self in Smith's false self for the force to feed on; in time, it fed on dead aspects of the true–false self too.

The force plays both ends against the middle and plans for the future. While it focused on Smith's personality, it also made inroads on his body. By the time Smith got around to using a true self counterpart to free sparks of true self, the whole psychosomatic system was ready to collapse. There was not enough viable psyche-soma left to support the true self engagement he reached. The house of cards collapsed around the place where the fire that never goes out might have been.

One can imagine the force feeding on the fire as a new world opens. Smith and his counterparts don shapes called choices or habits to try to do a better job. They do not merely start over from the same place. Their wink and twinkle and smile seem a bit wiser, a little more open and caring. They feel good to be on the move.

REFERENCES

Balint, M. (1965). *The Basic Fault*. London: Tavistock.
Bion, W. R. (1965). *Transformations*. London: Heinemann.
——— (1970). *Attention and Interpretation*. London: Tavistock.
Bollas, C. (1989). *Forces* of *Destiny: Psychoanalysis and Human Idiom*. London: Free Association Books.
Eigen, M. (1984). On demonized aspects of the self. In *Evil Self and Culture*, ed. M. C. Nelson and M. Eigen. New York: Human Sciences.
——— (1986). *The Psychotic Core*. Northvale, NJ: Jason Aronson.
——— (1992). *Coming through the Whirlwind*. Wilmette, IL: Chiron.
Fairbairn, W. R. D. (1954). *An Object-Relations Theory of the Personality*. New York: Basic Books.
Khan, M. (1979). *Alienation in Perversion*. New York: International Universities Press.
Klein, M. (1946). Notes on some schizoid mechanisms. In *Developments in Psycho-Analysis*, ed. M. Klein, P. Heimann, S. Isaacs, and J. Riviere. London: Hogarth, 1952.
Rodman, F. R. (1987). *The Spontaneous Gesture: Selected Letters of D. W. Winnicott*. Cambridge, MA: Harvard University Press.
Weil, E. (1958). The origin and vicissitudes of the self-image. *Psychoanalysis* 6:3–19.

10

Counterparts in a Couple

Ben was a therapist who loved psychological truth. He wrapped truths around himself like armor and used them as weapons to bludgeon others. I have written about Ben in *Coming through the Whirlwind* (1992b) and "The Immoral Conscience" (1991), and use bits of recent material for this chapter (see also Chapter 8). Our work continues well into its second decade.

Ben's upbringing was chronically traumatic. His mother idolized him and flew into wild rages. She was alternately spoiling and stormy. Ben's father knotted him with threats of violence and displays of self-pity and sentimental emotionality. Both parents were damaged people who poured themselves into unrewarding work and scarred their children with intensely demanding, crazy love. Ben would never recover from years of trauma, no matter how much analysis he had.

Analysis helped Ben make and maintain a marriage filled with real possibilities and enabled him to become a father. Having his own family enabled Ben to reach levels of living previously closed to him, but his gains were not without cost. Ben's gains in personal living were always threatened by his narcissistic rage coupled with a misuse of truth to persecute himself and dominate loved ones. At any moment the complexities of living might misfire and trigger a fall into a warp, where life is hellish. Periodic somatic breakdowns, which were not life threatening, resulted from the strain. A congenital heart problem, which would worsen with age, loomed in the background.

Ben was furious with analysis because it did not cure his physical problems. He cited psychological texts suggesting that analysis might build his psyche so he would not have to somaticize. He took seminars with writers he quoted and even consulted some of them. So far none of them told him to leave me. I pointed out to him that, in addition to not curing his physical problems, analysis did not even cure his psychological problems, and this must be disappointing as well as infuriating. It meant that Ben must grapple with necessary loss, including the loss of the omnipotence of analysis, the loss of the demand, expectation, or hope of an ideal cure on this earth.

Lucy, Ben's wife, was a good container for his morass, but had problems of her own. She felt more or less comfortable staying at home and taking care of their child, Ron. However, she was chronically depressed. She functioned well enough as a mother, but dangerously neglected her own self. She gave up on her ambitions in order to build a home.

Lucy's depression kept her in contact with herself. She hugged herself with her blue feelings, and depression gave her a sense of inferiority. Her pace was slower than Ben's, and she could not be stampeded easily. By holding on to her depression, she held on to her own mind. Depression gave her space. Through it she maintained a certain degree of freedom and autonomy from Ben's demands and domineering ways. Ben could not bully her blues away.

In time Ron entered middle childhood, and the family's economic condition worsened. The need for Lucy to join the workforce increased, not only for family finances (although this was nearly a necessity) but also for her own self. Ron was away all day at school, and Lucy could not justify spending so much time on housework, even if the chores comforted her. She spent hours sitting around feeling bad about herself or throwing herself into compulsive, mind-obliterating work.

For years Lucy had withstood Ben's attacks on her for her failure to make money. Now she joined them. During her first marriage, to an artist, she had gone to art school and painted. When her marriage broke up, art school died out and she did not paint for years. When she married Ben, she went through a program to become a psychotherapist. She was an excellent therapist, but hated the work. She could not bear her own intensity and did not want to have to bear the responsibility for life-and-death situations. She was so serious about what she did that she was almost crushed by her own sincerity.

For a time Lucy and Ben had shared a fantasy about working together: two therapists sharing life, truth, a calling. They would discuss cases, co-lead groups, enjoy colleagues, and learn and teach together. It took a lot of strength for Lucy to stop practicing without breaking up the marriage. When she did, it meant one more dream of oneness dashed.

You can imagine Ben's outrage at the money, time, and hard work "thrown out." For Lucy, throwing away what she had worked for was an act of discovery, but also of stagnation. She discovered who she was not: she was not a therapist, she was not Ben or his satellite. She was not Lucy either, whoever Lucy might be. She was someone who was stagnant, perhaps someone who *needed* to be stagnant. Yet she was appalled at her own stagnant state. It seemed endless, bottomless. She would never stop sinking.

It was a wonder she kept on with life, family, and the household. Ben chronically raged against her depression, but was deeply frightened by it. Lucy scared herself, but she also felt deeply filled with satisfaction at being a mother again.

(She had mothered a child two decades earlier in her first marriage.) Perhaps this time things might go better. Her first marriage had been devastating, but she found strength in surviving it. Then again, perhaps she didn't survive it, although a kind of mute strength did.

Lucy felt a wonderful fullness at being the center of the household and building family life. The fullness was at least as great as the bottomless sinking: neither nulled nor compromised the other. Both were basic, irreducible realities that took Lucy years to grow into. She was bewildered by this double capacity. It gradually dawned on her that doubleness pervaded her life. She had been unable to admit it or, perhaps more accurately, lacked the equipment and frame of reference to accommodate such pervasive doubleness.

For Lucy, family life also meant years of fatigue. It was more than enough just to get through the day: exhaustion was a daily fact. Ben would never know the full meaning of the fatigue attached to staying in one place, at home with baby. Baby and me, alone together: this was Lucy's specialty. She wouldn't have missed it for the world. What could be more precious! But now baby was a child in school, and her cover was blown.

She sat with herself and saw that she had never made a living, or not for long. She was alone with herself and could not move. For long spaces between marriages, she had drifted, doing a bit of this or that or nothing. Things didn't build or evolve. She barely got by. Ben couldn't bear Lucy's easy acceptance of deprivation. He ridiculed her for being a "deprivation addict." He wanted her to want more, to get more, to show more, to do more.

Lucy sat, and one thing she got out of sitting was just *being*. Ben could not sit or just be, except in front of a television. He always had to be moving and doing. Even in front of a television he was not merely empty or vacuous, but gorging on grandiose fantasies. Lucy could empty out, something that Ben never could do. Lucy could be still and taste being that was now empty, now full. She immersed herself in contentless being. Ben was forever restlessly filling spaces.

One day it hit Lucy and me at virtually the same time with crystal clarity: she, a woman who can't move, married a man who can't sit still. Lucy had reached a place where movement seemed impossible.

WHY I WAS SEEING LUCY

Ben's and Lucy's previous therapists had committed suicide within a couple of years of each other. Ben's therapist ran a car off a mountain road, and Lucy's jumped out of a window. I mentioned Lucy's therapist in *The Psychotic Core* (1986, pp. 338–339). Both were prominent and well-respected men in the mental health world. Both were in the forefront of the humanistic psychology movement, the "third force" of the 1960s. Many would be envious of their achievements.

I did a few months of couples work with Ben and Lucy before and soon after their marriage, so it was natural for Lucy to see me when her therapist died. It was I who called to break the news of his death to her. We had already established a connection and liked and respected each other. In time she began work with another therapist.

Apparently her new therapist was unable to bear her immobility. He was a competent, well-meaning man who urged her to be more active. Lucy appreciated his support, but could not make use of his suggestions. She would not push past herself. In time she began to question whether his approach was right for her, and after several years he abruptly dismissed her. For awhile therapy had given her faith in herself, but in the end she felt punished for not doing better.

After the hurtful end of her therapy, Lucy nursed her wounds and her failure. She kept functioning as mother and housewife, while her inner being was collapsing and dying: she was losing herself as a *person* more than ever. She knew she was there somewhere, but paralysis spiraled. At great cost she reached out to me and I saw her.

At our first meeting she showed me how panicky she was. The idea of seeing a therapist terrified her. First a suicide and then a rejection: What was she exposing herself to now? What struck me most was the color in her face. Terror enlivened her. I felt person-to-person contact as fears tumbled out of her guts. I could see her open and open: tears, grief, rage, fears upon fears. Years of sitting poured out in moments.

The relief was palpable. Lucy was not a loud person, but she was not withdrawn. There was a direct line between her deeper self and her face and voice. Ben was a fast thinker and fast mover. Lucy was slower. She chewed her cud and let things brew. Ben could not stand her slowness, and his speed sometimes frightened and bewildered her. But they were both highly expressive people. They were just alive in different registers.

In spite of years of humanist and feminist ideology, you could see the lines of a traditional couple in them. He was the hunter, with his faster, skillfully impulsive pace. She was the anchor, slow and steady, holding the ground together. However, he tended to fly off, and the ground opened beneath her. Both were caught in the modern vertigo.

The fact that Lucy and I began working from the moment we saw each other swept past thoughts I had about risking a referral to another therapist. Not every psychotherapist would agree to see a husband and wife separately, and I might not do so myself. But life is bigger than categories. I felt it would be a betrayal of life to stop the flow now.

Lucy thanked me for what I had done and continued to do for Ben and their marriage. We spoke about the difficulties her seeing me might cause. One would expect that husband and wife sharing one therapist might involve some nasty business. There were also unanticipated difficulties. At first, Ben felt deep relief at Lucy's seeking help, and my work with both of them moved along with its own impetus. We rolled along with therapy's momentum.

BACK AND FORTH

Within a few weeks of Lucy coming to see me, Ben's happiness at her getting help was joined by an increase in anger. He fell back into verbally pounding her for her faults. It was not only his anger at sharing me, although this was bad enough. It was also a feeling that, since Lucy had someone to help her, he did not have to be so patient. He could lash out, because someone would help her nurse her wounds, the same person who helped him with his.

The triangle reached deep into primal parenting and involved questions concerning the foundations of support. Could more than one child be supported by a parent? For Ben this was partly a question of whether his parents could nurture two children, his sister and himself. His experience was that one got at the other's expense. It was not simply a matter of whether or not there was enough to go around; each got, each lost. The problem was not quantity, but the method of distribution. There was a dire fault in parental structure that made it impossible for more than one to get at the same time. One got only through opposition, through one pitted against the other. There was always a versus with one up and one down.

There was a radical dysfunction between the one and two. The gradient was toward oneness, a succession of ones at the maternal center. First you, then me; first me, then you. Never two at a time, never three. The two existed within the one as a versus, an irritant, a permanent restlessness. There was no easy one, no peaceful one. One was permeated by the struggle of exclusion: one as center of all, one against all. Two and three were swallowed by one, a one maintained by maternal giddiness.

Going deeper than siblings, the versus within oneness referred to parent and child. Ben's mother would do anything for him, but this justified her right to abuse him. Ben and his mother were latrines and suns for each other, victims of maimed psychic structures that had been passed on for generations. Parent gets at the expense of the child's loss and vice versa. Together they were one against all, yet each drew strength from the other's loss of self. They slid between star–audience roles in hideous ways and looked down at ordinary reciprocity. Ben's anger was never ordinary. Instead, it was massive, plugged into the parental warp.

It is unlikely that Ben's mother *could* be passive. For Ben she was a wild lady with a comeback for everything. In her old age she was a live wire, a raw nerve, wild, self-absorbed and demanding, with a mate to share her crazy oneness. In contrast, Lucy's mother had to reach to find activity. Left to herself, she sat vegetating. Lucy feared her mother's stillness, passivity, and inertia. She had dreadful visions of her mother going under, wasting away, and being unable to take care of herself. Lucy was terrified that she was like her mother, as Ben was like his.

Yet when things *had* to be done, Lucy's mother roused herself and did them. That her mother *could* take care of herself amazed Lucy. What a difference between the family photos of a young, beautiful, lively woman and the aged, empty sitter! Yet the sitter *did* take care of herself. And the fact is Lucy took care of herself too, and she took care of a whole family. She moved even if it felt as if she did not move, just as her mother moved even though Lucy did not believe she would. Perhaps it was not movement that was lacking, but a feeling link with movement.

However, Ben's anger at me and Lucy's hatred of herself made sure we all understood that in some deep way Lucy was immobile. She did not move out into the work world. Each time she tried, terror drove her back. To Ben, Lucy seemed a stubborn mule. He got leads for possible jobs for her, one as a therapist, another as a teacher. She could not reach out for them. Ben's empathic tolerance was exhausted. He did not see the flaming angels that barred her way.

Was it simply that they came from traditional families in which the man went out into the world and the woman took care of the home and each was carrying on the tradition? Surely this was part of it, but Lucy also felt this was a dangerous alibi, an excuse. She needed more and demanded more. She had to do more. She could not be a person if she settled for less. The pressure Ben exerted on her was also pressure she exerted on herself. She identified with, as well as fought, his angry voice, because it spoke truths that were her own. Ben's voice was, in part, the still, small voice in her writ large. He had his own reasons for demanding she do more, but the demand was also hers.

Lucy resented being rushed and resisted the push for years. The fact that Ben and her therapist anxiously, angrily, and perhaps indifferently pushed her had enabled her to bounce off outside barriers and postpone the moment of reckoning. Her own impetus to grow fused with their demand and drove her to a standstill. Ben's voice might be hers writ large, but it was hard for her to hear and believe her own when she had to fight his.

Ben turned his wrath on me when Lucy's therapy did not get anywhere. For months there was no apparent movement. Lucy was the same as always. Ben could be rational and knew that therapy took a long time. He knew many forces worked against it. He could perhaps adopt a make-believe tolerance and shape himself in terms of rationality. However, the truth was that he was angry at Lucy's lack of movement. He learned he had to hold back with her or risk losing his marriage. But now he could let me have it for her paralysis. Hadn't he helped get her into treatment, hadn't he urged her to see me, hadn't he steered her to me? Now, if she didn't move it was my fault. He had me to blame, and he lost no time taking advantage of this situation.

I could imagine how Lucy must have felt in the face of Ben's insistence that she move. What a temptation to freeze, to pull into oneself, to hide! My job was to do my job in spite of the pressure, neither rushing nor retarding the therapy. There is a main line of therapeutic work that keeps ticking through storms and dry spells. My job is to keep locating these main lines of processes, to find places that count. Ben lost it out of impatience and anger, and Lucy spent too much time building arks against the floods of his rage and her terror. Ben feared losing himself if he slowed down, and Lucy feared losing herself if she sped up. Therapy finds places where different speeds and fears begin to connect and make room for each other. For that to happen I needed to withstand Lucy's fear of movement and her lack of a feeling link with her movement, as well as Ben's demand for it and his dread of stillness.

It always amazes me when the right attitude or stance or place emerges (sometimes it doesn't; see Chapter 18, "Boa and Flowers"). It emerges out of a combination of letting disturbances and pressures have an impact and build and at the same time letting go. An invisible range finder works out useful ways of being for a time; then conditions shift and one starts again.

I genuinely respected and cared for, and, let me say it, loved Lucy's still spot, her immobility. I *felt* something positive in it. I also sensed "pathological" abysses of inertia and collapse. This was more than double vision: it was a quivering of experiencing now this way, now that, now both at once. As I got to know Lucy, it began to dawn on me that she had reached a remarkable place.

The force that goes on working after destroying time, space, and existence (Bion 1965, p. 101, Eigen 1991, 1992a,b, see Chapter 4) did its work. Lucy was "gone," "out of it," "killed off." There was a blank where *she* might have been. Lucy knew what it was to die out. Yet there she was also radiantly being and alive in her terror. All dead, all alive, and so many variations between. She *lived* through nothing, everything, and so much in between. The in between was the medium of her existence: positive and negative no-things and every-things, positive and negative mixed textures.

My glimpse of the place Lucy reached triggered shocks of recognition. It was not that she never recognized where she lived, but her surprise at finding me there too enabled her to own her recognition. Meeting me in the place she lived let her relax a bit more into this place–no-place instead of judging and fighting it. A new intimacy with herself was beginning. Everyone in her life tried to get her out of it; everyone was afraid of it. Surely she would sink, vanish without a trace, and never come back. The truth is that one never is the same after this trip to the other side of the moon, to the blank side of being.

One of the most amazing and basic facts about Lucy was the fullness and completeness with which she lived with affective deadness and heightened affective aliveness at the same time. It was as if I discovered a being with an extra arm or leg or head, with an extra sense. For Lucy it was an everyday thing, the "point" of her existence. I don't think she realized that most other people did not share this point or had not reached it yet. Perhaps for them it was unconscious or less conscious. For her it was consciousness itself. She had never quite realized that this was the point that made her different and set her apart.

Perhaps it was not until she met me there that she could let herself feel just how different she was: the extent of her underlying sense of difference otherwise might have been overly devastating. Now at last she could relax into this difference. We were partners in difference. She could begin to let the tension inherent in singleness–doubleness do its work.

After all my talk about appreciating, even loving, Lucy's stillness and immobility, it may sound odd to hear that I, like Ben, was also restless and agitated for change. I identified with both positions; both are valuable to me. I am neither simply stillness nor motion, but love both. My agitation and restlessness did not grow mainly from the fear of stillness. Both poles are real and basic parts of our experiential equipment as we know it now. I think because of my deep appreciation of Lucy's stillness, my restlessness was contagious. She began bits of movement into the world without losing touch with her alone self. Her movements were tentative, but palpable. She began thinking of what she *could* do to make money and what she might like doing, and she began to find a possible point of meeting between must and like.

It was at this point, when Lucy actually was getting ready to *do* something, that an amazing thing happened. Ben began getting physically ill: a short trip to the hospital with one problem that came and went in a week; panic about his chronic heart problem, which turned out to be no worse than earlier; and finally, the painful urethral passing of a stone. A few years earlier, Lucy also had passed stones painfully.

Perhaps shared symptoms were a matter of shared diet or coincidence. But I could not avoid feeling that Ben needed to feel more like Lucy, so that he could be cared for more by me. Also, he secretly envied her life at home, alone with their child. She didn't have to work and carry financial burdens such as inflations, recessions, patients coming and going, mortgages, or taxes. She could be with their boy and share his growth more intimately and fully than Ben. How wonderful it must be to be a woman, at home with the most precious charge on earth, living a feeling life. How good to give up the fight and be one with existence.

Perhaps Ben was missing out on the most precious thing of all. Was illness the only way he could be passive and stay home? Still, illness did not make him a mother; it made him a baby. Lucy took care of Ben and of Ron, their son. She nursed Ben through the worst of his illness. Ben could be a mother only by proxy, through identification with Lucy. He was terrified that his body was failing him, and that in the end he could count on it to fail. He became desperate for nurturance and, to an extent, got what he wanted.

At the same time it was the threat of Lucy's doing something that had precipitated Ben's partial somatic breakdown. He did not fully realize how much he counted on her to be the background object, the stay-at-home, the one who would be there when he returned. He had been hiding his essential passive element through his anger at her staying home. Yet when she showed signs of really moving out, he got sick. If she went into the work world, he would have nothing wholly his own.

A wish coming true tends to bring about a crisis.

UNCONSCIOUS PROCESSING

A crisis can stimulate the growth of unconscious processing.

Psychoanalysis is more than making the unconscious conscious. It helps unconscious processing reset itself so that it can do its work better. We rely on unconscious processing to support us and help keep us in life. We rely on it for new ideas and feelings. If something is wrong with the unconscious processing of affects and ideas, if there is a warp or chronic blockage in primary process work, no amount of secondary process compensations or hypertrophy of consciousness will correct the sense of basic wrongness.

A bit of growth of unconscious processing between Ben and Lucy can be seen in their dreams. As Ben was recovering from illness, he dreamt the following: Ben's balls (testicles) were made of shit. They began inflating like balloons until they exploded, a shit explosion. Then they were flat. The flatness especially frightened and mystified Ben, although the whole dream was scary and deflating.

The dream constituted a narcissistic injury, since it rubbed Ben's nose in his shit, here as his shitty balls. There was panic linked with the explosive loss of control, but the mortification of having shitty balls was more cutting. Many things can be said about this dream, and I can only touch on some of them.

Massive self-hate and lack of self-worth were circumscribed by a specific image: the shit or garbage self was channeled through shitty balls. For Ben it was humiliating to face having shitty balls. He'd like to think his balls were wonderful, that they were family jewels. How can he trust his unconscious if it shoots him down this way?

Ben's unconscious was not nice to him, but it told him truth. One could say that his shitty balls were a heritage from his parents. His father had shitty balls too. He was filled with a sense of failure, self-pity, and rage. Ben's mother was chaotic. She alternately idealized and emotionally violated Ben in myriad ways, so that Ben became a sort of shitty deity. This distortion of self was permanent. It ran through the family and had been passed on through generations.

The unconscious tends to speak truth in an exaggerated, reduced way: something is blown up; something else is left out. The truth of the unconscious is not the whole or only truth. Unconscious truths qualify one another. Different states of self compete with, offset, and feed each other. Ben's whole self is not merely explosive, flattened, inflated–deflated shit. But this state or attitude or feeling or process or structure or thread or theme must be included in the overall picture: it is a real part of experience that is sometimes denied and sometimes is taken as the whole.

The discovery that one can be ill and feel physically shitty may make the whole self feel shitty for a time. Ben was healthy and felt healthy most of the time. The realization that his body was simply a body, prone to such things as health and illness to which bodies are prone, aroused anxiety. The temptation is to devalue the body and for this devaluation to spread through the whole self.

In Ben's case his partial physical breakdown was coupled with a broader threat to his psychic economy. His wife's new psychosocial movement disrupted Ben's equilibrium, which he maintained partly by being able to put her down for not moving. The loss of an inner–outer scapegoat increased his anxiety and vulnerability and threw him into an uproar approaching mayhem. It may be that his middle-aged body was prone to ailments it might have withstood at an earlier time. One might envision a complex psychosomatic complicity, in which an older body finds it more difficult to contain threats to self and self is more easily affected by physical frailties. Body and character wear each other down.

Considerations of family, history, and body set the stage for his coming to grips with self. Ben felt with special urgency that something about *himself* needed to be faced. He was the fact he most needed to meet. Shitty parents, shitty history, shitty body, shitty self: he could not simply wipe all this away; he could not create himself or his background all over again as if the shittiness didn't exist. The shittiness *did* exist, and *he was* it, or partly it. Wallowing in it would not help. He had to find the right slant on it, an attitude that would help move things along. It is too easy to get swallowed up by shit.

The dream image was specific: shitty balls, not simply global shittiness. This dream had bite to it. This dream had balls. It helped Ben to think that he had misused his generativity, that he had misused his creative capacities. This thought made him feel more at one with himself for the moment. He applied it not only to his verbal ability to bind and dominate others and yoke them into admiring him for his breathtaking insights but also to his capacity for friendship.

Ben's life was littered with failed friendships, and the stream of losses pained him. It dawned on me that Ben did not use his God-given powers to cultivate ball-to-ball, heart-to-heart relationships with people he *really* liked. Instead he used his powers to win images. He went after people who were quick-witted (hostile bright), on top of things, and more highly positioned. He wouldn't be caught dead with someone who wasn't flashy or "pizazzy." He had never liked or befriended an ordinary, good-hearted person (a slob, a *shlep*, a *shmo*). He never had had a heart-to-heart relationship with anyone, except perhaps Lucy and me. The bright relationships he had were "show-offy." The brightness was not used for mutual impact and growth. Shit balls, shit truths, not truth balls used for real development.

Ben felt something like a moment of repentance. His life flashed before him and he wept. His unspoken, unconscious prayer was answered by Lucy's dream.

LUCY'S DREAM

Lucy dreamt she was sitting astride Ben, his erect penis deep inside her. She showed him where it came up to on her belly, pointing out how big it was with a sense of profound affirmation.

Did Lucy dream this for Ben? Did she respond to his shitty, explosive-flattened balls by showing how valuable and good he was? Did she contain and transform his bad self-feelings?

This dream came immediately after Lucy told me how her father put rope on the top of her crib so she couldn't climb out. He inhibited her movement in many ways. Both her parents were frightened and inconvenienced by normal baby motility. When she was a bit older her father intimidated Lucy with exaggerated portrayals of diseases she would get if she allowed her body free play.

The penis in her dream was not only Ben's but also her own. She was mother to her own baby (penis = baby) self. She was affirming the value of her own phallic might, activity, and aliveness. She could *be* and *do*. The image of Ben's penis inside her completed a circuit. For the moment there was a reciprocity of container–contained, the erect and enfolding, a moment of wholeness. The contribution of both partners was needed. The interweaving was beautiful, in fact redemptive.

If Lucy's dream answered Ben's terror, his dream showed why she needed him. He was movement itself. Spoiled movement perhaps, but movement. He was the soiling, splattering baby, exploding all over the place, the opposite of the imprisoning restraint that had been imposed on her. Together they shared the experience of getting flattened out. But Ben kept the possibility of exploding alive. In contrast, Lucy's depression (flattening) was steadier. Ben's was more apt to be the downside of an exploding manic, grandiose position.

In Ben and Lucy's marriage, terror met terror. With therapeutic help, unconscious could interweave with unconscious to the benefit of both. Ben's parents were more explosively chaotic than Lucy's, who were on the side of exaggerated restraint. As they grew up, Ben and Lucy had rebelled against parental warps—yet ironically and in spite of themselves, each lived out these warps in new, refined keys (more sophisticated, better educated). They could not wish or will the warp away, but they could experience it more deeply. They could grow around it, sometimes through it, and perhaps melt bits of it now and then.

Ben's and Lucy's dreams represent a growth of teamwork. Together they portrayed shitty aspects of self and a kind of *tantric* cleansing. Shit did not simply trigger shit. I don't think Lucy's or Ben's parents could have dreamt her dream. The joy of natural unity grew in the midst of peril and fragmentariness. Shit was not denied, but was not the last word. The loveliness of coming together was real.

Ben quickly recovered his physical health and had several dreams involving friendly women. These women were neither seductive nor competitive, but were genuinely *friendly* and *good willed*. As may be seen in my extended account of Ben in *Coming Through the Whirlwind* (1992b), this was no easy achievement. Experiencing *simple good will* was not something Ben could take for granted. Ben grew up in a seductive–competitive atmosphere ruled by the will to control and a sense of helplessness. His life was permeated by mistrust. It was nearly impossible for him to believe that goodness was happening to him of its own accord, with no strings attached. Lucy brought simple goodness into his life and at the same time drove him crazy and made him work.

If there was a shit circle, there was also a good circle. Lucy and Ben mediated goodness for each other, and I for both of them, and both of them for me. The good stood the test of the shittiness. The friendly women in Ben's dreams were new growth elements, as was Lucy's tantric scene of fulfilling sexual interlocking. In the midst of anxieties, terrors, and arrays of god-awful feelings, something beautiful was growing in Ben and Lucy, something more fulfilling than either knew before. Their own true selves were growing through it all. With all their never-ceasing difficulties, life was opening up for them.

REFERENCES

Bion, W. R. (1965). *Transformations*. London: Heinemann.

Eigen, M. (1986). *The Psychotic Core*. Northvale, NJ: Jason Aronson.

———— (1991). The immoral conscience. In *The Psychotherapy Patient*, ed. J. Travers. Binghamton, NY: Haworth.

———— (1992a). Notes on the Counterpart. In *Clinical Series*, ed. N. Schwartz-Salant and M. Stein. Wilmette, IL: Chiron.

———— (1992b). *Coming through the Whirlwind*. Wilmette, IL: Chiron.

11

From Attraction
to Meditation

"From attraction to meditation." These were the words the I-Ching answered a woman, Marion, who wanted to know whether analysis with me would be "emotionally enriching and spiritually rewarding."

She had heard me give a talk on counterparts in a couple (see Chapter 10) and reverberated to the way I spoke from my insides. She also took satisfaction in feeling that she understood me implicitly while some of her colleagues found me baffling.

After two sessions with me, Marion decided to leave her woman therapist of nine years who had helped her immensely. I was surprised because I was given to think I was one of a stream of intermittent flirtations or affairs that had enabled her to endure the frustrations of her analysis. Her analysis seemed to have reached the point of diminishing returns and beat on because nothing better came along.

Marion said several times that her therapist's office never changed. It was immaculate, perfectly orderly. Her analyst's stockings never had a run; her hair was always right. Marion breathed with relief at my disheveled appearance and messy office. When her analyst asked for more sessions to "tidy things up," so much was left hanging that Marion replied, "That's your way, not mine. You're tidy, in control, and want things cleaned up. I'm messy, a slob."

What relief Marion felt. She breathed easier. She had wanted to say something like that for years without realizing it. She felt put down by her analyst for being the sort of person she was. Apparently her analyst wanted to help Marion be more in control, on top of it, but Marion just wanted to be herself.

So much happened in our first sessions that I felt deeply enriched by them. Our conversation spanned many levels—spiritual, emotional, intellectual, and sexual. During our second session, I became sexually aroused and wondered what to do. Within a minute or two, Marion said she felt sexual stirrings for me. Who stimulated whom?

Marion felt ashamed of her sexual stirrings, but was also afraid of them and perhaps afraid of my rejection of her. I stayed with my arousal, and gradually words formed. My sexual feelings translated into the question, "I'm not sure if you're more afraid I'll be aroused by you, or more afraid I won't." Being able to formulate this question gave me relief. I somehow felt I was able to do justice to my arousal without disclosing it directly and perhaps precipitously.

"I'm more afraid you won't want me," Marion answered.

I sat there smiling broadly, enjoying the stream of body tinglings, as blood rushed upward, filling my face. It was a nice moment for both of us.

I don't think the explicitly sexual part of the session lasted more than a few minutes. Marion's pain returned, and we dove into the pain of existence. Where did sex go when pain returned? Where did sex come from when pain subsided?

OUR SECRET

The pain was immense. Marion had twice been hospitalized for depression. I think Marion came in after several sessions and glowered, in order to drive this home. "I'm depressed. I want to kill myself." I felt her words sink into me like depth charges.

My vision blurred. It occurred to me that it was important for me not to see her. She was showing me something I was not supposed to see. Her face was menacing. I relaxed into the horrible feeling and thought of all the monster movies I saw as a child. They fed my nightmares and dread of the dark. I must have looked under my bed and checked my closet well into my teens.

Marion's horror and menace washed through me. My mind blurred. When I came to, her face softened. I think she was surprised at the impact she had on me. Our interaction was subtle and wordless, yet I could see she read it. She looked at me through the impact we were having on each other and was touched by the fact we could do this. It was our secret, that we could feel each other so deeply, in so many ways.

SINKING–SWIMMING

When Marion first called, she had asked for a supervisory consultation. She is a fine therapist and an intriguing psychoanalyst. I remember her asking questions at my talk. She was incisive and searching. Her probes got between seams of psychoanalytic concepts. She seemed especially interested in Lacan and Melanie Klein and made fascinating mixtures of their concepts. Her dogmatism frightened me, but I appreciated her creativeness.

She began our first meeting asking questions about concepts in some of my papers. I wasn't tempted to answer. I would have felt oddly out of contact had

I begun an elaboration of something I wrote years ago. More importantly, Marion's face told me something more was needed. She was looking for something that escaped her. Her desperation and need could not be satisfied by a lecture. Maybe all she wanted to know was that I respected her mind, and I conveyed this respect.

The main thing was that I kept sinking. I sank into myself, past Marion's intellectual overtures. I sank into the pain I felt when she spoke to me, when I looked at her. I sank into the pain of our eye contact, into the bliss and pain of our skin contact. Yes, skin contact, although our bodies never touched. I felt our eye–skin contact was very strong. We sat in chairs across a small room, separated by several feet. I was keenly aware of how permeable our skin was. We swam in and out of each other through our skin.

I sank past Marion's talk of her former therapist, a competent, dedicated, helpful woman with firm boundaries. Perhaps Marion needed firm boundaries—or perhaps they starved her. Is it a choice of one or the other? First, Marion organized our meeting with an invitation to an intellectual feast and then continued with a critique of her therapy. I was aware that whatever Marion said of her old therapist she might say of me someday. Perhaps she'll find new, more awful things to say of me. Her old therapist got off fairly well.

Perhaps her old therapist was afraid of this sinking–swimming in and through each other. Perhaps she found it irrelevant, a distraction, primitive. Is there a prejudice in the mental health field that sinking–swimming means the destruction of boundaries? How far would we sink? How thoroughly would we swim in each other's abysses? How much permeability ought two people stand?

Natural boundaries were set partly by our eyes. We bathed in each other's stare. Are eyes permeable and porous? Yes, I think so. Lovers swim in each other's eyes, as well as arms. One flies into and with the Other by seeing and being seen. There are eye baths, as well as arrows and snares. Narcissus was devoured by his stare: he drowned in the eyes of his mirror.

But along with eye-heart, eye-skin, and eye-genital connections, there is eye-brain. Porousness comes up against visual hardness, the need to see exactly, objective vision, the seeing of the heartless bird that eats its prey alive. Marion and I bathed in each other's stares, but also came up against each other's visual shields and swords. We saw ourselves seeing each other and, at times, delighted in this supraconsciousness. The knowing brain-I places a sort of limit on fusion by catching it in the act.

It is a matter of attitude and mood, this kaleidoscopic play of capacities. An appreciative steel-trapped brain-eye can let fusion spread. The more, the better. There is fusional knowing, as well as detached knowing. Fusion can go places that detachment cannot. The two can link up with each other, share each other's findings, intensify each other's experiences. A meanly critical attitude freezes fusion. One becomes too afraid, mistrustful, devaluing. Fusion does not stop, but becomes more diffuse, sneaky, monstrous.

Fusion can be detached too, becoming detached fusion. Sexual addicts know this only too well. The fusional capacity can respond like an open gate, divorced from the personal, open to everything and anything, a promiscuity of stimulation. We do not like to think that we ride a sea of anonymous capacities. It is scary to realize how much our thoughts think us and how little we think them. The same is true with streams of feelings, sensations, imaginings, willings. Our little I-feeling mounts them and says, I think, I see, I want: I, I, I. Isn't there something anonymous about our I too? The I-feeling: Isn't that also given to us by an anonymous Donor, by anonymous processes?

It is amazing how the anonymous and personal permeate each other, break apart, reconnect ceaselessly. I suspect one of the things that glued Marion and I together was our appreciation of this sort of fireworks display. We experienced our personalities falling apart and coming together in all sorts of ways. Now an I-feeling shoots like a meteorite across heavens/hells, with this or that bit of sensation-feeling-imagining-willing-believing-thinking mixture. The kaleidoscope turns and the I-feeling fades. We are left staring at nothing, or there is a rude, naked ticking of capacities. It can be frightening, staring into nothing. It also can be wonderful. What a relief to be free of the tyrant I that is so self-referential about everything that happens.

SHE COULDN'T WAIT

I was amazed when Marion picked me as her therapist. I thought I was a transient consultant who would serve his purpose and then be discarded. At best, I imagined I was a curiosity, someone a little different. Marion would satisfy her appetite, then return to the tried-and-true. I could scarcely believe she would let go of a safe nine-year-old relationship for the offbeat and unknown.

I have two sets of feelings about such matters. One is my amazement at being picked: I expect to be rejected. Yet I feel sad at not being picked when I feel I might have helped someone. A quiet voice whispers, "Couldn't they see I could help? Yes, they had reasons for not staying, but. . . . " From greedy self-depreciation to therapeutic megalomania.

Marion told me that her therapist said I ought not have spoken the way I did when I gave my talk. Her therapist and many therapists, according to Marion, felt my language was too informal, too naked, too open; that I was baffling, provocative, and embarrassing. I was trying to be simple, exact, evocative, to convey the sense and atmosphere of a bit of work I hoped would be useful. One never quite knows oneself and hopes to create an impression different from the one actually conveyed. It is sobering to realize how irrelevant one is to many, yet worth it for the few who find one's voice moving or freeing.

The unfortunate result of speaking for the few can be a shared sense of secret superiority that isolates one and makes one immune to ordinary criticism. Was there the danger of Marion and I forming such a bond? Was the fact that my craziness spoke to her craziness (and vice versa) alarming or healing? Would the language and concerns we shared isolate and injure us or bring us more deeply into life?

The contingencies of life broke fantasies of oneness and brought us to our first real crisis. I was out shopping with my children and came back five minutes late for Marion's appointment. By my reckoning, I was only three minutes late (five minutes by the time I was on the phone calling her). I understood that she could think I was almost fifteen minutes late, since her new time was ten minutes later than her original time. She could say that she forgot her time was changed or that it was not changed ten minutes. If it was changed five minutes, then I was eight to ten minutes late. My eyes searched anxiously for her on the porch but I knew she would not be there. I half expected her to come back any moment. Perhaps she was late and soon would ring the bell. I looked out the window on and off, but knew she had left.

I remember my happy feeling driving home with my kids thinking I would be only a few minutes late and would make my appointment. I was a few blocks from my house when the sinking feeling hit and it dawned on me: she would not wait. The fact that I would arrive and she would not be there somehow set things in order. There would be no secret society. She was right to slap my grandiosity in the face. Her leaving kept things honest. We were not in a love nest or ivory tower or bell jar.

What a way to keep things honest: I am not there for her, nor she for me. We come and go before and after each other. Perfect! In an instant we said everything! Wound for wound, modern talion. Hole meets hole, abyss meets abyss. We offer each other the Great Zero. We create the Great Zero and enter it together. It is our action painting, our bloody comedy.

It is common courtesy for patient and therapist to give each other fifteen minutes to show up before going about their business. Marion could not give me fifteen minutes. I called and left a message on her machine, letting her know I was there and was sorry she didn't wait. I offered to see her after my next appointment. While I was with my next patient, she called to say she was on her way over. We would try again.

I felt it a sacrifice to give Marion another session. My wife was away seeing her ill mother. I was home taking care of the kids. The kids would take care of themselves during the two sessions I scheduled. Now we had to change plans because of the additional time I had offered Marion.

Perhaps sacrifice is the wrong word. Perhaps it was more an imposition than sacrifice, but imposition is too weak. After all, I offered the extra time; no one forced me to. The fact that this was our next-to-last meeting before my two-week vacation must have played a role in my offer. Was I afraid of losing Marion, tipping her over the edge, wrecking our relationship? Our relationship was new. We were still finding each other, getting each other's range.

I do not think being a few minutes late is a terrible thing. Most people absorb this. More important than objective facts were the *shock* waves I felt. I was late, she left: *shock* waves. In the great waves were little waves of fear-anxiety-panic guilt. Why didn't I take the time of our appointment more seriously? I wanted to make it up to Marion, make it better, repair the rift, re-establish harmony, undo disconnection and upheaval. But the great shock waves involved more than momentary panicky guilt.

To say I was furious or resentful is an understatement that misses the mark. It is crucial to do justice to the extra sum of intensity that blasted the day, the intensity that Marion and I generated. A disruptive force smashed and battered our day. I am tempted to say an uncontrollable upheaval ruined our day. It *almost* ruined the day or *might* have ruined the day. It also saved the day. By damaging the niceness of the day, it brought our day to another level.

Every day has its disruptions, its serious disruptions. It was not enough for Marion and I to be nice to each other. If our relationship could not work with disruptive forces, it was not worth anything. Therapy is a highly distilled version of two people working with the disruptions that a relationship generates. To say that Marion and I generated disruptions partly misses the mark. It may be truer to say that we had to find our way around-with-through the disruptions and uncontrollable upheavals that mark emotional life.

The shock of Marion's not being there and of my not being there for her acted like a magnet that melded together other shocks I experienced in our relationship, such as her announcing she wanted to kill herself, or her menacing glower. It was important to let this impact build, to experience it fully, as best I could. I needed to be true to what was happening between us. It would not devastate my being for long. My day would re-form around it. Yet I had to admit that what was happening involved a sense of devastation. Was it my devastation? Marion's devastation? A free-floating devastation that we happened to run into? It felt like it would go on forever, that we could never recover. It felt like it had always been there and would never go away.

We coil around and swallow events too big to handle, then stretch to digest them to whatever extent we are able. We coil around some segment of shock and try to metabolize it. Our impact on each other matters and requires fidelity and cultivation, even if that impact is devastating. Perhaps what matters most is the elasticity we exercise in response to the devastating impacts we have on each other. It is as if we must test our capacity to stretch to the limit and then draw back to a workable area. We repeat the process and grow or snap.

I felt Marion's hurt feelings at my lateness, her panic that I forgot about her. I half hoped she would say no when I offered an extra hour, but I knew she must say yes. I was glad she did, not merely sorry. An important ingredient in the steps of this episode was a sense of inevitability. She *had* to go through this and so did I. We had to inflict certain sorts of injury on each other, endure suspense, and then enjoy the relief of momentary resolution.

Being a bit late triggered the sense of catastrophe. That the circumstances were not really catastrophic gave us a chance to work with the sense of catastrophe in a nearly tolerable dose. In ordinary life the sense of catastrophe paralyzes Marion, warps the tone of her days, forces her to provoke more suffering than need be, strangles her efforts at living. The sense of catastrophe can never be fully encompassed by our personalities. In every life there is more catastrophe than a being can handle.

We constrict ourselves to areas we imagine we can handle. We bite off a bit of reality and plunge in, mold it, learn to feel at ease with it: our little nest, workplace, home, sets of relationships. We metabolize what little bit of the catastrophic sense we can and make the best of it.

Marion had her home, her marriage, her work, her family, her world. She progressed as an analyst, a mother, a wife, a person. Yet nothing felt satisfactory. She did not get where she wanted to be professionally, nor in her marriage, nor as a mother, nor as a person. Something pulverized her life, poisoned her relationships, shattered and deformed her sense of self. The sense of catastrophe pervaded every bit of her life, so that her capacities felt like spider's legs wriggling helplessly, ceaselessly, every which way, under the impact of an injury to the center, an injury too immense to heal, too pervasive to locate.

Marion's mother also was depressed; an overwhelming depression was passed on through generations. Marion grew on psychic grounds that were shaky. Whatever she built could be destroyed by a shift of the emotional weather. She lived between earthquakes. Catastrophe was part of the taste of her milk. She spent so much time learning to survive catastrophe that she did not have much time for herself.

Marion's mother alternately supported her and tore her down. Women were not supposed to get educated. Being a professional broke the mold. In a sense, Marion rode her depression past her mother. Her depression catapulted her into the therapeutic world, where her mind found food that fit her. She could think about herself through others and about others through herself. Her mental gifts nested in her depressive sensitivity. Her mind pirouetted through the psychoanalytic kingdom in search of treasures. Here she could be herself, exercise herself. Working with severe disturbances in others came naturally to her. Her own therapy was a place she could let down and let her yucky self out. It was also a place she could let her best self shine.

I knew all this and appreciated Marion's real strengths, her battle against odds, her real triumphs. I empathized with her panicky vulnerability and sense of fragility as well. I was able to ask, "Why didn't you wait for me?" We openly touched in's and out's of no mother, no other, no ground, a subzero world. It thus came as a surprise when the word that formed in my mind was "merciless." I would not escape the growing sense (accusation?) that Marion's not waiting for me, whatever else it was, was merciless, an act of cruelty.

She meant to devastate me. We created a bit of shared devastation. Perhaps I tasted what she lived with, what she had to contend with. To go through a devastating time was like breaking bread together, the bread of catastrophe. We would break catastrophe together and metabolize bits at a time.

"How merciless, not to wait for me," I said.

She could not believe her ears.

Was I being hostile, letting out my anger at Marion for messing up part of my day? I had to risk it. The word *merciless* formed in big red letters in my mind. It was inescapable. I lived with it for a little while before saying it, a mountain of a word, unbudgeable. If I didn't say it, the moment would die, an opportunity lost. We were alive together in a difficult, almost horrible way. There was no compromising the moment. "Merciless. You are merciless."

She was surprised, interested, relieved. There was also disbelief, a "What-do-you-mean?" glance. The menacing glower was not absent, but not dominant.

"Your not giving me a chance to show up was merciless."

Was I doing this for her or for me? I felt freer, less intimidated by her illness, her glower. I could locate cruelty in the glower. I saw a cruel tyrant. Leaving so precipitously was tyrannical. The fact she was weak, vulnerable, needy, and fragile ought not excuse cruelty and tyranny; needy and cruel aspects of personality often interweave.

There was a silence in which I felt we were sinking more deeply into, through, past ourselves. I did not know what would happen. Would she be hurt? Enraged? How much would I have to pay for my transgression? We kept sinking past our situation, deeper into our lives, past our lives.

"Merciless," said Marion. "I've often thought I was merciless. That's a word that would come to me. I would see myself do something to someone, my husband, my child, and think I was being merciless. It never passed my lips. It was never said."

Marion spoke resonantly, fully, a bit shakily. I felt we shared a moment of transcendence. In a breath it could slip away. As she spoke she saw and sensed the icy cruelty that is part of life. A hair's-breadth shift of spirit and she would no longer encompass this icy cruelty but be it. It does not take much to feel maligned, injured, to feel the full scope of the evil done to one, the real deprivations and horrors that deform the self. Being abused by existence justifies abusing existence; torture justifies torture.

Marion repeated the word *merciless* a few times, mulling it over, trying it on for size. She spoke it as a confession, a subtitle to so many actions that ran off automatically and baffled her. She dared not let the other in on her mercilessness, lest it be used against her or dismissed. Such an admission would give the other an unfair advantage. If her mercilessness was admitted as evidence against her, she would lose the imaginary advantage conferred by secrecy. She would no longer feel she had the right to prosecute her case.

She gave me a "How-did-you-know?" glance. I could see it was not a question, but an appreciative acknowledgment of a shared capacity. Things often came to her that turned out to be accurate. In sessions she would think or say things that reflected the depths of her patients' beings. They would come out of the blue, little birds of meaning from nowhere. Such words carried the authority of unconscious work, a taking in and processing of the patient's impact.

My saying something that had often stained her awareness validated the reality of unconscious transmission, valorized the fact of permeability and porousness. We are porous and permeable beings who transmit intuitions to each other. We may deny or abuse this capacity, milk it for all its worth, or pretend it isn't there, but it *is* there, ticking messages of felt significance. My saying what Marion thought suggested that she was part of a community that respectfully worked with porousness. She was not an isolated freak or weirdo. Unconscious processing of attitudes-affects was part of a real job by real people, she and I among them.

ON BEING MERCILESS AND
A TALENT FOR DEPTH PSYCHOLOGY

In the next session Marion said she thought a lot about my calling her merciless. She felt accused, put down, ashamed, worthless. I made her feel among the lowest of the low. She hated me for this. She went into a depressive spin.

These were not new feelings. She was used to feeling worthless.

Abjection was home; to be a worm was business as usual. What was important was that she pulled out of it.

She pictured herself as merciless-worthless and felt more backbone. It felt good to stop making believe she wasn't cruel. She was suffocated by her role as the weak one, the one to whom bad things happened. It was a relief to own up to doing bad things to others, as well as others doing bad things to her.

Marion pulled out of her depressive spin by sticking with a bit of psychic truth, the same truth that plunged her into it. She said the word "merciless" over and over, like a mantra. She rode out her depression on this mantra.

Marion had long loved psychic truth: her sensibility craved it. Some people have a talent for psychic life. They are at home swimming in the psyche. Nothing fills them more than visions of psychical reality. Marion's tragedy was that she could not get this talent to work for her. She used it to decimate herself and others. She also used it to enrich life, to link up with others, but the dangers were great. She picked wounds, and when they opened, she jumped in and vanished. Wounds took on a life of their own; they gorged on her and she on them.

What we needed to do was create a context that enabled her to use her talent without destroying herself and others. That context or background or horizon was stimulated and sustained by the quality of our interplay. In the depths of my being I could say, "Wow, Marion! You really can destroy me; you can destroy my day. We can destroy each other's day. And we *do!* But we somehow bounce back. We find ways of contacting each other. We reconnect. We destroy our connections and reconnect. We really do this repeatedly. Our relationship survives us, and we survive it. More than survive: we are hell for each other, and through hell, radiance for each other."

An important element in this porridge is that I really respected Marion's psychic talent, her contact with psychic life. I did not simply view it as a secondary or compensatory offshoot of personality problems, a schizoid, borderline, or narcissistic sensitivity, although it also may be that. I know the deep joys this talent can bring, and I know its pitfalls too. There is such a thing as a talent for psychic life, a gift for psychological intuition, sensing, or construction. It can take many forms, including being a therapist. It is a talent that needs to be accepted as part of daily life, not devalued as something that ought not be there if one were healthier.

I would not be surprised if Marion's past therapists tended to fear or play down her psychological sensitivity. Marion was expert at tuning into psychical reality in devastating ways. One could be devastated, as she herself was, by her abilities. One could see the need for firm therapeutic boundaries, distance, and self-protectiveness, although the result would be lasting fear of Marion's psychical foundations and greatest gifts.

According to Marion, her past therapists assumed the role of the ones who had the right to live, as the carriers of self-worth. Their job was to encourage Marion to become one of the worthy. There was an unbridgeable gulf: they healthy, she sick. They were what she was supposed to be. They tried to help her past the barrier of herself. They were encouraging, warm, and supportive (although one also was supercilious, self-justifying, and testy). They invited her to jump to the other side of the healthy–ill line, their line, perhaps Marion's imaginary line.

Perhaps Marion was attracted to me because I was further along in accepting my offbeat sensibility and in learning to use it less destructively. Perhaps I conveyed to her the sense that it was okay to be the sort of person she was. There were no lines to cross. It was a matter of practice and experience.

A few sessions ago Marion commented on what she called my "healthy indifference." She felt lifted into a new dimension of psychological care by my minute attention to nuances of shifts in her moment-to-moment states of being. She felt I registered shifts in mood and intention: she could see and feel her impact on me. Yet she could see that my own life ticked on, that my lifeline was not deflected by hers. I could pay attention to her, then drop her or let her go.

Marion said she respected my sparse use of words; she respected my competence. She used the term *respect* several times. Apparently the word was growing in meaning for her. Surely her past therapists respected and helped her. But now it seemed as if a lifelong dream were coming true. Her naked psychic life was respected for its own sake, and she did not have to do anything to earn this respect, not even get better. Psyche called to psyche, psyche resonated to psyche. The psyche has its own range finder, tendrils, ways of knowing. Marion scarcely believed her luck in stepping into a world where sensitivity reverberated to sensitivity in a raw, respectful way.

Marion liked the fact that I could pay attention to her, yet let her go: my own brand of mercilessness. It irritated, enraged, and depressed her. It also made her breathe easier. At times she could be jealous of her own psyche: Was I more interested in her psyche than in her? She needed the reassurance that I worried about her, that I cared. Indeed, I did. I was aware she could drown in depression, that injury and rage could do her in. The new dimension of psychic care I offered might not be enough. In time she would get used to it, use me up. What then?

Meanwhile, Marion enjoyed contact with a flow of double capacities that matched her own. I could be upset, yet immune to being upset; attuned to suffering yet not done in by it. I could worry, yet follow the psychic threads of the worry. Like her, I could let vagueness and clarity alternate without favoring either, although she tended to favor clarity and I vagueness.

We were merciless in our own ways. Psychotherapy has a merciless aspect. One experiences the pain of the other, and one's own pain, and does what one has to do. One follows the lines of psychic interplay to the end. Psychoanalysis is an operation without anesthesia, although one does not spit in the face of merciful lies. Can one do this work without faith and a lust for psychic reality?

Who does what to whom? I was a bit late, and Marion left. I called, and she came back. I said the word *merciless*. She said she wanted to say it. Time stood still, and we were nothing but mercilessness, totally absorbed by the mercilessness that runs through life. The word *merciless* consumed us for a time and became our primary link. The merciful thing to do was to experience our mercilessness. For the moment, the most heartfelt thing to do was to sense our heartlessness.

Our mental and sexual arousal brought us to this cold spot, from heat to ice. Passion and coldness inform the exercise of capacities. We were making room for the mercilessness we tried to hide from, the mercilessness that we tried to wish away. Could the heat of our relationship metabolize a bit of cruelty?

Cruelty can never be fully metabolized. We will be cruel to each other, to ourselves. We learn to make better use of cruelty. We keep reworking our relationship to what is cruel in ourselves. We become creative partners with our merciful–merciless attitudes and moods.

I am grateful that my relationship with Marion gave me a chance to rework some of my own coldness, indifference, mercilessness. My contact with this dimension, through Marion, chilled me and warmed me. Wasn't there something cool and casual in showing up late? I could have made the effort to come on time. I could have planned better, not done so many things, rushed a bit more. If I had taken the time of our appointment more seriously, I would have been there as expected. If I had taken Marion's expectation to heart, I would have been there.

There was a dismissive, self-absorbed aspect to my casualness. The world could wait for me. I refused to be dominated so totally by schedule, by time, by the other. I was angry at the regimented aspect of my life. For the moment, it was Marion's fault. She was to blame for my having to make a living, for my having to go to my office when I was shopping with my kids. Well, damn it! The hell with it! I'll go at my own pace, not hers. I'll show up when I show up. She'll wait, she'll be there.

I raced home, and Marion raced away and raced back. Together we faced our self-absorption, our self-protectiveness, our inability to sustain life's tensions and contraries, our need to be and not to be with each other. Our therapy is only a few months old. It will take a lot of growing or ingenuity or genius for us to stick with the situations we must find our way through, the states we create with each other. That is part of the glory of this work, a glory that radiates through mercilessness.

12

Primary Process and Shock

Sam is a young, handsome man, a poet who looks like he lifts weights. He reminds me of certain actors who have fresh, well-packaged looks, faces composed as they wish, a sense of control running through facial as well as bodily muscles. He is in command of his functioning. He is affable and warm, altogether pleasant and engaging. He *ought* to be likable and actually is. Yet there is something uncomfortable and jittery about him, as if his muscles do not quite work as a shell, and the sensitive underside is exposed. His face seems very naked, yet nothing seems to be there except raw nervousness.

I am interested in Sam and glad he is seeing me. I am in my late fifties, he in his twenties. In some ways he is living the kind of life I might have liked to live in my twenties. He is a gifted writer enjoying affairs with numerous women. My relationships with women, especially in my twenties, were tormented, if also joyous. I went from hell to hell, as well as heaven to heaven. Sam aroused my envy with his great affairs with great women and the pleasures he got from writing (writing: one of my favorite torments). Everything Sam did was fun and pleasurable. He seemed to have a right to pleasure. Where was Sam's hell?

Sam dated his death from a moment in college when his father walked out of a restaurant in a fury, leaving Sam and his mother in a state of shock. At that moment Sam split off from himself and never came together again. A vast emptiness arose between his feelings and a seeing eye above. This emptiness pervaded his pleasures. Living was marred and canceled itself. Nothing developed in significant ways.

Nevertheless, there were moments in sex and writing when Sam came together and was lifted beyond himself. These moments were short-lived and dwindled into insignificance, but they made him feel that life ought to be different and that he must not settle for the status quo. The odd thing for me was the way Sam reduced his best moments to an ideology of pleasure.

In my twenties the best moments stood out against torment and banality, lifted life to another level, shook me into the faith dimension. Intense pleasure catapulted me past itself through an open heart toward the face of God. A light beyond the fires of hell pierced shell after shell of oblivion. Yet Sam was willing to settle for pleasure, to call life at its best pleasure rather than glory. Did he take for granted what was most meaningful to me, or did he suffer from massive amnesia? As a writer he certainly must know the age-old association of pleasure with emptiness. Did Sam's emptiness, linked with shock, use pleasure to soothe or wash the shock away? Did pleasure grow out of emptiness or emptiness out of pleasure? Were both part of a reduced field connected with shock?

Furious Father left Sam and Mother in shock. The shock of being left by Father is one image of a shock that has no beginning or end. Shock runs through the psyche and molds life and character. I wonder if I have ever met a person who was not in some state of shock. Perhaps one's personality or character is a sort of shock dealing with shocks. The fact of shock is never outgrown. But what is Sam's shock?

I repeatedly ask Sam about the fateful moment from which he dates his greatest difficulties. I encourage him to get into or taste or explore the shock. He is mostly blank, but we learn his father was short-tempered. Sam remembers him as impatient and irritable from the outset. As years went by he let himself go and became a fat, morose, loving, angry man.

I see a shocked baby when I look at Sam. Actually, a number of different shocked babies, representing a geology of shocks. I can't help it. It's my indoctrination, my style. I see shocked babies when I think of Sam's father and mother, and their fathers and mothers. The shock with no name takes on a history. You and I are unique bits of shock waves, contributing our own ripples, pulsations, bits of quakes and floods.

So-called oedipal and preoedipal shocks are prismatic reflections of shock itself, the generic shock beyond names. We share the capacity for shock with other creatures, perhaps all matter. Maybe every particle and subparticle that ever existed has a capacity for shock, a capacity encoded in every bit of universe. Our unconscious/conscious mind infinitizes shock. Our psychic life raises experiencing to an infinite power, blows up extremes. It is normal to exaggerate.

We are partly arrested shocks, shock funnels, homo- and heteroerotic shock filters. States of shock take on a certain stability. As I travel through Sam I come upon bits and pieces of congealed shock and then an enormous mountain range topped by the highest peak of all, Mount Shock. Somewhere in the distance I hear Sam talking about his mother. He is saying that she is submissive but deeply manipulative. She appears to be in the right and uses this fact to get her way.

Sam is grateful that she does not blow up. Her patience and perseverance create an illusion of understanding contact. The shock of shocks is Sam's realization that she does not *really* understand him. What he took as understanding was simple maternal regard: a generic maternal love, mixed with narcissism, blind and mute attachment to a body with emotions, a face with a smile, devotion to an essence, a soul, without a freeing apprehension of the face on that soul. Sam felt his mother insinuating herself into him. They were snakes intertwined against the father. He fears he will never wake up from this spell. He fears he is waking up.

His father's fury meant to shock him out of maternal fusion, but only made Mt. Shock grow. Sam's personality cracked along its fault lines. Years of conflicts within and between parents wore Sam down. Just at the moment when Sam looked strong and old enough and big enough to bear his father's fury, his father let go, and Sam was severed from himself.

The words I hear in the distance do not surprise me. We recite our versions of wounds, our stories or myths. The contents of Shock Mountain can be boring, but I am never bored by the thawing out of mountains of shock. Contents are necessary parts or conduits of processes that go far beyond them. I keep my eye on shocks and thawing. How wonderful therapy is when the shocks we are begin to thaw.

I wonder why Sam picked me. He went through obligatory auditions of therapists. Maybe he felt understood as a writer. I imagine he looks at me and sees the 20-year-old still fucking and writing like mad in the basement of my personality. Can he also see the pools of hell? Doesn't he know I don't think that pleasure can paste personality together? Sam baffled me. He thinks suffering is not essential, that it ought not be there. If only the fateful shock had not happened, he would be whole. His life would be a stream of pleasures. If only he could repeal the fateful moment, the traumatic dinner, and be one again.

Am I cynical to think of his fateful shock as a moment of destiny? From that moment, living as a pleasure machine would not do. It would take Sam years to approach this realization. All he knew was that he was not the same. His personality split or broke apart. Yet his whole being did not suffer breakdown. He functioned well. He wrote, dated, he made a living, he had experiences. Yet the break-up of his personality stayed with him. He poured pleasures into it, through it, around it. He tried to bliss it out with mental and physical orgasms. But the fact of unpleasure would not budge. He could not wish the pain of life away.

My vision/prejudice is that Sam's break-up will not go away unless he becomes the kind of person who can make room for and absorb his break-up. Sam's stuck point demands that he develop a new relationship with himself. He must develop an emotional context capable of absorbing and processing shock and divisions.

Sam needs to thaw from the ground up, as well as from the top down. My feeling is that rigidity of ideology is matched with rigidity of primary process work. Sam's belief that suffering is an accidental, not an essential, part of life reflects a constriction that is not merely cognitive. There is a narrowing of his ability to sustain and process affects and to link affect to thought. Shock covers incapacity, and incapacity covers shock.

Any analyst would suspect that Sam's problems did not date from the traumatic dinner. That must be a screen memory, a privileged moment that summarizes and encapsulates patterns and fault lines of self. Sam's memory of early events is barren. As a writer, he is startled by how little access he has to his early self. He is in contact only with raw facts of his history, not the living memory. When he tries to let himself go, he feels how far away from his life he is. Orgasms fill holes in the self for moments, but will not let pain associated with emptiness mount. Sam wants to be fixed without feeling agony. He wants an imaginary totality, without living through fragmentary processes.

PRIMARY PROCESS AS A CAPACITY

The traditional portrayal of secondary process doing the binding work, while primary process aims at discharge, is exaggerated and misleading. Primary process does work too. It begins the processing of affects, particularly catastrophic affective impacts. Catastrophic affective globs undergo processes of transformation, via condensation and displacement and so on, and enter dream work. Bits of nameless, formless catastrophic impacts are reworked into moods, images, and narratives in dreams, myths and reveries and become psychic objects and parts of successive levels of thought.

One can envision primary process as serpentine, wiggling this way and that. Freud uses liquid and electrical imagery when speaking of its fluidity. Yet in primary process work uniting–dividing is going on. At least we picture it that way when we think of condensation–displacement. Divisions may be fluid, but they are made use of. We like to think that our associative streams mirror, in a glass darkly, what the unconscious may be doing.

I confess I am a primary process lover. In an important way, loving the flow of primary process meanings has made my life worthwhile. The unfolding of my life has been part of this flow.

Many elements help knit a life together. Pleasure can link personality together; so can pain, or power, or catastrophic dread, or a sense of persecution, or preoccupation with somatic or hysterical concerns. In this chapter, I want to celebrate the linking power of primary process work. Pour hardened meanings in a hot pot and melt them, liquefy them, pour the liquid into new molds, and do it again. Liquefy the molds and pots too.

It feels so good to be nothing, to liquefy identity, to be raw identity. I pop up again, just plain me, everyday me. I am aware of my link with a deeper unconscious flow that supports me, that throws me over. I dive again.

I think this is the flow that Sam tries to contact with orgasms, alcohol, drugs, writing. He would like to use pleasure to get to it, but the problem is deeper. It is not just a matter of getting to the flow. In an important way the flow has stopped. Perhaps the flow itself has become a barrier or hiatus.

Sam tries to rev up momentary intensity to jump-start the flow. It is not just that contact is broken. The underlying primary process snake is not well enough to do the job. It is not able to start metabolizing catastrophic bits of affect in ways that link a person with himself without being a menace to the community.

Primary process work links personality together. One can use many images to express this linkage. It is the blood of personality, circulating throughout personality structures, issuing nutrients throughout the psychic body. It stimulates, warms, inspires, scares, and incessantly breaks apart and puts together experience in startling ways. When it works well, it facilitates the overall growth of personality.

My feeling is that Sam's personality constriction and emptiness involved more than ego deficit. Ego constriction and rigidity often reflect constriction and rigidity of primary process functioning. Sam's shock affected psychic systems on many levels. It ran through his personality. It made his psychic blood colder, his psychic skin more colorless. A numb chill was where a warm flow might have been.

What does one do to help Sam's primary processor thaw out and develop? How does one enable the psychic intake-digestive system to work better?

IMPACT AND MOVEMENT

A core ingredient in the kind of work I have in mind is the impact of the patient on the therapist. Impact is the primary raw datum. It is the most private, intimate fact of a meeting. The therapist may hide yet secretly nurse the deep impact the patient has on him. To put the impact into words and share it too soon may spoil its unfolding. An impact needs time to take root and grow. It occurs instantaneously, but needs the analyst's faith, time, and loyalty in order to prosper.

The analyst must be true to the patient's impact. Yet many times he may speak away from the impact to keep things going. For example, the therapist can keep the patient busy with mapping out early object relations and traumas and discussing current problems, conflicts, deficits, the in's–out's of patient–therapist interactions. All this activity can be helpful and bring relief. Bits of the patient's hidden impact may be used in the therapist's formulations. But full disclosure of the impact may be destructive. One plays for time and protects and nurses the impact. In some instances it may be years before an impact can be revealed, and by that time the patient has a different impact, although something of the original impact remains.

Different therapists have different styles in dealing with impact. Some spray bits and pieces of it, shotgun style, musing aloud. Others channel it with laser clarity and intensity. Some oscillate between extremes, and most are probably somewhere in between.

One cannot know ahead of time what parts of an impact may or may not be usable. Parts of impacts remain outside the psyche's digestive ability, for better or worse. Other parts dissolve more readily and distribute themselves through affective currents that enrich living.

Most often, impacts are shocks, the shock of one personality impacting on another. Sometimes the shock is pleasant, sometimes not; often it is mixed, and usually mute. A monolithic shock soon becomes variegated. As one lives with a shock, one comes to know different parts of it. One becomes more familiar with its colors, tonalities, textures, tensions. There are blue, white, red, and black shocks, and sometimes one sees stars or hears ringing or voices or music.

One's personality may contract or constrict itself around the shock of the Other, the point of impact. If the shock is great, stiffening may be widespread.

One goes blank and waits. The mind may race to get its bearings. If the shock is unpleasant, the chest may freeze. It takes moments to realize the danger is psychical, not physical, so that the primary processor can come out of hiding and work.

If the shock is wonderful (e.g., the shock of joy), one can't open enough. The tuning fork rings and sound carries. If the shock is horrible, one can't close enough, and sound flattens as fast as possible. The taste of a shock comes through in a micro-moment, although sometimes one wades through layers of numbness to get the taste.

In this chapter, I do not try to delineate the full impact of Sam's personality and being on me. Some of it was pleasant, some not. A curious part of it was the odd sense that this affable. warm, verbal, and competent man was an exoskeleton, that he wore his insides on his skin like a shell or crust. We had enjoyable moments together chatting about life and literature. Yet my chatting was informed by the deeper impact he had on me and by the not yet verbalizable impression that he wore his insides outside like a shell, that his insides had become a shell.

Now and then he might wait, and I might note that he seemed more intent on not being like his parents than being like himself: he did *not* want to be remote and angry like his father, he did *not* want to be submissive and controlling like his mother. He vanished in his *not*. There ought not be suffering, like there ought not be parents. Sam's drinking, drugs, and women increased.

I noted that he lacked a processor for his experience; nothing stuck to him or built on itself. We spoke about what it might take to grow a processor, to really have insides. His drinking subsided, and he wondered about himself. Perhaps wonder would stretch to reverie and dreaming.

ONE PROCESSOR TO ANOTHER

A traditional psychoanalytic view is that the analyst acts as a model for the observing ego, which somehow stimulates growth of the patient's ego through identification with that of the analyst. This idea is too top heavy. For tip of iceberg changes to be truly effective, changes must also occur in the psychic substratum.

What the traditional model means, yet takes for granted and obscures, is that the analyst is a model for processing psychical states that stymie the patient. This processing is not confined to observational functions, but involves conscious/unconscious transformational processes on many levels. For one thing, the analyst's primary processor works over the patient's affective impact, so that this impact begins to be metabolized.

The analyst's processing of the patient's impact is multidimensional and conveys many messages. For example, it gives the patient a sense of being taken seriously. More deeply, the patient *experiences,* if initially through the analyst, the possibility of *someone* processing what could not be processed. The patient learns that he is not entirely indigestible nor entirely digestible, that partial transformational movement is possible and necessary. This movement goes on bottom–up as well as top–down, and involves evolution of the deep processor, not only upper story functions. Without the growth of unconscious processing ability, upper story changes feel shallow and narrow, even besides the point. The analyst is not only an *auxiliary* ego for the patient, but an *auxiliary deep processor,* including an *auxiliary primary processor,* for a time.

For example, Sam refused to experience emptiness because his parents were empty (in his view). Yet emptiness plagued him. He could not dip into his own emptiness and savor it fully, in part, because he did not feel it belonged to *him.* Since he associated emptiness with his parents, to give himself over to emptiness meant to lose himself in them. One might wonder about projective–introjective aspects of emptiness. To what extent was emptiness introjected from the parents, projected into the parents, projected by the parents into Sam, and so on? To what extent did emptiness reflect the failure of environmental provision?

Such questions provide material to fuel an analysis for years, and I do not want to minimize their importance. However, my emphasis here is on a missing or deficient function or capacity, a lack of equipment. *Deficit of equipment can be experienced as emptiness.* Unconscious identification with parental emptiness and emptiness owing to the failure of environmental provision can be used to mask emptiness linked with a deficit of equipment.

One works with projective–introjective emptiness and real emptiness, but it is also important to realize when equipment to support emptiness is missing. One needs to be careful about encouraging a person to experience emptiness (or pain) more openly and fully. For some individuals, to go into emptiness is to go off the edge of the psychic universe. This is not simply because emptiness is endless (which it is), but because the individual lacks the capacity to process the experience. He not only gets lost in emptiness but also falls through a hole in his psyche. In this instance, emptiness fills the place where a primary processor might have been.

Sam did not merely refuse or deny emptiness: he was unable to tolerate and process it. The emptiness itself was a sign of this lack. Thus I did not ask Sam to go into his emptiness more fully—to own the disowned—but wondered how much of it he could or could not take at a given moment. This question is both quantitative and qualitative. How much can you take raises the issue of what sort of relationship you have with experience; it is a matter of quality.

The focus is less on experience than on the capacity to support and process experience. In Sam's case, no amount of writing or sexual orgasms could make up for the missing or deficient processor. By degrees, gently, playfully, deeply, and systematically, I help Sam realize that what he lacks is not experience, but the ability to do justice to experience. He cannot dwell with experience or with himself. A long-term challenge is set that whets Sam's appetite. His love of life makes him want to be the kind of person who does justice to his beloved, and a reorientation to what it means to be alive begins.

FRAGMENTARY WHOLENESS

Freud's fantasy that the infant hallucinates a breast when it is absent suggests how hallucination satisfies needs and drives, closes gaps, and covers deficits. A totality is substituted for a fragmentary state, an end for a process, a beatific moment for the missing Other or thing that is not there.

Sam finally came for help because orgasms failed to take the place of missing functions. A string of moments of wholeness is not the same as experience building on itself. Structural deficits involve deficits in the ability to process experiencing that run through the psychic body.

In response to Sam's wish for everything at once, I felt, all too keenly, the piecemeal, fragmentary nature of my remarks. I had to battle to be just plain me. What pressure there was to be the hallucinated totality, the breast, the filling Other! What pressure there was to be another of Sam's orgasms! To be everything at once is okay for awhile, but takes away from another kind of ecstasy. I love to pour myself into samples of experience, bits and pieces, fragments.

There are therapeutic ecstasies that include letting depressive affects build, or letting emptiness build. There is a tough ecstasy in letting Sam's impact build. So many images, ideas, and possibilities grow out of it. It is important to stay with the void in the middle of Sam's orgasms, in the middle of the orgasms he gives me. The void marks the place where relationship might grow.

Bits of processing grow by pulling on loose threads. Loose threads are real links, ecstatic links. I wonder if Sam saw me because he felt that my lust for loose threads complemented his lust for totality? Maybe he saw me as a loose wire and felt a shock of relief.

Maybe Sam saw me because I knew about shock. I was a sort of agent of shock, not just a hallucinated breast. Psychoanalysis is a matter not only of dosing feeds but also of dosing shocks. Freud was shocking. Has there been a shift in ideology from psychoanalysis as shock to psychoanalysis as soother, from soothsaying to soothing? Is that why psychoanalysis is bored with itself?

My relationship with Sam initiated a new kind of desire or perhaps stimulated a dormant one. Sam wanted to metabolize our interactions. He wanted what took place between us to become a part of him, he wanted more to happen, he wanted the process to build. He was interested in the kinds of things we did, our serious play together with elements of personality, our personalities.

To some degree, the growing intensity of Sam's desire to get more out of what we did stimulated the ability to do so. Therapy lust stimulated growth of the processing ability. Sam's personality was starved for good primary process work. In this regard, I could help support movement his parents could not. They were driven to make Sam their hallucinated totality, whereas I mainly wanted to help stimulate and share a process, the fragmentary hallucinations of psychoanalysis.

13

Being Too Good

Some difficulties that therapists and patients face arise when either one in the pair seems too good for the other. The painful consequences of such a situation was brought home when a therapist (Elaine) sought help with the serious suicide attempt of her patient (Susan).

Elaine was lovely, well dressed, well spoken, a pleasure to see and be with. She described her patient as extremely disturbed, unpleasant, and ugly. Elaine felt she had done wonders with Susan. Susan was becoming a therapist like Elaine, but she never seemed far from breakdown or suicide. She pushed herself every step of the way. What seemed to come easily to Elaine was a series of impossible hardships for Susan.

As Elaine spoke, I felt sympathy with Susan. Elaine depicted a tormented being, always near zero, somehow managing to keep going with a blind persistence that kept splattering and starting again. Susan's suffering was immense. What a sensitive, determined person she must be to come through her difficulties, battling enormous odds. I wondered if her difficulties made her more sensitive with patients.

How taken back I was when Elaine responded to my thoughts with emphatic negation. Elaine was exasperated with Susan's demanding anger, low self-esteem, hysterical clutching, fragmentation. She was tired of Susan incessantly drowning in a raging, bottomless pit of worthlessness. She wanted more for her patient. She felt Susan should and could be doing better, that there was a hump to get over that Susan was pulling back from. Susan was afraid to give up suffering and leap into and sustain a better existence. Elaine was angry at Susan for still being so tortured after all their work.

Elaine felt that her impatience was on the side of life. She did not want to sink into the cesspool of self-loathing that sucked Susan down. Elaine's was the voice of health. She extended a hand to lift Susan out of the muck. Susan took that hand, but could hold on only for short bursts. Elaine feared my sympathy with Susan's suffering was an invitation for Susan to regress and die out. Elaine's tendency was to be actively encouraging, hoping Susan would latch onto the taste of life and not let go.

Ostensibly, Elaine seemed to have more faith in her patient than I. She appealed to Susan's strengths, while I seemed sympathetic to her weakness. Elaine and I were in danger of becoming polarized against each other. We could cut her patient up and throw pieces at each other. I felt defensive. I didn't mean to succumb to weakness so much as acknowledge how tough it was for Susan and how courageous she was to persistently come through such suffering. Elaine and I quickly felt unjustly picked on by the other. She felt my sympathy with Susan as criticism of herself. She wanted me on her side, not her patient's. She attacked me because she felt attacked or in the cold, as she feared I felt she somehow left Susan in the cold. She came to me for help, not to be picked on.

I shut up and sat with my feelings awhile, awash in self-doubt. I felt badly that I jumped in too quickly on the side of her patient's pain. I felt a flaw or hole in my own personality, my impatience and inability to let build. I started going down the tubes, angry at myself for messing up the consultation. Maybe there was time to recoup and start over. Maybe we could give each other another chance.

But when I opened up and tried to start from scratch, the same thing began to happen again. Elaine was beautiful and gifted, but seemed filled with herself. Again my sympathies shifted to her suffering patient. In a few moments Elaine and I would be polarized again. She would feel left out, rejected, judged.

We would not be able to work together. Couldn't I identify with both Elaine and Susan at the same time? What about Elaine's suffering and struggles? Elaine worked hard on herself and had come a long way. Surely I appreciated her love of creativeness. Was I threatened by a beautiful and bright woman? Did I become hostile/defensive to cover my fear? I struggled to stay open.

Still, the more I listened to Elaine, the more the gap between Elaine and Susan grew. Susan was taxing, inaccessible, unappreciative, eternally frustrated and frustrating. Elaine was nourishing, creative, emotionally honest, present. Elaine brought the good stuff into the room and Susan the bad stuff. Susan kept falling through a hole in herself; Elaine kept bringing her back. Elaine wondered how long she could go on picking Susan up in face of the undertow.

Elaine did not seem very ruffled, scared, or worried, as I might have been. Rather, she seemed more exasperated and exhausted, as if Susan were trying the limits of endurance. She realized she was Susan's lifeline. Her resources in bringing Susan back to life (or keeping Susan in life) were being tested. Perhaps she was doing a little of what Susan did, looking for support and encouragement to get back in the ring.

My offering support and encouragement prompted Elaine to unleash her negativism against Susan and to voice her weariness fully. Would life triumph over destructiveness? Was all their work for nothing? The depths of Susan's self-hate and worthlessness consumed whatever Elaine offered. Susan felt too badly about herself to use a good relationship. Yet she did use it. Susan and Elaine kept coming back for more, even if the tie between them broke down and seemed ruined for a time. Actually, Elaine felt the tie was always there, although sometimes they couldn't find it. Perhaps all Elaine wanted from our session was a chance for faith to regenerate.

I could let it go at that, and that would be enough. But the distance between Elaine and Susan nagged me. I don't mean distance in the usual sense. Elaine was not a distant, cold person. She was easy and comfortable to be with. She kept things flowing. She always had something to say and was brimming with experience; she was a warmly rich and full person, optimistic, supportive, creative. Yet I felt left out. It gradually dawned on me that I was one of the sick ones, and she was one of the healthy ones. The earlier part of our session seemed thousands of years away, but now I began to get a sense of why I jumped the gun, why I had sided with Susan prematurely. Susan was *sick me*. I did not get the sense that Elaine knew in her bones who sick me was. Elaine was on the other side of the line that divided the healthy ones from the sick ones, like Susan and me. I wondered if Elaine expected sick souls to grow like healthy ones. Perhaps we sick ones have our own ways of growing. Did Elaine really expect Susan (or me) to be like her?

I needed to know if there was any way Elaine wanted to be like Susan. What in Susan did Elaine find valuable? I usually can find something in every patient that I need more of. What did Susan have that Elaine needed?

The shock waves from the earlier part of the session had died down, although not entirely. Without quite realizing it, I had been trying to keep things calm, trying to give Elaine and me a chance. Superficially, things had been going better. But if shock is there, one cannot keep it under the carpet indefinitely. The impact of the last part of the session was even greater than the first. I was blown away by Elaine's strong assertion that there was absolutely no way at all that she wanted to be like Susan and absolutely nothing of Susan's that she wanted to have.

My question was foreign to her. Why on earth would she want to be like Susan or want anything of Susan's? Susan's life was horrible. What on earth could Susan offer her? I wondered if something was wrong with me for imagining that Susan might have something to offer Elaine. What was wrong with me that I could find something to admire in Susan's struggle? The distance between Elaine and me seemed greater than ever. Instead of two professionals establishing a helpful supervisory relationship, we were inhabitants of different universes that had not yet discovered each other's signal systems.

Elaine's basic position was clear. She had something to offer Susan, but Susan had nothing to offer her. Susan could only bring her down, and she could only bring Susan up. We had gotten back to where the session started, from another route.

I was dumbfounded and wondered how to be tactful, honest, helpful. At some point I said something like "I can't help feeling that Susan feels you're too good for her. She can never be you, or like you enough. She'll always fall short. She's another kind of person. She's the kind you can't identify with and don't want to be like. She offers you nothing of value for yourself and is forever outside your desire. She can never get in, unless she becomes like you."

Elaine and Susan could analyze this gap forever, but Susan would always drown in it, because it was real and Elaine's feelings reinforced it. Susan was in the bind of getting help from a person who somehow experienced her as an untouchable. The helper was kind and caring and warm—one of the good ones. I could *feel* the problem, because Elaine's goodness made me feel more of a pariah too, even though I knew Elaine liked me and wanted affirmation from me. She wanted me to affirm her together self, but in doing so, my sick self felt all the more left out. When Elaine spoke to me, I felt she was speaking to the wrong person, to her picture of creative me that fit creative her. But I was somewhere else, like Susan.

Susan must be baffled by this duality. She is with a dedicated therapist whose work is superior. She is with someone who wants to help her and has very real ability. Yet Susan cannot locate herself in her therapist. She cannot find herself in her therapist's psyche. Her therapist does not have a Susan she values in the depths of her being, at least not yet, not consciously. For Elaine, Susan is a not-me element, an element of revulsion. There is no point of attraction or use she can find for the Susan in her soul.

I haplessly suggested that Elaine try to find some way to lessen the distance between Susan and herself. Maybe she should try to meditate on Susan's virtues. Can she find something of use or value for herself in Susan's being? Must Susan be forever foreign? Elaine is honest. She could not see anything in Susan that is exemplary. Susan needs help. She needs to move to another level. To be Susan would be a downward spin for Elaine. What value could there be in *that?*

Our session ended without solving the problem of how Elaine and I might communicate. I felt I had failed her. She probably left feeling criticized. She wanted to feel close to me, but I needed to include sick me, sick Susan. Elaine was too good for us, I feared. I don't think I'll kill myself over that, but it might be a lot of pressure for someone like Susan.

Jackie consulted me about her patient, Tina. Tina sounded a lot like Susan, except she was less suicidal. Tina periodically fell apart and could not function. She was anxious about diseases and needed frequent reassurance that her brain or other body parts were not disintegrating. Her social life was almost nil, and she had intermittent sexual contact with an otherwise unavailable man.

Jackie, like Elaine, was picture-perfect, elegantly dressed, tenaciously intact, warm, and caring. She feared her patient's periods of disintegration and felt a little guilty over the incessant reassurances she provided. Yet she did what her patient needed, and Tina improved.

Tina grappled with issues of self-respect, and her life grew. She took better care of herself and her apartment (positive identification with Jackie), got more satisfaction from work, and began experimenting with some dating. To Jackie's relief, Tina's periods of disintegration diminished in intensity and frequency. Things were going well enough.

My problem was that I felt I could not *find* Jackie. I did not *feel* any real contact with her, or any sense that I knew who she was. I could not *feel* her insides from my insides. When I inquired about this, she insisted she was easy to find. So therefore it was my problem.

Things were going well with Tina. Why should I upset the applecart with my problem? If I became insistent, I would become traumatizing. Things went along swimmingly. Why should I bother? As with Elaine, I felt left out somehow. Jackie's presentations of sessions were coherent, complete, competent. Whatever I might say seemed tangential, superfluous. I did not find vital loose ends to pull on. Was my main function to be reassuring and enhance Jackie's good feeling about herself and her work?

Jackie, like Elaine, was much better dressed than I. She was more together than I and took pride in her warm elegance. She spoke fluently about her work. She did not seem to have to struggle with what she felt or said, even when she voiced difficulties. She seemed immaculately on top of things.

The fault lines of my personality showed more than hers. I felt more flawed than she. But perhaps the fact that I saw her as a sort of perfect jewel was my problem. Maybe I was making her into something better than she meant to be. Perhaps my self-esteem was simply lower than hers, my personality less intact. Maybe I was feeling the inevitable exclusion of the less socially adept person. It wasn't her fault if she was better than I.

Yet the feeling that I could not find her nagged at me, although I got nowhere sharing it. Then an incident occurred that did not establish real contact between us, but which gave me some indication that I was not altogether crazy. Jackie came in and anxiously reported that Tina was disintegrating again. Perhaps Jackie was not really anxious, but simply frustrated, a bit stalled, uncomprehending. Maybe she was angry at Tina for disintegrating again. Jackie went over her checklist of things Tina fell apart about, but could not figure out what did it.

Jackie looked different to me this week. She had a different glow and tone. I couldn't put my finger on it but something felt different, so I asked. Jackie broke into a big smile and said she was in love. Her life changed since I last saw her. She seemed delighted with what was happening with her. It was easy for me to say something like, "I guess Tina couldn't take your being in love."

"Noooo. . . . Is that it? Could it be?" Jackie said, as if a light had gone on. She made the connection between her changed emotional state and that of her patient.

I became dramatic. "Your patient had a new therapist this week, one she never saw before." It was the first time I felt I could be of some use to Jackie. I could feel her experiencing the link between herself and her patient in a new way. At the same time, it seemed important that she had so utterly left herself out of the equation.

What a gap existed between Jackie and Tina! Tina must have experienced the change in Jackie, although neither mentioned it. Tina's loveless life seemed more acutely empty next to Jackie's love-filled one. The gains Tina made paled by comparison with Jackie's radiance. Jackie's *more* made Tina's *less* unendurable.

It would take a little time for Tina to get used to the new Jackie and for Jackie to get used to herself. Tina would spontaneously come back together, as soon as she realized that she and Jackie could continue contact, in spite of the latter's change of state. It was a matter of giving each other time to regroup and come through a major affective shift in the therapist.

In this case, Jackie was more bubbly and bright, so that Tina's light seemed dimmer by comparison. The distance between them need not only stimulate envy and torment, although it might if the therapist fails to recognize the real impact that her changes have. If rightly handled, Jackie's movement can provide a model for the possibility of opening and change. Changes in the analyst generate changes in the patient, for better or worse.

Jackie's breakthrough triggered waves of affect that were too much, too fast for Tina to handle. There was too much splendor in the room for Tina to take. Yet it was good for Tina to feel that such splendor was possible. It existed. Its effects were palpable. Would she be excluded from it forever? Was she banished from the kingdom? She tasted it in the room. Could she share some of Jackie's? Would she only get it through identifying with her therapist, or dare she get some of her own?

Many months later Jackie came in and started weeping. Something in her life had gone wrong and she was scared. She spoke about her fears and aspirations through her tears. Her life *might* be better than Tina's, but somehow *better* was irrelevant. Jackie suffered. She had her own dreads and worries, as well as joys. She may not go all the way down the tubes, like Tina. She does not disintegrate like Tina, nor feel so totally damaged. But she can identify with Tina. Tina's lows are not alien to her. They are not signals from another planet. She *can* see herself in Tina, and Tina in herself. They are very much part of the same soup, fellow travelers facing shared obstacles, one journeywoman further along than the other, but both in it together. The distance between Jackie's and Tina's lives is immense, but from Jackie's view, it is not alien.

What is the function of the supervisor in instances like the above? One function is to let the impact of the therapist and her presentation grow. In the two cases described in this chapter, the impact included a sense of discrepancy between therapist and patient. In each case, the therapist was much better off than the patient. Elaine appeared to experience Susan as more alien than Jackie experienced Tina. Nevertheless, there were moments when the differences between therapist and patient peaked, and therapist seemed too good for patient. What was possible for the therapist was impossible for the patient.

It is important for the supervisor to hold and metabolize the difference between analyst and patient. Neither Elaine nor Jackie fully took in the extent that their better condition had an impact on Susan and Tina. For some reason, they could not bear to realize that everything they worked so hard for in their own lives could increase their patient's suffering. Elaine and Jackie had made something of themselves. Now they had to deal with how their achievements might torment others, especially those they tried to help.

Another way of describing the difference between Elaine and Jackie and their patients is in terms of aliveness–deadness. Elaine and Jackie appeared to be more alive than Susan and Tina, not simply more successful, healthy, and attractive. The more one works with deprived and fragmented individuals, the more one realizes how important it is to modulate therapeutic aliveness. A too-alive therapist easily floods the patient without meaning to.

Elaine and Jackie were proud of their aliveness. Jackie worked at becoming more alive; she felt an inner deadness. Elaine flaunted her aliveness: aliveness was her *credo*, and she waved it like a banner. Both assumed their patients would be glad to have alive therapists: Susan and Tina wanted to be more alive. What Elaine and Jackie failed to take to heart was that Susan and Tina could not tolerate too much aliveness, not their own and not their therapist's. They might want and envy it, but could not take it. The sudden increase of aliveness that Elaine and Jackie stimulated was as fragmenting, overwhelming, and depressing as it was relieving. There were moments that therapist aliveness made Susan and Tina more hopeful, but it could evoke despair and a sense of impossibility.

The double-edged effect of aliveness is something a therapist must catch onto as time goes on. With experience, one may learn to adapt one's intensity level to what the patient can use. A therapist can either be too alive or dead for a particular individual at a given time. As one grows in attunement, one finds one's psycho-organism automatically regulates emotional volume, turning it lower or higher as situations change.

It is difficult for many therapists to recognize that they may be too much or not enough for their patients and that turning oneself on–off is an important parameter. An individual who chronically numbs or deadens herself in order to survive lacks experience and resources to deal with the full range of emotional aliveness. Therapists who work with dead and fragmented patients (or parts of many patients) need to develop sensitivity to the impact their own fluctuating aliveness–deadness is having.

The theme of envied aliveness, power, and goodness is ancient. Murder is part of the experience of exclusion. Biblical psychology can be cruelly honest: to those with more, more will be given; to those with less, even that will be taken away. Therapy is concerned with how to shift the balance of lives to the more track. More what? Aliveness? Good living? Use of capacity? Use of self? Still, there will be more, sometimes less differences in quality; there will be inequities.

Empathic recognition of the suffering that differences bring helps soften the outrage. Outrage and envy can be useful as motivating spurs. But in Susan's and Tina's cases, fury too often became destructive. Outrage boomeranged and increased their sense of damage, despair, inability. The carrot that therapy held out made them feel more helpless and hopeless at the same time that therapy helped them. Elaine and Susan needed to recognize how helping someone can be galling and increase destructiveness for the one needing and getting help.

Suppose Elaine included in her repertoire, and made a systematic part of therapy, references to how it must feel getting help from one who seems to be more alive or on top of it. Elaine *really* did feel better than Susan. I can imagine her saying something like, "It galls you being helped by someone better off than you." A remark like that may seem harsh and wounding, but there are many ways to put it that may soften the blow. Variations of the theme of being wounded by the helper must get played out and taken for granted. If the patient bites the hand that feeds, the hurtful helping hand also must be acknowledged.

My own personal suffering has been immense, so that it is hard to imagine placing myself above anyone else's distress. I *feel* myself a partner in suffering with those who see me. Nevertheless, I *know* I may appear better off to some or worse off to others and that perceptions of better–worse are vexing. It is one of the cruelties of idealization to imagine the "better" to be less tormented. In contrast with Elaine, I might have to say, "I fear your feeling that I am better than you so torments you that getting something through me makes you feel like dying." We need to find remarks that fit our subjective states. How to be helpful by being true to ourselves taxes human ability.

If Elaine really *felt* how much her goodness and aliveness hurt Susan, something in her touch might soften. A different tone or atmosphere might evolve, one in which Susan needn't feel quite so horrible about herself when she looked at Elaine or one in which she could share more readily the horror and pain of being propelled farther and farther away.

Creative Elaine came to join with creative me, but sick and dead me screamed for recognition. Sick/dead me felt unwelcomed by Elaine, and Elaine felt rejected if sick me was not happy with her creative self. Elaine did not have a category for sick me linking with sick Susan. Susan and me formed a community of sick ones that Elaine did not want to join. Who excluded whom? My ability to help Elaine with Susan was taxed. My perception of Elaine's superiority made me more defensive, less available to *her*. It was my job to begin metabolizing the difference between Elaine and me, between Elaine and Susan, between creative me and sick me. Elaine did not give me time to begin metabolizing my defensiveness, so as to work better with hers and Susan's. Differences propelled us apart, instead of creating possibilities for a varied relationship.

The propulsive element was an important part of what happened between Susan and Elaine. Elaine was propelled away from me by my sickness, as Susan was propelled away from Elaine by her health. The propulsion away from the excluding object, if unchecked and unmitigated, can be suicidal. What died between Elaine and me was the possibility of working together.

What happened or failed to happen with Elaine, Susan, and me is a good example of selective recognition processes. I could not recognize Elaine's creative self unless she recognized my sick self. My sick self was outraged by Elaine's undervaluation of the sick me in life (Susan's, mine, hers, anyone's). I would have needed time to grow around my outrage and find ways of establishing communication between the best in Elaine and the worst in Susan and me (and perhaps, Elaine?). I would have needed time to live my way into the propulsive force that our differences ignited. Perhaps in time we could soften together and find ways to connect in the face of seemingly unsolvable differences. Surely, something like this needs to happen between Susan and Elaine, in a way that Elaine has not yet been able to recognize and suffer.

Elaine and I acted out, in brief, what lacerated her work with Susan over the long haul. The gap between sick self and creative self became a propulsive force, with abruptly violent possibilities (our quick end). Elaine could not give me time enough. Let us hope Susan gives her time enough.

Jackie ran through a wider range of states. She had more patience with me than Elaine. Nevertheless, there was a blankness or lack of connection between us. We somehow did not really *feel* each other. I think this blankness was part of what needed to be metabolized. I don't know where it came from or what purpose it served. Jackie spoke of sealing over a horribly traumatic background, and I suspect it partly had to do with that. However, we were not fully honest with each other, at least not yet. For the time being, I tolerate our partial holding back, our testing the waters, our sparring.

Jackie speaks of holding back with her patient. She fears the loss of control if she is too expressive. She is afraid she will become too emotional and lose everything. Being the competent doctor protects her patient and herself. What good would showing too much of herself do her patient or herself? Thus, in spite of her warmth and good will, an emotional blank spot substitutes for expressiveness, partly out of fear. She fears her anger and tears. I hope she is not too angry at herself for the little she showed me. Perhaps next week I'll be the weepy, frightened, angry one. It's never far away.

ADDENDUM

After I wrote this chapter, I began to feel Jackie from the inside. The inner bell jar disappeared. Now she seems exquisitely expressive to me. I can feel her moment-to-moment shifts of feeling, infinite modulations of grief, fear, joy. She surely runs away from her feelings and deflects into intellectual considerations. She keeps something of a hard edge and hangs tough. But I can feel *her,* and I was not able to before. What happened?

Was she there all along? Was it me who was not there? Or did something thaw—in her, me, or Tina? Did writing this chapter sensitize me to her? Was this chapter a sort of proxy attempt at metabolizing my (her, Tina's) defensiveness?

Jackie is more open to considering how her mood shifts affect her patient. She inwardly feels the connection between her joy and Tina's disintegration, and she is aware that her depressive feelings, if they are not excessive, make Tina more comfortable. The possibility opens of her and Tina traversing a wider range of states together and learning how they affect each other in a variety of ways.

How much of Jackie dare I let in now? I can feel her *feeling self.* What a quiveringly ecstatic sense! I don't know how much I can take at a time. Life is always given in excess, more than we can use or handle. We bite little bits to chew on—enough, enough!

I can *see* Jackie opening to what happens between her and Tina. How much can she and Tina take? They are discovering that there is the direct transmission of feeling between them. How will the discovery of this kind of openness transform or fail to transform them? The flow between us is real. What will we do with it, it with us? It spreads in waves between Jackie, Tina, and me and now, also, you.

14

In Praise
of Gender Uncertainty

GREG

There are individuals who decide what sex they are too quickly. In extreme instances, the outcome can be tragic. I am thinking of a young man, Greg, who consulted me years ago to help him get started in life. He was a lively, tormented, sensitive person who lacked the confidence to develop friendships and follow his heart's desire. A lot of his energy was diverted into battling with parents who could not take his being gay. Yet they had consented to a partial sex change operation when he was 16, at the advice of a psychiatrist-physician team.

Apparently Greg and the medical team convinced each other that Greg was really a woman in a man's body. Greg long felt himself to be a woman. He imagined himself as one sort of female or another, but rarely as male. There was no doubt in his mind that nature gave him the wrong body. He found a medical team that specialized in sex change operations, with a mission to correct nature's errors. I was appalled that the adult world around Greg enabled him to carry out his wish to change his body.

Still more stunning was the fact that Greg had started to realize that the operation was a mistake, that really he *was* and *felt* like a male. It came to him as a revelation that he dared not think, that he dared not live out: he was really a *man*. This was an unbelievable sensation that went against everything he ever felt. He had not even remotely anticipated that some day he would come to feel and be a man. He came to therapy for support in his anguished state.

Greg was horrified that he had done something so final and that adults had mediated it. Yet the dawning sense of being male was his new truth. Greg's life was excruciatingly painful. He oscillated between male–female sensations, but there was no doubt his self-image was changing. He liked dressing as a woman, but now felt that he was a *male* dressing as female, a male being female. This was new. Previously he felt all female. He wished he could undo the sex change operation. He wanted to act and dress like a female sometimes, but not simply be one. It is impossible to exaggerate the momentous, cataclysmic states Greg suffered through.

I liked being with Greg. He had a crazy, flamboyant charm. He was, as they say, outrageous. One moment my heart would be touched by an innocent vulnerability. The next I would be catapulted into a weird world where megalomania reigned. Once he spent two months of sessions creating the universe anew. He was Great God Ego doing a better job than the seven-day God. He could not live in a world he did not create. I went through this with him with a mixture of awe, curiosity, delight, apprehension, and occasional repulsion. I never got used to riding bareback all the combinations of megalomania/vulnerability he would produce.

This two-month period was the most intense and systematic God enactment he performed, although sometimes he would get up in sessions and act like a God Magician, creating some bit of reality he needed to control or make real. It was easier to imagine controlling bits of social-physical reality than controlling the flow of truth. The discovery that truth could change blew Greg's world away, and he needed to create another one.

My fear that Greg would seal himself off in his self-created universe was naive. He *had been* sealed off in a hallucinated universe that was exploding. For years he hallucinated himself as a female with absolute certainty. Now his hallucinated universe cracked, and he actually shared with me the process by which he created alternate realities, worlds of his own. The surprising news was that the new worlds he created were meant for adventure. They were filled with intriguing people and opportunities that Greg must explore.

I supported his experience of oscillating identities, now more male, now more female. Now a male with female elements, now a female with male elements. The hybrid nature of sexuality opened possibilities not conceived before. Perhaps increased uncertainty precipitated the sustained God creation. In any case, the new oscillation and creation went along with a breakthrough of social activity and vocational quest.

Greg's focus shifted from battling his parents to the puzzle of who he was. He *wanted* to be an actor, possibly a director. He wanted to go to bars and clubs where theater men went. He easily met people, got into wild adventures, began acting in plays and taking drama classes. It seemed like he could do a million things at once; he was full of boundless energy. Yet what seemed easy from the outside (I could never do all he did) was filled with anguish inside. Every step of the way felt catastrophic.

His sessions eventually became recitations of inferiority feelings, inadequacies, who would be good for him and who wouldn't, and musings on how to make his way without destroying himself. His roller-coaster swings, sense of catastrophe, and round of activities and adventures seemed good enough to him for the time being. More than good enough. He had begun to live a life he could say yes to. After nearly two years he left therapy. I'd love to know what happened to Greg. I hope he didn't get AIDS and die just as he was getting to enjoy himself and his mess of misery and joy.

Greg got the main thing he wanted out of therapy: he started his life. He was springing loose. But what a blood-curdling time he went through and what a sense of loss he faced. He had made precipitous changes to his body with which he would have to live. It seemed that he was destined to go through life feeling his body did not fit him or that he and his body only partly fit each other. Are we not all in Greg's situation one way or another?

I could speculate at length about Greg's history, family, object relations, identifications, and the like. In this chapter I must pick only a few bits from this speculative flow. Contradictions characterized Greg's background. His father was both passive and violent. He could be weak, quiet, gentle, sweet, and charming, but also given to explosive fits. His mother was self-effacing, but ran the household. He was the provider, she the organizer. She dominated from inside, he from outside. Greg bounced from one dominant parent to the other, one weak parent to another, tossed by changing combinations of parental strengths and weaknesses.

To an extent, he used the woman's body as a cocoon. Perhaps in the face of Father's violence, he placed himself in the image of woman for safekeeping, where he could ride out the storm of his life. The explicit threat of paternal violence made maternal threats less visible. His father mirrored life's castrating-annihilating aspect, but also was castrated-annihilated. His mother's castrating-annihilating aspect was overshadowed by her function as background-inside support. Cracks, shakiness, or violence in the background-inside support would be tantamount to the ground opening beneath/within him, the threat of totally falling apart and disappearing from within. Greg was caught between annihilation outside and disappearance inside.

Greg sealed cracks in the background-inside support by hallucinating himself into the external accoutrements of woman. The woman Greg hallucinated himself to be was not especially sexual (at least not sexuality that welled up from within). Greg was captivated more by the way he imagined a woman to move, speak, and dress, the adornments of a woman, than by her sexuality. The background-inside support became an external shell. Greg became a flamboyant, outrageous image of woman, not a deeply feeling sexual woman.

In the family Greg came from, the mother stayed at home, and the father worked. In this household mothers were not supposed to be very sexual, but were to take care of home and family. The Madonna image played an important role in this Italian-Catholic family, reinforcing its emphasis on supportive, maternal, authoritarian qualities. Yet the flamboyant, made-up woman Greg became was unlike the exterior of his plain, supportive, controlling mother. It was a sort of plaster of Paris woman, not a personality-less, mindless church Madonna but an exaggerated, loud, screaming version of a life his mother didn't lead.

Becoming Gay, Becoming Male

Greg remained a woman from childhood through adolescence. After he was 18 the idea that he was really male began taking hold. Was it the shift from adolescence to young manhood that brought about this shift, a need to find and redefine himself in terms of the larger world?

The Greg I met was tortured and despondent, but bubbling with energy. He needed places to pour himself into. The theater world titillated him. He wanted to connect with it. But to do this he would have to work hard and be more than the exteriorized female version of himself he was used to. He would have to play different roles, take chances.

For one thing, he would have to get out of his house, out of the world of his immediate family. He would have to go to studios, bars, and rehearsals and meet people. This drive to get out of the house and into the world ruptured the female kingdom, ruptured the family. Why did his parents let him have a sex change operation? Part of the odd answer has to be to keep him in the family, to keep a hold on him.

The family was ingrown, a world to itself. As female, Greg would be Daddy–Mommy's little girl forever. As female, Greg was sexless. The family stifled individuating tendencies. Never mind that he turned into a monster female. He was *theirs*, he belonged to them, and that's what mattered.

The one thing they could not take was his drive to get out. This went along with sex, leaving them out, leaving them behind. This is when the idea of Greg's being gay hit home. The idea of being female (another homebound creature) didn't get to them. Being gay did. Being female somehow fit the family psychosis, whereas being gay ruptured it.

Being gay went along with living his own life, being himself. This had the unpredictable consequence of discovering he was male. Being gay meant being male. Getting out into the theater world and gay bars gave Greg a rush of freedom. He pursued acting roles and different sorts of relationships. He began sexual explorations. In the gay theater world he discovered a home away from home, a truer home than his family in spirit. For the first time in his life, he felt a sense of fitting in, of being with like-minded souls. He did not leave his torment behind, but found a more fitting arena in which to enact it.

By becoming male and gay, he broke the shell of his mother that had grown around him. The exteriorized version of a woman he had become was an attempt to get his mother outside him. He became a woman who only had outsides, rather than a woman with insides. Becoming gay meant stepping through the female crust into a world of like-minded men.

When Greg was totally a woman, he was not gay. He was not sexual. The breakthrough into gay life was an act of individuation.

SANDY

Sandy was a woman who felt she was a man. She had partial sex change procedures that took away female breasts and gave her male secondary characteristics. He then passed as a man at work and social life. In daily life no one knew he was female.

Sandy was lonely and isolated. He spent years in group therapy and never told anyone she was a woman who had become a man. He wanted everyone to take him as a man, as he took himself. He did not want anyone to know his secret. He wanted to live as a man, or not at all.

It would be easy for Sandy to establish a lesbian relationship, with himself in the male role. But he wanted to be a man with a heterosexual woman. He wanted a true heterosexual relationship, nothing else. From time to time he dated women who liked him, but he could not culminate the relationship without revealing he had no penis. He dared not be honest. Above all, he wanted to be a real man and to be perceived as a real man. In time he would seem strange to his partner, and the relationship would end. Hiddenness and loneliness were his true partners in life.

Sandy, so different from Greg, spent years in therapy. It is remarkable that he kept his secret from group members and that his therapist let him do so. In individual therapy he lay bare the depths of his loneliness. In group he looked for support in seeking and being with others. Group members tried to help him, but his attempts to reach them fell short. They could not feel his pain in an immediate way, since he reached out to them across a barrier, a secret. He felt injured by their perception of him as distant, abstract, strange. No amount of encouragement from his therapist enabled him to open up. He could not cry from the heart.

Unlike Greg, Sandy failed to find a milieu of like-minded souls. Greg cried from the heart, laid bare the roots of torment, dared to change identities. Sandy placed his dual status (partly female–male) out of bounds. The fact that he was once a female who partly changed to male was not a subject for exploration. Discussion of the problematic nature of sexuality was banished from therapy.

Attempts by the therapist to explore what it was like for Sandy to have a psyche that felt wholly male in a body that was partly both sexes (neither fully one nor the other) were experienced by Sandy as an empathic failure. The therapist was allowed to empathize with Sandy's loneliness, but not explore it. Sandy spent a good deal of time talking about why it was impossible to trust the therapist (or anyone), since trust led to injury.

The issue of trust was a dangling carrot that tyrannized and tantalized therapist and patient alike. Sandy's picture of trust was that the trusted one would never hurt him. Yet it is not possible for two people to be close to each other without hurting each other. For Sandy, the idea that pain was part of intimacy was intolerable. He had been hurt so severely from childhood on that injury was equated with villainy.

Sandy's mother was a witch who had abused and abandoned him. The road toward identifying with Mother was closed. In order to survive, Sandy defined himself in opposition to Mother. He would be everything Mother was not: gentle, sensitive, kind. Sandy found pockets of warmth with his father, who was nice at times but was weak and unable to protect him. Sandy formed the nucleus of his identity around pockets of paternal warmth, but also defined himself in opposition to his father: he failed to protect Sandy, but Sandy would protect himself.

I learned about Sandy from a European colleague who was genuinely involved in helping him. I was touched by her sensitivity to Sandy's pain. She was fearful of hurting Sandy, yet managed to maintain her boundaries. How Sandy's vulnerability tyrannized him! His therapist walked on eggshells, but a wrong move made her either the bad mother or the pointless father. Therapy was always on the verge of triggering unbearable pain and furious accusations.

Sandy could not get past his sense that he was totally vulnerable, afraid to open up because of pain and injury. Any onset of pain or hint of injury was a signal to close off. The idea that the analyst might also be vulnerable, or that the two might come through hurting each other together, did not seem to register.

Sandy's mother was not the sort of person who could empathize with a child's pain, yet she inflicted plenty of it. She could not tolerate Sandy or his pain. Parents who are especially good at inflicting pain on children often cannot take any sign of the pain inflicted. They cannot handle distress in themselves or others. So often such individuals try to stop pain by causing more of it. Perhaps there is a sense that more pain obliterates the painful situation. Sandy's dread of empathic failure had a real basis. He learned that vulnerability triggers abuse.

Sandy's life was an endless series of Catch-22s. He could not open up because he feared abuse. He could not have the heterosexual life he wanted because he lacked a penis. Therapy seemed to hold out a promise of contact with self and other that it could not deliver. It required an honesty Sandy could not get to, yet Sandy *was* as honest as he *could* be. He spoke honestly of his pain, fear of vulnerability, certainty of the Other's and his own failure. He was honest about feeling he was a man.

Therapy, like life, was self-defeating. Sandy used therapy's emphasis on honesty against it and himself. In a way, Sandy was *too* honest. He closed his emotional truth around him like a straitjacket. His truths were the pain of emotional vulnerability, the Other's failure, and his sense of being a heterosexual male. These were unshakable certainties. Any therapeutic invitation to extend the field of experiencing seemed an invitation to dishonesty. Sandy's very honesty about the way he felt stopped him from letting feelings grow.

Sandy read deeply in psychology and philosophy. He was searching for some way to make sense of his condition. Yet his intellectual probing could not budge the certainties of his emotional universe. It was as if he had been thrown up on a little island of self after shipwreck, and this bit of self was all he knew. His island personality closed around him, leaving no trace of ambiguities and oscillations antedating his *certain self*. What a painful gap existed between the therapist's wish to expand experiential possibilities and Sandy's need to assess all possibilities in terms of what he *knew*.

I can imagine several alternative lives Sandy might find more satisfactory than his present one. What would happen if Sandy could complete his sex change? What stops Sandy from being the male in a lesbian relationship? What stops Sandy from coming clean, telling all, perhaps finding (or starting) a group with others like him? If he were moved to do so, Sandy probably could become a therapist for others with problems like his. The list could be extended.

The point is I can imagine possibilities for Sandy that would feel dishonest and unreal to *him*. I can imagine alternative lives for *myself*. My sex life is heterosexual and I relish it. But there also are doubts. I can *imagine* falling in love with a man. I can entertain the possibility. One never knows what life brings, the conditions one finds oneself in, where an emotion will take one. I can ask myself, like Schreber, what it might be like to be a woman in sexual intercourse. Isn't imagining this possibility a part of sexual pleasure? My sexuality can be shaky, fearful, modest, uncertain, funky, confident, playful, tender, raunchy, so many things, as the kaleidoscope turns. I would not want to miss any of it. Shifting nuances add color to life.

The tragedy is that Sandy, insisting on one thing, gets nothing. He could not tolerate the degree of uncertainty and shakiness of self I've felt. I could imagine being Sandy, but he could not imagine being me. He could not imagine being me drifting around not knowing who I am or what I want. He never went through a period of unknowing in his conscious life. Sandy seems determined to bend life to his conditions, rather than working with and being worked over by the materials at hand.

In writing about Sandy I go back and forth, not quite sure whether to call him–her female or male. In my mind I use feminine, sometimes masculine pronouns. I suspect my oscillation reflects a sense that Sandy has not dealt with the doubleness of his sexual being, but has whisked multiplicity under the carpet of a single identity. He has closed off alternate selves. In my feeling, at least, I keep the possibility of multiple identities open. In the end, I respect his truth and use the masculine pronoun. Nevertheless, I cannot help feeling that my going back and forth inwardly expresses a shakiness, ambiguity, and oscillation he needs to experience.

Certainty and Deadness

Sandy's life tightened around him, and he felt increasingly empty. As the years passed, the pain of isolation and loneliness competed with an even worse state: a growing deadness and meaninglessness. How much pain can one take before numbness sets in? The pleasure he got from intellectual activity could not keep pace with the growing deadness.

Sandy's deadness was not painless. His deadness was horrifying to him. Life crushed his hope that he would find a woman who would love him as a man. Yet he could not modify his game plan. His true self feeling told him he was a man who needed a heterosexual woman. He could not change his true self feeling. True self feeling can be tyrannical. Sandy's true self feeling was killing him.

It is useful to have the capacity for uncertainty and self-doubt built into true self feeling. It is a wonderful moment when one can say, "Aha, so that's who I really am." What a relief to catch on, to have a sense of knowing. Such moments can be definitive, and one can build on them. But they may fade and be qualified by other moments, other revelations of self. One may feel that an earlier version of self was wrong, or partly right and wrong, or right for that time but not for this.

Editing is part of the pleasure of life. One edits oneself as one goes along. Life edits one. Sandy does not seem to value self-editing or revision processes. He takes a version of self as *the* final version, which repeats facets of original traumas in abbreviated forms. Sandy's true self is organized in such a way that it keeps crashing into reality. The original Smash, Pain or Ouch keeps getting replayed, without the qualifying variations that would change the self.

It is wonderfully freeing to realize that moderating and modulating oneself can enable one to *be* more fully and truly. One grows in appreciation of the zigzag, wiggle, detour. The more one lets overtones and undertones of self and Other resonate, the more thrilling life becomes. To try to coincide with one version of self is akin to vanishing, just as sound dies without multiples.

I am a heterosexual male, but not the same heterosexual male I was thirty or twenty or ten years ago. My sense of maleness has changed more in the past ten years than in the last three decades together. What it means to be a man has gone through enormous changes in my lifetime. I don't get the feeling that Sandy has thought much about what it means to be a man or experimented with different ways of being male. Sandy's true self configuration prevents him from undergoing experiences that would amplify, qualify, open his sense of self, and open him sexually.

I wonder if Sandy ever felt deeply wrong about anything, or if he ever subjected his vision of life to serious questioning. Being who he is is agonizing, but the agony does not seem to precipitate an overturning of self, a change of vision. Life is wrong; the Other is wrong. Life has treated him badly; the Other has failed him, treated him badly. Of course he is right. But the rigid quality of addiction to rightness seals him off from thoughts, images, feelings, and experiences that might make a difference.

Some people complain about being too chameleonlike, but it is also possible not to be chameleonlike enough. There are many possibilities between diffusion and immobility. Sandy seems overly caught up in the idea that one ought to coincide with oneself. But one needs to be different from oneself too. The self moves between sameness–difference, distinction–union, never solely one nor the other. Sandy seems to have stopped this movement. He seems to have substituted onethingness for everythingness. He has pitted himself against the movement of life and pays the price of torment without change.

Truth

Who can predict or control the flow of truth? For years Greg was sure he was female in a male body. As he neared adulthood, the truth that he was male began to dawn on him—that he was now male in a partly female body. Greg's predicament brings home a dilemma we all face. A truth that we believe one moment destroys us the next.

Isn't this one reason why Freud advised not acting out during analysis? In analysis truth keeps changing. We can hurt ourselves and others by acting too quickly on what we are discovering. It is precisely the mobility of truth that is one of the important lessons analysis teaches. The subject stays open to transformations of affect, thought, and object choices; it dips into streams of consciousness, streams of life. One learns from experience how one truth qualifies another. We are never one truth but many, in wiggly, wobbly ways.

We learn we are not only entitled but also obligated not to reduce ourselves to one version of ourselves. We turn ourselves over this way and that. The turning never stops. We put it aside to rest, to do something else, to recover from the movement. But when we are ready, we dip in and ride the rapids as best we can. We do not know ahead of time what current will take us where.

We may live out/explore some female element, or male element. We are a sort of male-in-female ↔ female-in-male Taoist Chinese box. If we look closely at any moment, we see male ↔ female elements turning into each other, interweaving, pushing against each other, subtly shifting direction, energy, and meaning. Freud's writings show every psychic fiber alive with the play of opposites, restless dualities, multiplicities, clashes ↔ mixtures ↔ fusions ↔ reversals of this tendency with that.

Truth comes in waves. We select some or some select us to spend time with. We turn a truth (systems of truths) this way and that, walk around it, see it from a number of perspectives, different profiles. Sometimes a truth seems very big but shrinks as we live with it. It doesn't take washing well. Truths we didn't think much of can grow and we may grow with them. There are innumerable flirtations with this or that truth, fun for awhile, uplifting for a time. Sometimes there are good marriages, truths that sustain and surprise us for decades. A good set of truths enables us to keep turning our identities around. Each moment of truth enables us to experience another facet of who we are (or aren't). To work on our truths is to work on our identities (*vice versa*), like a potter or sculptor.

To be an *artist of identity truths* must be an alien idea for Sandy. The stiffness of his true self is a measure of the catastrophe it binds and is itself a catastrophe. What does therapy need to do in order to free him from the pressure of trying to be one thing, one way? His therapist is trying. Will she find and lead him to the place where alternatives are ceaselessly born, the place his own swerving came from? Salvation, partly, is learning the art of swerving from oneself in time. At times swerving leads to derailment, but often one swerves into unseen openings and pours oneself into them with all one's might. What a delight such swervings can be; how lucky we are to go with them!

The art of self, in part, is the art of distance–closeness. How to be the optimal distance from oneself at any moment, not too far but not too close, is an ever-changing task. If we coincide with ourselves we may enjoy a moment of mystical fusion, but we also may be fanatic, one-eyed, or no-eyed. To be too one with ourselves may be to take ourselves too seriously, to not leave enough room for the otherness in us. If we are too far from ourselves, we may lose ourselves in echoes: by the time we hear ourselves, we are light years away from the voice. To freely move closer to the moment to give us ourselves.

By the time Greg left therapy, he was somewhat able to appreciate and use the internal range finder of self, that inner gesture or psychic body English that moves us farther–nearer to ourselves. Sandy's range-finder seemed stuck in one position. One sees how important was Freud's (1937) concern with psychic immobility. What conditions make for more or less mobility and what sorts of mobility–immobility? Psychoanalysis is still a study of movement and its barriers.

A COP: STRONG MAN—WEAK MAN

Every human being is actually many males, many females. If we took this as an axiom of daily life, we might get along better. We might make room for ourselves and each other. We ought not assume we know too much about the capacities that constitute us, who we are, and what we are made of. We are and remain mysteries all our lives. If we are lucky, we learn a little about being partners with ourselves.

We are protected from getting too close to ourselves, perhaps for good reason. Our systems of defenses and barriers act as filters for the radiating light within, like the ozone layer shields us from too much radiation. When Moses became contaminated by God's radiation, he put a veil over his face to protect others from the glow. We cannot take too much of ourselves or get enough of ourselves. Part of maturation is learning how to dose oneself and others out.

At times our filter systems get the better of us, and we vanish in or are broken by defenses that ought to mediate us. Jim, a policeman, lived his life as a good-natured, strong man. As long as he felt strong and his strength was appreciated, he could afford to be good natured. He got along well with community and family.

What worked as a younger man did not work so well as Jim got older. His body could not keep up with his image of strength. Jim lived a full, rich, successful life, one busy with relationships, pleasures, and adventures. In time, his children left home to live their lives, and he could no longer imagine himself central to their existence. Younger men in the department did the things he once did. He suffered several serious illnesses, including a heart attack, but could not make room for the changes that were taking place. He started to drink heavily and become angry with himself and others. His body could no longer support his self-image, and his self-image refused or was unable to make the necessary shifts.

Jim, the strong, good-natured cop, would have to make room for weakness if he did not want to die prematurely. There is a strong man–weak man dialectic in every personality, especially in males. Too often the strong man has contempt for the weak man, and the gap between them grows. The weak man becomes a nucleus for a bad self-image that drags the personality down. Instead of being able to enjoy the pleasures of weakness, the weak man is consigned to secrecy and feeds on inferiority, shame, and self-hate, a loathing that grows through sneaky moral superiority and passive–aggressive vengefulness.

The polarity of strength–weakness is heavily charged in society. It is good to be strong and bad to be weak. In order to compensate for this one-sided viewpoint, religions have emphasized virtue in weakness. Mastery and dominance for the strong, surrender for the weak. Yet there is strength in weakness and weakness in strength. "In the storm, the oak breaks, the reed bends," suggests the *Tao Te Ching*. And perhaps one of the greatest war cries of all times is, "The meek [weak] shall inherit the earth."

We need to meditate on the worm. When we think of weakness, we think of the worm. "You worm!" we cry in disgust, a cry of derisive repudiation. The worm is associated with humiliation, baseness, sneaky aggression, a sense of unworthiness. It spoils some of our food and feeds on our bodies when we're gone. Yet it does not seem to harm living creatures and for eons has helped the soil. The lowly worm precedes us by millions of years. It apparently can survive in dark underground places, although it whitens without sunlight. It bothers us that a creature crawls without a backbone all its life long. We only crawl a short while before we stand and grow up, higher and higher.

Poor Jim must fear becoming worm-like! He is having trouble maintaining his straight and tall mount above his backbone. If he cannot look down at worm-like creatures supporting life, he may become one of *them*. Something in his psyche whispers he is better off dead than weak. The idea of becoming a worm after living a life of integrity is too much to bear.

I want to praise the worm. We need to let the worm into our self-image more openly. It is not so bad being a worm. There are many good points to it. Too much pride in who one is can be as stifling as too little. We need the worm for balance. We need to taste the earth, let it go through us. We need to be close to the ground, not just high above it. Jim's pride in strong manhood is killing him. Perhaps it also is killing society. To play down strength is malicious or silly; to play down weakness is delusional.

In one way or another, a strong man–weak man dialogue plays a role in many therapies. Any man is many men. We also need to hear more about the strong woman–weak woman dialogue. If the repressive force of the strong man image lessens somewhat, dialogues between and within males and females and male–female elements may become more creative. Social realism teaches that if the strong let up, the weak tear them apart. We need to find ways into processes of mutual interplay that really work. We do not know if this is possible, but we cannot wish the messy turmoil away.

Jim lived a clean life. Sandy tries too hard to live a clean life. Greg dipped into the mess. He let himself be surprised by who he was and wasn't. He couldn't avoid it. Shouldn't we all take the plunge, in our own ways, in our own measure?

A NOTE ON IMAGE AND BODY

Is the human psyche too much for the human body? We can imagine anything, but we can not be whatever we imagine. Our visions and perceptions often outstrip our ability to act. We can imagine ourselves both sexes, but only be one. I can imagine more sexual possibilities in five minutes than I am likely to realize in five years.

We have a bisexual psyche in a monosexual body, more or less. Such a statement needs qualifications, but it conveys the immensity of what we are about. Psychoanalysis teaches that sexuality has many currents and subcurrents, dominants and subdominants. Our identity includes many subidentities. As a species, we tend to try what we imagine. If we can imagine it, someone is trying to do it. And, probably, there is also someone speaking against it.

This is part of the glory and hardship of having the sorts of minds we do, of being the sorts of beings we are. There is a gap between what we think and do. I can think of many more sentences to put down on this page than the ones I select. I try for a reasonable fit between what is trying to be expressed and what actually does. Writing is a frustrating pleasure, a pleasurable frustration.

Our sexuality also is a teeming ocean of possibilities, but we tend to make do with a mixture that fits us. We edit and re-edit our sexuality in order to connect with it so that we can live it in a way that uplifts rather than damages us. In clinical practice we discover that not everyone connects with his or her sexuality. The key is finding an identity (sets of identities) that work for a particular individual at a particular time. Freud taught that every micro-strand of identity is a plethora of multiples, alive with contrasting possibilities. One might conclude that a certain amount of confusion, uncertainty, and self-doubt is normal, that the lack of confusion is artificial.

We speak of the true self. We ask, is this my true self, is this? An individual may feel he has found it. He develops certainty about his true self feeling. In Greg's case, true self feeling (or the form of it) changed, and he was able to go with it. Jim's and Sandy's remained constant, with accelerating damage.

Wouldn't it be good if our true self feelings passed through our systems like soil through a worm? Perhaps as a society we need to emphasize more the difficulties involved in metabolizing true self feelings, not simply finding them. When do true self feelings pass into our psychic bloodstream as nutrients, when do they kill the flow? We need to find ways, and keep finding ways, to link true self feelings to real processes of living.

REFERENCE

Freud, S. (1937). Analysis terminable and interminable. *Standard Edition* 23:216–253.

15

Emotional Starvation

Many people are starving to death emotionally. Emotional starvation takes many forms and is part of a wide range of disorders. The images of starving bodies in Somalia so lacerated us, not only because their essential horror assaulted our sense of humanity but also because they reflected a hidden part of our own inner condition. We hide our starved beings from ourselves.

An obese woman, Sheila, complains about overeating. She tells me she is going to quit therapy if I do not help her control herself. She is quite demanding and impatient. I almost say, "You have to be in therapy to quit it." She is not close to starting therapy, and she is already leaving.

A few months later she still threatens to quit if I don't help her soon. By this time I know that she grew up with a psychotic mother and alcoholic father. I can feel the pain she must have felt as a child, but she gives no hint of it. I picture her child soul falling through ghastly abysses of maternal madness and traumatized by paternal violence. She shrugs it off. "What good will talking about *that* do now? You've got to help me stop eating now!" She gets angry if I say anything about *then*. She berates me, "Talking about the past is a waste of time." Her tone contains a menacing warning: "If you waste my time, I'll leave. Do better, or else."

The way she talked about wasting time rocketed through me. I was on the verge of feeling unreal and getting lost in self-doubt. The sense of waste gathered momentum. I felt how horribly wasted *she* must have been from early on. I could not let go of the pain of her life. I pictured a little girl ripped apart by her mother's paranoid depressive attacks, alternately exploited, devoured, attacked, and abandoned. I pictured her cowering in the face of her father's raging erruptions and the dreadful relief that stuporous obliteration brought. Yet I didn't only talk about the past. I talked about now, the living moment. She picked on my empathic remarks about her past to wipe out what might happen between us in the present. Our chance for a relationship was being wasted.

The word "wasted" makes waves! To be wasted, blown away, destroyed without a trace. To be waste material, a child's soul turned to shit, a shit-self, shitting itself out, treated like gold one moment and shit the next by out of control, golden-shitty, brutal, sentimental, uncomprehending parents. To be wasting away, undernourished, ravaged, stuffed with emotional toxins, flooded with eye-popping horrors that eat one's insides out.

Her fat winds like insulation around unendurable pain. Inside she is starving, wasting away. She does not know she is starving. She did not just starve as a child. She is starving now. A process has been set in motion and mushrooms. I look at her enormous body and am lacerated by *seeing* a skin-and-bones concentration camp self. I *see* a starving self. My rational self knows this is imaginative vision. Yet I see and feel it, as if a direct transmission is being made from her inner being to mine. Her body gets more and more bloated, as her inner self reaches a vanishing point. My gaze is riveted to the vanishing point.

I have an eerie sense that I am witnessing a life rhythm gone wrong, that I am being let in on a secret. We expand–contract, grow bigger–smaller on a daily basis: emotions rise–fall, fill–empty. We may all be millionaires in emotions, but we need to be able to let them come and go, and there are ways we come and go with them. What has happened to Sheila's emotional flow, its rise–fall, expansion–contraction? It is as if the contraction has turned into an invisible starving self, forever vanishing, while the expansion has turned into an outer covering of growing fat.

She cannot tolerate any hint of inner starvation. Emotional starvation is converted into physical hunger, which she fights and gives into. She cannot withstand the urge to gorge. It is an addiction. The bloated, stuporous content she feels after an orgy of bingeing is a macabre caricature of the infant's sleepy satisfaction on being filled by a good feed. Her constant demand that I help her immediately caricatures the infant's urgency. Yet unlike the healthy infant, she can not truly be satisfied nor helped, not immediately.

I wish she would gorge on me or on what I might offer. Yet I do not seem to be able to give her anything digestible, even in small doses. I am irrelevant to her because I cannot give her *everything now*. I cannot fill her up, partly because I do not know how to get through to her, nor does she have ability to use me as I am. Our interactions are uncomfortable and unsatisfactory. Yet she keeps coming. Something *must* be getting through.

As time goes on, I feel I am starving to death with her. Apparently unlike her, I feel the *pain* of not making contact, of the lack of flow, of the inability to communicate. Her potential pain seems immediately translated into anger at me for not helping her control herself. She fills up with anger like she gorges on food. Her anger occupies too much space in her emotional life and leaves little room for other feelings.

She wants me to help her control her anger like she wants me to help control her eating. She wants help in controlling what she cannot experience. She can be filled with anger without tolerating the feeling long enough to taste it and know what it is about. Anger, like eating, becomes part of a blank stuffing–emptying cycle.

After a year I begin to get the idea that her wish for control is a vestige of her wish to have a full psychic life. She no longer (if ever she did) knows what a full psychic life might be. Our earlier meetings made it clear that control is so important to her because she could not control parental madness and violence. Her wish for control is partly an indicator of chaotic helplessness and vulnerability. Yet the idea of control, at least, refers to mind, so that there is something she wants that is not only physical. Some idea of internality persists, if only as a reduced, displaced lack.

The idea of control is vastly overrated, but is easy to grasp and disseminate. Destruction and control of destruction provide enough material to fill our days with anxious preoccupations. It is easy to organize ourselves around desperate concerns. The idea that we should be in control feeds our vanity and flatters us with the illusion that we can control our control. But the preoccupation with control obscures other avenues of growth.

Leaders get bad press if they do not seem strong and decisive. Yet the need to appear strong and decisive can cause trouble for multitudes. There are times when it pays to oscillate, to wiggle-wobble, to curve this way and that. There is something good in human weakness and indecisiveness, something undeveloped that leaves room for creativeness. Passivity plays an important role in healthy development. Perhaps the weak will inherit the earth, after the strong kill each other off.

The idea of partnership offers more promise than control. How do we become partners with our capacities, ourselves, each other? Control, strength, decisiveness enter into the equation as variables with shifting values, depending on the moment. Weakness and passivity must be given their due as necessary parts of generative processes in public as well as private domains. The word "part" is part of partner: separating–joining go together. The media's greed for action stuffs us with cyclopean images that destroy the need for intricacy. Intimacy is always intricate.

Can we be on intimate terms with ourselves? Can the public domain survive without intimate input? Is intimacy possible? What *is* intimacy? Where intimacy is concerned, we are always beginning. Part of getting to know ourselves and each other involves making room for being a beginner.

There seems to be little tolerance for learning how to begin in either public or private domains. Leaders are criticized for not already knowing what to do and how to do it, when actually learning and self-questioning are necessary. They are frequently impelled to do *something* when waiting might be better. Things happen too fast to let actions ripen. Sheila too cannot wait. She is impelled to act. She *must* stuff herself with food and anger. Whereas waiting might be experienced as weakness for a leader, it would be strength for Sheila. She cannot let actions ripen.

"You are starving to death," I tell her.

"Why do I come here? You don't help me. I need help controlling myself. Stop me from eating." Anger stuffs the room. She is needy, pleading, weak, and demanding, but her fury obliterates everything.

"You are starving to death," I say many times, many months: this is my litany, my chant. Those are the words that come, that fit my emotional center, that make me feel connected. I say many other things over the course of time, but the navel is a sense of starvation.

I am frightened the first time these words pulse out of me. Am I crazy? Here she is stuffing herself into oblivion, and I speak of starvation. Am I maliciously defiant, relishing taunting her with paradoxical communication? I can tune into the sardonic satisfaction of the transcendent therapist, always inverting realities and mentally outfoxing the patient. But when the words come out of me, I feel deeply linked with myself, with Sheila's inner self, with the way it feels to be together in the room. Above all, the words are heartfelt.

Sheila stares at me blankly. How can I say she is starving? The blankness gives way to puzzlement, even a little curiosity. What happens if she delays stuffing herself with food and anger for moments, seconds, or minutes? What happens between the urge to eat and obliteration? I encourage her to try to wait even micro-moments and tell me what she feels.

"I can't wait," she tells me. "I feel I'm dying, starving, suffocating. If I wait a moment more, I'll die." It is important for her to know that waiting will lead to other experiences, even if she can't wait. There are worlds of experiences she cannot have because she cannot wait.

For one thing, she cannot take the build-up of dying. As soon as she feels she's dying, she eats herself (or infuriates herself) into oblivion. She cannot live her dying, it scares her so.

"You substitute one death for another," I say. "Instead of starving or suffocating, you kill yourself with rage or food. You die a numb death instead of a live one."

"Words, words!" she screams. "Words can't help me!" Unlike writers or madmen, she cannot stuff herself with words. She needs food or rage.

After two years Sheila says, "You are trying to help." She begins to feel that waiting is not controlling. Something happens when she waits, although she can't take much of it. Something builds. She *must* give in to need, to demand. She cannot deny herself. Yet she sees me waiting. She *feels* me waiting. She *knows* something is happening in my waiting. She experiences the build-up of my feelings. She *sees-feels-knows* that she makes me feel something and that it mounts. "You are waiting for *me*," she says. That she can see and say this is monumental.

There is a moment of self-to-self contact, which makes it possible to realize that self-to-self contact usually is missing. Sheila abruptly says, "I'm waiting for me too." In the next months she can say, "I'm usually not there. I feel full when I stuff myself. Then I feel *something*. Satisfaction, satiation. Then disgust sets in. I can't bear myself and die. When I start coming back I get panicky. I eat or blow up."

"You can't take being there or not being there."

"Not being there is easier. But I hate myself."

Not many people can take very much of themselves. We tend to hide this or do not even recognize it. For Sheila, the increase in both aliveness and unaliveness is scary.

"I feel I'm there a little," she says, "More than when I first came here. I'm growing a little, and a little is a lot."

Such a statement marks an amazing turn. For Sheila, a lot has been too little. Once gorging starts, nothing is enough. She reaches a point of triumphant, malignant ecstasy, as she becomes bloated. I imagine a tic or some sort of parasite feeding on blood, like a baby on milk. She may puke so she can eat more. What is she pumping up inside her, inflating her stomach like a ballooning breast? The growth of fat and fury substitutes for emotional growth. That she now has a moment of happiness with a little taste of real growth is astonishing. Experiencing even a little growth provides another reference point for what life is about.

One thing that is beautiful about therapy is the value it places on growing the capacity to grow. A therapist has to experience this beauty in order to have faith in it and also perhaps needs faith in order to experience the power of this beauty. Sheila must have felt growth was impossible and so lost a sense of it and vice versa. What sort of nourishment did she find in life? She had to make do with toxic nourishment and was always ready to react to what she was not getting or to the noxious mixture available. She swallowed poisons to survive. She hated life, herself, and others for the degraded, reduced world that entombed her. She survived like a rodent on garbage.

Where but in therapy could the love of beauty outlast or outflank the garbage self? What a beautiful garbage dump therapy can be. Generations of psychic pollutants pour into therapy. The beauty of therapy survives them. How beautiful the ocean in spite of all the waste it metabolizes. Can it keep up with the toxins?

Let us not devalue our capacity to survive on toxic pollutants. We need it. But let us not reduce ourselves to it. Sheila was in danger of reducing herself to a small, mean, tight personality, one that lived on emotional yuck. She lost or never developed the ability to engage fully in more nourishing relationships.

Her capacity to find and sustain nourishing interchanges atrophied. She was used to no one being there, or someone attacking her or gorging on her in toxic ways. It was difficult for her to know what to do with relationships that were not toxic or empty or attacking enough.

What makes therapy special is that it appreciates psychic garbage. The therapist knows the importance of the garbage dump in human interactions. At the same time, there is a deep sense of what *can* happen between people, in and out of the dump. One hand in shit, one in beauty, and with two hands, new, undreamed-of circuits grow. The therapist in the shit is not too alien for the patient. The therapist in the beauty can then be uplifting.

The image of an ocean metabolizing waste is expressive of the unconscious processes metabolizing emotional pollutants. We describe the stoppage of emotional flow in terms of walls or holes. We are walled off. There are holes in us. We are rigid, tight, or amorphous, jelly. Something bad happens to us and we are hurt, afraid, angry. We stiffen, break, collapse. Unconscious processes attempt to metabolize injury and the results of injury, including our reactions to what hurts us. We keep reworking what bothers us.

We become depressed about the splits, walls, and holes that make us up and become parts of lasting psychic/social structures. But a certain fluidity remains. We keep trying to reset ourselves. Our experiences become part of a background tapestry, adding threads, colors, and designs as life goes on. We do not know how things will look as life continues.

The background tapestry is part of the ocean of unconscious processing that absorbs and incessantly reworks everything that happens to us. One hopes for alive unconscious processing that shapes things to our benefit, our special blend of truth, beauty, garbage. One labors to become partners with a processing capacity that aids further absorption, experiencing, reworking. There is no reason to think that we and our processor ever stop evolving, unless disease eats away this precious ability.

In time, Sheila sensed the background tapestry growing in me. She felt it grow in our sessions. Something she made me feel would dissolve into and link with other things she made me feel, so that a Sheila world of feelings grew in me. She heard this Sheila world in my voice, saw it in my face and body. There was nothing I wanted from this Sheila world other than its own existence. It gave me new, other-than-me nourishment. I grew from its growth. Its roots were deeper than anything I consciously experienced. Only intimations were possible and, now and then, flares.

This sort of immersion and reliance on the background tapestry of being was new for Sheila. It made control superfluous. Most people in her life associated growth with control of a bad, child self. In therapy, dependence on unconscious processing takes the place of the compulsion to control. Sheila's fat and fury were signals that unconscious processing was not working well. Emotional injury was not getting reworked as part of larger movements in life.

Sheila's life was incessantly reducing itself to the sum of her injuries and the reactive world that adhered to them.

The background tapestry of being failed to develop in ways that supported, enriched, and strengthened a sense of generative opening. One needs support to thaw and open. One needs actual experience that thawing and opening are possible. Sometimes this experience is only gotten by proxy through another person. Sheila's watching my growth—there came a point she could no longer escape the realization that I was growing before her eyes—brought home the reality of a way of growing that was not primarily based on control. That I could and would grow through her evolving impact on me was a revelation. For a time, the therapist is the patient's stand-in in the dangerous/thrilling moment of opening.

It takes years for Sheila to realize she cannot obtain from food the nourishment she wants from a person and that she cannot obtain from a person whatever she needs in order to fill holes in herself. There are people so badly damaged that no amount of contact with nourishing others may make a difference. Sheila is badly damaged, but is able to make use of therapy over time. To some extent, she is able to let the therapist survive her intimidation tactics and demands. I do not cave in too long, partly because she does not demand my permanent annihilation. After Sheila is satisfied that she can knock me out for a time, she lets me resurface and regroup. She is fascinated with my elasticity. She damages me, kills me, and I bounce back. Over time, she contacts her own *personal* elasticity by experiencing mine.

When Sheila entered therapy, she enacted elasticity by filling with food and emptying out, blowing up with rage and deflating. Therapy provided a psychic model for the functions that her behavior was caricaturing. One can be filled and emptied of meaning and of a wide range of feelings and imaginings, as well as food and fury. Two people can undergo many sorts of ruptures of communication and then reconnect. The quality of going through ruptures and reconnections is crucial. Therapy provides the place and impetus for the quality of rupture–reconnection to evolve.

Therapy too provides an alternate ideology to the self-defeating ideology of control that stamped Sheila's thinking since childhood. Therapy's focus is more on whether or not or to what extent one can tolerate the build-up of experiencing. How much feeling-thinking-imagining can one take? What happened to the equipment that makes a growing, feeling self possible? Therapy provides a shift of focus, a way of thinking-feeling-sensing-imagining that becomes skin and air for analyst and patient alike. For the time they are together, patient-analyst breathe therapy air, inhabit therapy skin. Therapy partly helps the patient–analyst tolerate experiencing therapy. Once the therapy self begins growing, it is felt as precious. It is no wonder many patients become therapists.

As years go by, Sheila's therapy self feeds her heart's desire, her wish to be an actress, She cannot sit still all day like therapists do. She needs to move.

Her experience of moving me enables her to feel she can move others. She gorges on feelings. Her fury gives her strength and power. Her hunger makes her appealing. Her range of feelings grow in depth and subtlety and expressive cunning. She allows herself to become a different person when she acts, more of who she really feels she is, a truer, transmuted self. The garbage dump self is real, but so is the taste of heaven.

Sandy (see Chapter 14) was born a woman but is a mentally man, and became as much a man in body as medical technology allows. He was unable to acquire a real penis, and his penisless state haunts him. He desperately wants to be a real man with a woman, but attempts at love relationships fall apart, since he dare not let his partners know he is penisless. Nevertheless, he passes for a man in everyday life. No one knows he is/was a woman, except his therapist. His parents are dead.

His upbringing was a horrible mixture of abandonment and abuse. His mother frequently left the family, and when she was present she was given to violent rages. Sandy received some warmth from his father, but the latter was too weak and unreliable to hold Sandy above the storm. In therapy, Sandy persistently voices longing and vulnerability, yet shuts his therapist out. He is terrified of being hurt if he lets her in. He verbally acknowledges that his therapist is there for him. But when he dips into actual feelings, he feels in danger of annihilation. His sense of injury is massive and overpowering, and he backs off from feeling anything.

His therapist, Mara, helped keep him in life for more than fifteen years. She consulted me because she felt guilty about such a long therapy that did not get anywhere. Sandy and Mara live in Europe. Mara has seen me several times over a five-year period when she visited the United States. I doubted I could help much. I felt that Sandy was too sealed off to permit what to Mara would be real contact. He monitors potential contact from a distance. He can see the possibility of contact, feel longing, imagine touching and being touched by another. But the actual happening of it is light-years away.

Sandy insists he must be secretive with people because he must keep his penisless state a secret. Yet he has no excuse with Mara. They are not going to make love. She knows about him. With her he cannot hide behind an organ lack; he must face his inability to make emotional contact without excuses, but is unable to do so. His eternal excuse is massive trauma. He is too traumatized to dare to open. He is too terrified of emotional injury

Mara is doomed to eternal frustration. She has done everything she can. She cajoles, respects, seduces, invites, empathizes, controls, surrenders–but she cannot unlock Sandy's hardened dread. It is as if she is the emotional self that Sandy fears to have. Sandy lives off Mara's emotional self without having to be it himself. He has been nourished by her for over fifteen years without acknowledging how much her emotional life has sustained him.

People who are emotionally starving to death may, paradoxically, feel that even a little emotion is too much, yet no matter how much they get, it is too little. This is Sandy's predicament. Any threat of emotional contact is too much. At the same time, whatever he gets from Mara feels puny in comparison with what he feels he needs. It is as if emotional life is simultaneously magnified–minified, too much–too little. Even a little emotion feels explosive. The wound is too great to tolerate feeling. The shut-off or reduction of feeling is constant and fast. Need makes anything too little, and vulnerability makes anything too much.

Yet Sandy *is* aware that Mara nourishes him. He keeps coming year after year. He does not give up. He is getting *something,* even if he is frustrated by what he cannot get. *Something* gets through. It is also important that Mara feels frustrated. She gets a little taste of what Sandy's feeling excluded from existence is like. She cannot establish with Sandy the kind of contact she values, that she feels would help him, and that she feels he wants. They both feel frustrated with each other and themselves. Neither experiences fully how much Sandy is getting because his complaints remain constant. The problems he sought help with do not seem to change. Sandy and Mara feel excluded from each other (as Sandy does from life), yet bound by Mara's flow of feeling that Sandy lacks and the secret nourishment and overt frustration this provides.

I picture Sandy as a baby secretly sucking Mara's emotional teat. A stuck baby. Clinging, tense, nearly rigid, frozen. This baby does not seem warmed by milk. It shuts out sight, taste, smell, and sound. Its muscles are so tight they shut out the feel of things. Yet the baby cannot let go. It is stuck to the teat in terror, glued by need. It neither starves to death nor is nourished. It cannot be transformed by emotional flow nor entirely let go hope of transformation.

I believe Sandy when he says his life is ruined by secrets. As I look at him through Mara, I see this secret baby, always on the verge of dying, nearly starving, never completely letting go of life. How frustrating it is to Mara that she is let in enough for Sandy to keep going, but not enough for him to be transformed. The whole point of his being in therapy is that he must keep his secret, that he must remain secretive and complain about the impoverishment that secretiveness brings.

When Mara tells me that Sandy is an avid reader of psychological writings I am taken aback. I ask her more about this and encourage her to tell me as much about his readings as she can. She reluctantly paints a picture of Sandy's passion for psychoanalytic literature. She disparages it, distrusts it. She feels it is escapist, an intellectualization, part of his avoidance of emotional contact with people. I have no doubt she is right, yet something quickens in me. It is a passion I share with Sandy, a passion Mara lacks. Mara is a down-to-earth, commonsensical person.

For the first time I begin to wonder if I am more like Sandy than Mara, although I feel I share something with each. I feel my walled-off, secret self, like Sandy. Yet I am emotionally permeable, like Mara. Mara mentions that Sandy reads my writings, is moved by them, is critical of them. I feel Sandy, light years away, tuned in to me. We are plugged into a common current. Mara is excluded. Did we exclude her, or did she by her nature exclude herself? I go deep into my Sandy feeling. We share a secret world of psychoanalytic (perhaps psycho-spiritual?) adventure.

I think of all the hours I spent alone in a secret psychoanalytic world of my own. Mara is more social. She has not experienced the same sort of anguished isolation Sandy and I have known. She spontaneously depreciates one of Sandy's most precious capacities. He *loves* psychoanalytic imagination. He *lives* it. He tries to find himself through it. It is a life-and-death matter for him. He reads with all his might and mind, a very emotional search. Yet all Mara sees is that he substitutes books for people.

It dawns on me that Mara's insistence on direct emotional contact between people as a criterion for successful therapeutic work is self-defeating for Sandy, at least as he is now. Such an attitude rubs his nose in his underlying defect or incapacity and insists that he does something he can't do. At the same time, what he *can* do is undervalued or put down. What he *might* share is neglected. How odd to think that the only thing Sandy might be able to share is exactly what Mara isn't really interested in: his secret intellectual life, which deals with emotional realities indirectly, several times removed.

To complicate matters, Sandy shares Mara's feeling that direct emotional contact is what counts, that his intellectual life is defensive. He depreciates what he most treasures, because of his fear of real contact. Year after year he casti-gates himself for not being able to do what he can't do: let down walls and enjoy emotional communion with another human being, get close to someone. He is imprisoned by his sense of vulnerability. He pours himself into readings. His analytic visions bring him moments of ecstasy. For periods he flies freely in the world of *emotional thinking,* as an individual with a muscular disease moves freely in water.

I think of Freud's remark to Fliess about psychoanalysis being like ancient mystery cults, with secret rites of transformation. Psychoanalysis lives off a sense of the secret. Its concepts are concerned with ways that human beings keep secrets from themselves. Its methods are ways of opening the secret self. Early psychoanalysis doubted that human beings can keep a secret and gambled on its ability to decipher secrets that words and behavior indirectly betray. Psycho-analytic confidentiality is another form of keeping (or failing to keep) secrets. In psychoanalysis we tell secrets secretly. Some version of psychoanalysis is here to stay, as long as secrets give children a thrill. Perhaps one reason psychoana-lysts seem more infantile than the general population is that the latter's work is more public, whereas psychoanalysts are like children doing secret things out of parental view.

Isn't it odd to have a secret psychoanalysis without a psychoanalyst? Such an analysis would not be a psychoanalysis at all—or would it? Sandy loves psychoanalysis. He idealizes the psychoanalysis of his dreams. Apparently he cannot risk being psychoanalyzed by another person. He cannot risk a real psychoanalysis. He engages in a sort of reading, rather than talking cure, which is no cure at all. His inability to make emotional contact with other people is intact. Yet is it fair to say nothing happens in his reading, that he merely reinforces a static position?

A writer's work holds not only his own voice but also the voices of others he writes to and the voices of others (for example, other writers) he hears or senses as he writes. One writes to/with others who are not there. Writing is longing. One writes with a voice more intimate than one's own. Writing is fulfillment, plenitude: lack and overflow. In writing one is closer to the Other (as inner presence) than one ever will be in real life. One hopes to draw the inner presence to one through veils of exteriority (the work), a real dream Other. Through reading, Sandy enters this bath of voices. He talks to Fairbairn, Winnicott, and Freud, and they speak with him, they and all the others encoded in the whispers of their works. He has been having conversations with me for years, and I have no doubt that the plethora of selves and others in my writings speak with him. I am probably more alive for him in my writings than I ever could be in real life.

This sort of aliveness is precious. It should not be put down. Thank God Sandy has it. Is it enough? God forbid! But where would he/I be without it? Writing opens worlds. Mara lives in a world that is closed to Sandy, but she has no inkling or appreciation of what he does have. Growth goes on in hidden mental universes, a secret growing. I go deep into and intensify my Sandy feeling. I glimpse a man–woman who finds in authors more than life offers, yet who needs something from life too. Reading is ecstasy, life pain, although reading is living too, and distinctions fade. But Sandy's pain brings him back to himself, forces him to feel *his* pain, alone and distinct. At moments, everything is outside the pain point, but writers infiltrate it and write from points of pain.

I stay with the Sandy feeling in me and find Mara supporting Sandy. Mara provides background support for Sandy's secret psychoanalysis. Neither she nor he realize how important her emotional self is to his mental activity. He would wither without it. My inner crystal says he is thriving in some way. His color tone is good. He has an intense inner life. He has some satisfaction in work. True, he is cut off from real encounter. But he has contacts and retires to his cave to work over impressions. He has areas of aliveness, along with barriers.

Yes, massive trauma drives him into secrecy. But my inner Sandy tells me things are more complicated. Secrecy is maintained *against* massive trauma, not simply because of it. Extremes of invasion–abandonment precipitate an electrified wall that Sandy cannot cross. But the wall also maintains islands of self that the traumatizing Other can't silence.

An area of secrecy is healthy and needs support in normal development. Sandy met with conditions that drove the secret self into ever greater secrecy.

He created an untellable secret in order to protect and save the more intangible intimation of secret (sacred) mystery. His partial sex change operation converted the inner sense of secrecy and hiding into a literal thing to be closed about. He could martial resources around a fixed thing–no-thing that must never be shared. The private, incognito dimension of self partly turns into a concrete dread, a symptom.

Sandy's walled-off secret self protects his sense of mystery. My inner Sandy tells me he is a deformed version of what he might have been, but he has not entirely lost the precious thread that links his secret self with God. The *incognito* self lives in God, but is supported by Mother. Mara urging Sandy past his barriers tempts him to break his incognito connection with God. His sense of secrecy has been driven so far back and become so rigidified that the movement toward embodiment takes on annihilating force.

Mara *lives* embodied life. She does not see Sandy's angels, his God connection. For her, his secret self–God connection is schizoid. If there is a God for her, it is a God of human relations, a God that lives through her and others being emotionally connected together. She does not want or know or care for a God of isolation.

Mara offers Sandy what he needs but cannot use, not overtly. There must be some secret connection between them, some invisible funnel she nourishes him with. Perhaps her feelings seep through his skin. He is porous, permeable. Just seeing her must be delightful. But she pushes him. She has a picture of how she wants him to be. She wants him to be more like her. She is uncomfortable with his secret life. Thus he feels pressure to be what he is not, even though he agrees he should be more the way she wishes. He would be better off her way. I wonder if she is jealous of his secret psychoanalysis, his psychoanalysis that excludes all psychoanalysts in the flesh, his Platonic analysis, his analysis beyond the pain that she might give him.

Mara is simply not interested in Platonic pain. She is into actual people. She does not have to hide the penis she does not have, nor worry about losing a secret God connection. She is living her life as fully as possible, through marriage, family, friends, and her profession. Sandy is signaling her from a very different world. In spite of the secret pipeline of nourishment and background support she gives him (without sufficient appreciation), the difference between them is enormous. Sandy reads her signal system better than she reads his. He understands what she has to say better than the reverse, and to commune with her he has to leave out vast areas of secret torture.

I try to let Mara know how far back Sandy has been driven in order to preserve an area of privacy, a secret sense of being. There is creativeness in his secrecy, though perhaps not any usual kind, not the creativeness ordained by collective values. His sense of secrecy itself involves something creative, if distorted. His Platonic analysis needs to be honored. Mara's good-willed invitation to more healthy living can't be accepted, no matter how hard he tries, since the equipment to live more like she does is lacking or damaged. I do not mean she should stop inviting him. The therapeutic trick is to play both ends at once. Mara is good with her end, but the elusive, schizoid self needs valorization for its own sake, before forays into embodiment can be risked.

To what extent did Sandy stymie and confuse his sexuality in order to push past his body? Sandy botched his attempt to have a body. He became a man without becoming a man. He stopped being a woman without grappling with what he might have learned from being a woman. He tried to transcend being one or the other sex by a mixture that prevents him from being sexual at all. In actual living he is asexual, but that is not transcendence. He is caught in a mixture of worlds that is no world, not even between. He needs a therapy that can follow the bouncing ball until something more begins to happen. Sexuality is now less important than preserving secrecy. Secrecy leads to mystery, the secret of the universe. My inner Sandy tells me that this is where his growth must come from, but he doesn't say how.

Four years later Mara consults me about Sandy and tells me he is studying at a seminary. This solves nothing, but I'm delighted. Something is beginning to grow. Sandy is starved for emotional contact. But for him now, emotional contact comes through God. For some individuals, the path to people is through God, although the reverse may be the rule. I have faith that as Sandy fills himself with God, his emotional life with people will grow. I can easily imagine Sandy developing a ministry for people like himself, caught between or outside the sexes, trapped by secret longing.

My discussions with colleagues suggest there are many people who share Sandy's predicament and feelings. I hope that communications like this chapter can do a little to encourage the hidden Sandys to come out, network, explore more possibilities of living. Whether this happens or not, my analytic crystal ball tells me one thing: Sandy's growth in capacity for emotional communion will not be quite what Mara—or he, or I, or you—can imagine now.

16

Disaster Anxiety

The sense of danger permeates life. Our joys are threaded over dread of catastrophe. Perhaps we ought to acknowledge how fearful we are about life's dangers by coining some generic term to make the fearful aspect of self explicit. In this chapter I use the term *disaster anxiety* as a loose marker, to make communication a little easier.

Freud and other psychoanalysts catalogue a host of disaster anxieties: birth anxiety, separation anxiety, abandonment-intrusion anxiety, incest and castration anxiety, annihilation and death anxiety, to name the most famous. Existential psychology subsumes Freudian anxieties under death anxiety, but emphasizes that growth itself is an anxious business. To grow or not to grow, the battle with the status quo or habit or what one is used to is *growth anxiety*.

There is free-floating disaster anxiety and free-floating growth anxiety. We are anxious about taking the next step. We might fall off the end of the universe. The recent news report of a New Jersey child sinking into a hole in the ground opening out of nowhere claimed so much attention, partly, because it fits our intimate dread of making the wrong move without knowing it and paying an unfathomable price. The child rushed along in his own energy flow, but the ground could not support him.

We complain about the recitation of daily disasters in the television news, yet there is a hunger for them. The stream of horrible shows and news reports seems to fill and promote an addictive craving, as if we need to bombard ourselves with fear. Newscasters even try to make us afraid of the weather. We feed on images of disaster like potato chips. We say to ourselves, "Look, these awful things *are* real. They *do* happen. I'm not making my fears up; I'm not imagining the dreadful side of life. Awful things *could* happen to me too. Some of them already have, and might again, or something even worse." We try to get inside fears outside, objectify terrors by pointing to images on a screen or reports in a paper. We try to match inside fears with outside realities.

In some ways having a psyche is too much for us. An older brother makes fun of a younger brother. In the night the younger one dreams of monsters and murderers and wakes in terror. Our psyche is a kind of magnifying machine, infinitizing wounds, fears, rage. Witches and devils replace the bad side of people, God the good side (although this is more complicated). We imagine disaster everywhere, where there are always disasters somewhere. Our mind generalizes, blows up, exaggerates, revs things to an infinite power. Dread becomes boundless. To what extent do evil imaginings and evil realities fit together?

We may overdo it in imagination, but reality is extravagant too. It is hard to imagine anything more extravagant than life and death, unless it is eternal or endless or boundless life and death. If it turns out that our universe was created by an explosion, it would not be surprising if explosiveness were part of life processes. The infant's scream testifies to our connection with explosiveness. We ought not pretend that explosiveness is something alien to our natures. It is an inherent part of our lives, and we need to learn what to do with it, not point a finger and try to shame it out of existence.

STILLNESS ↔ STORMINESS

Religions offer contemplation, meditation, or prayer as antidotes to explosiveness. These may work for some people in more or less satisfactory ways. But the explosiveness that marks collective affairs, including religious movements, does not speak kindly for attempts to erase explosiveness with stillness. Many gurus who come to our shores suffer erotic, power, and ego explosions. Stillness goes up in flames. Some of the most meaningful gurus of my time (such as Chongyam Trungpa and Bhagwan Rajneesh) were blown up and died young, unable to contain incendiary mixtures of Eros, ego, materialism, and spirit. Sometimes stillness exacerbates explosiveness.

Ken came for help with an abusive temper. He was appalled how easily his fuse blew with his baby daughter and was desperately afraid he would injure her. He was committed to Buddhist meditation and found that while meditating his anger would fade and he would open. But the contrast between states achieved during meditation and the demands of ordinary living was too great. Instead of meditative calm carrying over into family life, the latter exploded the former, and Ken would become helplessly furious.

When he sat (meditated), he felt renewed. Each time he went back to daily living, he felt this peacefulness would last. When he was in it, he felt it would last forever, such a fresh, unbreakable, full emptiness. But it would not take long for mindful awareness to break down. Reality would take him by surprise, hit a weak spot, pull the rug from under him. His wife and child had their own programs, their own needs, demands, and desires that pushed his buttons. Family life was guerrilla warfare.

Ken felt outraged that his family did not build their lives around his calm center. Why didn't they have calm centers too? Couldn't they see life would be wonderful if they lived from meditative stillness, if they let peace permeate their lives? Why did family life have to involve such turmoil? Turbulence, rather than calm, was the rule. Life was messy. Meditation was clean and clear.

Part of Ken's difficulty was his hidden wish to control his family and perhaps life itself with one mood. He was not content to enjoy calm and then pass into the tumult of real living. He wished to rule the latter by the former. An unconscious severity structured his tranquility. Meditation centered him, yet masked a tyrannical demand that life not be life, his wife not be his wife, his child not be his child.

We worked on building a capacity to move between states, a capacity for transitions. No mood lasts forever. One state passes over to another. Somehow Ken had gotten the idea that one state should be dominant, a sort of tyranny of enlightenment; this is a misuse or naive use of enlightenment ideology. Such holding of reality by a calm, embracing, transcendent consciousness did not work for Ken, at least not the way he wanted it to.

Nevertheless, the meditative calm that Ken experienced had important psychological functions. With therapeutic support, Ken dipped into chaotic and mad aspects of his upbringing, the violence done to him, the violence he felt. In time he realized that he tried to get from meditation the calm he never got from his parents. In part, he used meditation to calm his parents (in unconscious fantasy), as well as himself. Meditation was a way of creating calm parents, a calm self. That it did not work in daily living does not mean it did not work at all. Ken's sitting was extremely important to him. It gave him himself. It gave him moments that were his alone, expansive moments, moments of floating through existence without being crushed. It took the pain of life away and made him feel things could be different, that he did not have to give up on himself and others.

The fact that meditation was helpful to Ken in his own self increased his frustration at its failure to transform existence. He placed too great a burden on meditation as a transformational agent. He tried to make it work overtime as a cure-all, while too much wish-fulfillment, demandingness, and controllingness hid in meditative states. Ken felt caught between his allegiance to meditation and his allegiance to real life. He loved both, but more and more he began to hate real life. He was caught between different realities. The way he felt while sitting often seemed more real than the people who bothered him.

How does one open paths between meditation and daily life, so that stillness and storminess feed each other? In Ken's life they competed, tore him apart (like his parents). Can therapy provide a bridge, a two-way crossing? One of therapy's most important functions is enabling transitional flows between capacities, dimensions of experience, states of being. In Ken's life the gap between stillness and storminess increased, rather than lessened. Ken was unconsciously led by an ideology of mastery and dominance, a psychic imperialism, in which an elite capacity was to dominate (ever replace) others. His motto might be parodied, "Where storminess is, stillness will be."

Overworking a capacity backfires. Stillness cannot substitute for storminess nor vice versa. Both contribute to the texture of experience, the atmosphere and drama of our lives. If there is a working rule, perhaps it should be the placing of a double arrow between psychological capacities, functions, and experiences, e.g., stillness ↔ storminess. This leaves the relationship between terms open. Now the focus may be on ways that elemental terms of experience set each other off, or interpenetrate, or reverse. Stillness ↔ storminess may oppose and nourish each other, stand for each other, overflow into each other. As we dwell with stillness ↔ storminess, we may feel that the field of experience is more than the sum of its parts, at the same time that a variable mixture of stillness ↔ storminess informs every micro-particle of experience.

In time, Ken may move closer to a sense of partnership with capacities that constitute him and a partnership with capacities that constitute the fabric of experience generally. Can we say with assurance what stillness–storminess contribute to personality? Aren't the shifting relationships between terms of experience perennially open to imaginative exploration? Perhaps if Ken develops a more open attitude to the interplay of stillness–storminess, he will be less likely to use one as a club to beat the other.

Ken was smart enough to reach out for help when his situation became dangerous. For Ken, meditation and life were an explosive mixture. His attempt to cure himself via meditation added fuel to the fire. Ken was caught between loyalties to the meditative self and the family self, two selves or aspects of self that ripped him apart. Ken was loving enough to act on his fear of destructiveness. He spread therapy like a net between his violent outbursts and the harm to loved ones (and himself) that was fast approaching. Therapy was the place of last resort, an act of desperation. Its long-range job was to help an experiential field evolve in which stillness ↔ storminess contributed to a richer life.

Disaster is a blank to be filled in. Ken tried to dissolve disaster with stillness. This turned out to be a disaster, up to a point. He had to learn to work with the disaster of letting storminess in. Letting storminess in liberates stillness. Insofar as Ken can process disturbances of existence (bits of disaster), stillness need not function so defensively. Psychotherapy facilitates meditation by helping Ken process what bothers him. Processing bits of disaster does not make disaster go away. But one gains as the field of experience keeps opening. One thrills to opening, and opening on more than one front.

TANKS AND FIRE

Religions have always been close to disaster anxiety. They teach us that death is secondary, life primary. We can conquer death by a good life. Goodness takes the sting out of death. This places quite a burden on the sense of goodness. Goodness has to work overtime to bind the dread of disaster and violent surges. At times, goodness weakens or breaks down, and fascination with disaster runs amok.

Analysis of cult explosions sheds light on the pull toward disaster. The 1993 blow-out on Mount Carmel near Waco, Texas, provides food for thought. David Koresh and his followers courted violence. They expected the end of time and the coming of God's kingdom in a blast of annihilation. There were reports of abusive conduct within the group, and they were ready for armed confrontation. David Koresh was especially fascinated with biblical writings involving violent transformation processes.

On some of the television news clips I saw, David seemed like a gentle, unassuming man who played a guitar and sang. Perhaps he was nastier than he seemed in these scenes. One has to take media reports with a grain of salt. Perhaps he used religious experience to offset low self-esteem. Perhaps he was authoritarian and tyrannical, and exploited erotic possibilities, a mixture of love and delusional egoism. He seemed spiritually naive. His psychophysical being could not contain the messianic ideology that inflated him, and he was blown away by a visionary violence that was too much for him. He may have exploited elements of messianic experience, but I do not think he knew what hit him.

We know from the Bible that God is dangerous. No man can see or touch God and live. Aaron's sons were burnt to a crisp because they approached God the wrong way. It is important to have filter systems for God—laws, angels, rituals, a messiah. Our mystical selves claim immediate contact with God. We have to live with our mystical selves a long time to get some sense of how to use that contact. What to do with mystical experience is a lifelong learning process. How can we use contact with God to enrich, not destroy?

It is easy to see that we have to handle scientific-technological productions with care. We can bomb or poison ourselves out of existence. It is harder to realize that we have a lot to learn about the use of our experiential capacities. Poets have recognized the destructive and inspiring aspects of emotions, and psychoanalysis has made a business of working with them. But we must keep telling ourselves we are *learners,* no more or less. No matter how overwhelming an experience we have, no matter how *sure* we are of it, we have to remind ourselves that it may take years or lifetimes to grow into what we experience and to learn something from or about it.

Can you imagine David Koresh and his followers thinking they had something to learn from the F.B.I. or the F.B.I. thinking they had something to learn from David Koresh? Each side was sure it was right, and the other was wrong. Neither could admit wrongdoing. Their relationship was purely adversarial and combative.

It would seem that David procrastinated, played for time. He could not keep the conditions he set for giving up. Each time the moment for surrender came, he thought of something more he needed to do. This prevarication was not deliberate. Children procrastinate this way, thinking of something else to do when the parent makes a demand. Obsessive and psychotic individuals also show this sort of vacillation: they may feel the fate of the cosmos depends on whether they read a particular sign right or whether they act this way or that. When one is in such a state, the act of deciphering signs is unending. David kept postponing bedtime until the night swallowed him.

Did the F.B.I., finally, act something like impatient parents? At some point they said, "Enough is enough. This is it!" The situation was closed. No more thought would be given to it. The tanks rammed the walls and shot gas, but the children, rather than give in, shot or set fire to themselves. Sometimes parents miscalculate and make things worse by tightening the screws. They imagine the child will give in, only to be horrified when the child is willing to hurt himself to escape submission.

I cannot believe that the F.B.I. didn't think of this possibility. Perhaps they reached the point of the parent who needs a total blow-out. There comes a point where parent and child know that one more turn of the screw will lead to explosive screams and a total dissolution of the situation, but they can't help themselves. They just do it. They can't bear waiting and beating around the bush any longer. Each side feels abused by the other and feels justified by their actions.

The situation gets reduced to utter thoughtlessness. The time for thinking is over. Action triggers reaction. Mindlessness prevails. Will short-circuits thought. Each side refuses to be controlled by the other. All that is left is a vicious spiral: stubborn control versus stubborn control. Such a situation is always explosive. It is explosive in infancy and early childhood, and it remains explosive all life long.

The cult gave no indication that invasion would meet with anything but stiffened resistance. It demonstrated that it was not shy of violence. Media reports gave no signal that it would give in to force. Psychoanalysis teaches there is a double arrow between in and out. If there is sufficient prompting toward violence in a system, it can flow in either or both directions. If David Koresh felt that violence toward invaders would be useless, rather than be violated and reduced to helpless submission, it seems a serious likelihood that violence would turn against himself.

If the F.B.I. did not know this, it is guilty of amazing naiveté. I do not have access to the data base the F.B.I. used in making its decision, so my remarks are impressionistic, to be taken with a grain of salt. The F.B.I. struck out in its first invasion. There was no reason to think it would not stimulate a violent response in its second. Where would the violence go? Against armored tanks? There would be no satisfaction in that. Violence seeks unprotected, weak spots, so it can have an effect. The only unprotected weak spot available to the cult was its own person.

It was odd to keep hearing the F.B.I. refer to the cult's fortified position as a hostage situation. Was it so lacking in empathy and judgment that it could not bear to use the right name for what it faced? It was dealing with a cult that had its back to the wall; all avenues of escape were blocked but one: its own annihilation. Associate annihilation with an ideology of messianic transcendence, and you have an incendiary moment at hand. Many people following this situation would have been more surprised if cult members had responded to force by giving up and filing out than by going up in flames. One almost expected the latter and wondered when and how it would happen.

I do not know what the F.B.I. ought to have done, but sometimes we have to admit that some situations have no obvious solution. There is a temptation to adopt a solution that cannot work, rather than do nothing. However, it is important to be able to do nothing. Perhaps another path will open; some lucky thought will appear. Thinking takes time. Part of thinking is trying this and that possibility out in one's mind, and this involves work. Part of thinking is letting thought go, being blank, doing other things.

Sometimes in therapy one has a patient who does not seem to be getting anywhere. All roads are blocked, and the impasse goes on and on. One can get impatient and precipitate an end of therapy and even make it look like the patient ended it. Or one can do nothing but let the impact of the situation build. One can sit as openly as possible and feel its awfulness. If one sticks with the awfulness long and thoroughly enough, one may get to know something about just what sort of awfulness it is. It takes time to get to know an awful situation well. It is easier to get rid of it while the awfulness is building. Perhaps it is awful to think of therapists as "experts" in awfulness. But it is part of one's job to turn awful situations around and around, until unexpected pathways begin to open. In some instances this happens relatively soon, but there are instances when decades are needed (see Eigen 1993, especially Chapter 4 and the Afterword).

When things work well enough, patient and therapist give each other time for something to happen. Apparently the F.B.I. was unable to sit long enough with David Koresh for thinking or life to open unanticipated pathways. The situation seemed too costly or intolerable. There comes a breaking point when going on seems fruitless, to be too much work for too little return. One cannot tolerate doing nothing one second longer. It does not seem that thinking or life will come up with anything worthwhile. It seems like the impasse will go on forever. One does not give the situation any more time.

Yet isn't *time* God's most precious gift, God's most pervasive filter? To do away with time is to do away with life. The psyche needs time to work, the mind needs time to think, the soul needs time to feel, life needs time to evolve. David Koresh expected the end of time, and the F.B.I. joined him. The F.B.I. felt that waiting would get nowhere and felt provoked. Language betrays the issue: the F.B.I. would *give* the cult *no more time*. What an odd locution: to give or not give time, as if one owned time, as if time was a commodity. How much time ought one give a situation? What elements go into making such a life-and-death decision? The F.B.I. reached a point where giving felt like giving in. Macho impatience found time unbearable, unbearably timeless.

What a fateful phrase: *to give no more time* is to take time away, to end time, to finish it off. To give time became intolerable, and so psychic processes that need time—thinking, feeling, imagining, empathic sensing—ended. Time went up in flames.

A MARRIED COUPLE

A supervisee recently told me about a couple he was seeing for two years. The couple had been married for ten years and survived by fighting. The whole marriage seemed to be one fight after another. That was how they got along. They came to therapy because they were killing each other. My supervisee spoke about them because they felt therapy was not helping them and wanted to quit. They were as abusive to each other as ever.

To me it sounded like the level of abuse had lessened somewhat, but that the main pattern was still in place. They lived by fighting. Fighting fed them and made them miserable. They complained about it, but kept doing it. My supervisee tried "everything." Nothing slowed them down for long. A glance, a word, a gesture would precipitate an explosion. It happened instantaneously. They could not tolerate giving themselves or each other time to mull things over. Reaction fed reaction. They were always blowing up at each other and blowing each other up.

They could recite chapter and verse from their early upbringing and speak of abusive, neglectful, injurious parents who made them this way. They had individual therapy with different therapists for many years. The woman started therapy nearly two decades ago, when her first husband killed himself. Therapy helped her feel she had a right to live, to do the best she could for herself. The man was in therapy most of his adult life. He felt that his violent emotionality and bad feelings about himself would have done him in, if not for therapy. He became an extremely successful businessman.

The fact that this couple survived the worst they could give each other made each feel less destructive. Each blamed the other. Neither felt heard by the other, and neither heard the other. What they needed from the other was someone to fight, and someone to survive the fighting.

The therapist who presented this couple to me was an experienced, competent man at his wit's end. I was supposed to be the super expert who would save the day. There must be someone with wisdom to find the right move, to fix things. I felt a pressure to react, to find a solution while knowing no solution was viable. He did not want to lose the case, to give up, to admit the limits of therapy. He knew his wish for me to do what he could not was a fantasy. Now in supervision he presented a situation with no more time. The couple was not willing to give him more time, and he anxiously passed me a now-or-never ultimatum.

An odd thing was that this couple gave each other all the time in the world, without giving each other any time. They spent years together, but did not find time to really feel the other's being, to process the other and their feelings about the other. They were now pulling the plug on my supervisee because he was insisting that they make time for processing their impact on each other, rather than simply exploding. He was asking them to do something they could not. They lacked the ability to sustain and process bits of mutual impact.

People function as filters for one another. We have an impact on each other and respond to another's impact. If we are lucky, we let the other's impact play on us; we feel it, dream it, think about it, and let it give rise to creative musings. We give the other's impact time. A couple that lets this mutual filtering process take place grows in resonance.

This can be true of therapy couples too. A patient and therapist who have acted as filters for each other's personality and pain share a sense of richness. They have gone through something together and feel the appreciation that comes with surviving each other's personality. They know the freedom of surviving therapy together. Unfortunately, no such lucky experience occurred with my supervisee and the couple he told me about. He bounced off them, and they off him. They did not seem to become part of each other. Accusation, complaint, demand, mutual frustration, and intolerance left no space for being touched by one another. Explosiveness substituted for permeability.

I noted the pressure passed to me by my supervisee. For a time I lost myself in the feeling of pressure, tasting it and smelling it. I did not feel I could come up with anything useful, since this couple found nothing useful. That in itself was freeing. At least I could luxuriate in the impossible situation presented to me, and just savor the particular horror of the moment. I could empathize with my supervisee, who was sinking in pressure. But something told me to let go of him, and jump into the exploding morass that got nowhere.

I felt bad leaving my supervisee mad, anxious, dissatisfied. There he was in the room without a supervisor. There was every chance I would not return before he left. Yet I could not resist diving into the pressure that was taking his space away, the pressure he hoped I could deal with.

Do explosive moments keep exploding until they find good-enough filter systems? My supervisee's couple was an explosion that went on and on, passing through him or off him to me. Will the explosion pass through or off me to the next therapist-supervisor couple? Will it pass through the therapy field entirely, out of the therapy cosmos, through other worlds that cannot satisfy it? Perhaps this couple has become part of an explosion that never ends, an explosive element in the human condition that becomes more highly constellated in one or another situation, but never fully goes away.

I am gone, feeling what it must be like, being an explosion that never ends. Somewhere along the line I get a thought or word picture I want to share with my supervisee. I don't expect it to help, but it might be fun to share. It occurs to me that his couple are not two people, but one person, mirror images, doubles, proxies: they are reflections of each other. They have blown him up too, swept him into the explosion. There is an explosion where marriage and therapy might have been. There is simply an explosion mirroring itself. There probably are no longer any *people* in the room. I see them all as one or no persons blowing up forever. Psychic processing has ceased to exist, or failed to begin. Their one-two-three-way hell is always to have just enough psyche left to feed explosions, never enough to begin processing them: psyche ever going up in flames.

My supervisee and I may not be able to help his patients, but perhaps we can help each other. His patients pretty much blew him away. After all, the case was his. I wasn't in the room with them on the field of battle. I was safely in my office, discussing back-room logistics. Still, my room shook from the shells. I was a filter twice removed. I felt the impact filtered through my supervisee. Here he was, a bloody mess, wounded in war, a fighter between rounds, and we had to help him stay in the line of fire. He needed nursing. I might not help his patients, but at least I could help *him*.

I *knew* my supervisee would survive his patients, although it did *not feel* that way to him. While he was in it, worry consumed him. They would leave, his practice would go down the tubes, he would not be able to support his family or keep his life afloat. On a pure body-count level, if this couple left, sooner or later other patients would replace them; but this was useless knowledge. Anxiety blew his psyche away. The fear that his life would zero out was part of the obliterating movement his patients were caught in. In a situation like this, supervision functions to restore the supervisee's psyche.

The supervision couple survives the patient–therapist couple. At first, my supervisee tried passing the anxiety and pressure to me, but I could not get as caught up in it. I was farther from the point of impact than he. I was still able to lose myself in psychic functioning, whereas he lost his psyche. I could go away, dip into dream and reverie, lose myself in the explosion, let it work on me, and see what images, states, and ideas got set off. It is important to be able to lose oneself in an experience, to give it room to develop.

My supervisee pressured me to respond and come up with something to stop him and his case from hemorrhaging. But I slipped into dreamland. l didn't plan it. I just stayed with the experience he was describing or transmitting. The fact that I let go, vanished in the experience, and came back with something, added to his anxiety at first, but was comforting in the long run. He was mad that I didn't seem as worried as he was. It was his life and practice, not mine. His psychic blood pressure was skyrocketing. Yet it was important for someone's psyche to begin processing his patients' and therapy's explosion. I just happened to be the supervisor that was there and went with it.

The fact that I came back with the notion that there was no one, or perhaps one person in the therapy room, meant that someone's psyche (it happened to be "mine") began processing some aspect of the catastrophic reality my supervisee and his patients suffered. I passed it on to God. I told God, "Look. This is more than any of us can handle. I'm passing it to you. You got us into this, you get us out." Of course "God" is only a name. What the reality is I do not know. But a bit of processing started. My supervisee began thawing out and coming back. Before our session ended, he could tell the difference between worry time and immersion time. He could begin sensing what he was up against. Psychic life was being revived.

That I could give myself time to go away, to blank out, to do nothing was pivotal. The gift of time, the most precious gift: my patient and his couple lost it. He and I spent time, found time, and made time together. We went on working together in spite of pressures against it. The pressure that blew him and his couple away *was* the work. This pressure needed time, time to be, time for processing. Through "God" (or the unknown reality that feeds unconscious processing) a psyche arrived that began working over bits of catastrophe. The fact that I, immersed in unknown reality, worked over a bit of obliteration gave my supervisee time to come back and begin again.

Isn't this what colleagues do for each other? We survive our patients together. We survive therapy and the therapy field together. We give each other gifts of time, moments of self.

THE DANGEROUS THERAPIST

I do not think my supervisee was dangerous to his couple. They severed him from himself so thoroughly and turned him into such an anxious mess that they had little to fear from him. My supervisee sought coverage for himself and his case and did not simply succumb to therapy's annihilation. He brought the annihilating impact to supervision, to another human being outside the immediate situation.

Thus my supervisee was able to provide for himself the relief that comes through sharing distress. He remained communicative in face of his patients' obliteration of communication. They killed off communication, but he kept communication alive by seeking help. They were like screaming infants, so caught in their scream they did not know someone was trying to help them.

They could not feel anything outside their scream. Perhaps my supervisee was a bit like the child who goes to a parent, points to his wounds, and says, "Look what they did to me!" I think, to an extent, he wanted me to get them for him, to seek revenge.

What we were able to do together—it happened quite spontaneously, as if by chance—was to enable him to go back to the therapy room with them (the lions' den), to start fresh, to be himself once more. Our time together made him able to give more time to them. He feared it would come to nothing. They would make short work of him. But he was armed with the idea that there was no one or one person in the room, a single explosion mirroring itself. This was his koan or mantra. He could hold onto it for a time and not imagine he was working with two people.

If he tried to talk to two people, he was doomed. They would gang up on him and each other. If he acted like a therapist and treated them like separate people they would blow him away. With his mantra, he had something to hold onto, something to keep mind or psyche alive, a sort of respirator. Its function was to give him space and time, breathing room. How long could he maintain himself, before demise? Not very long, perhaps, but a bit longer than before. At least he was catching on to how pervasive and chronic an activity obliteration can be. At least he would be gazing at the thing that was happening as it made him go under. Whether or not his couple stayed or left, therapeutic capacity would survive them.

My supervisee *knew* he was injured and did something about it. He got protection from his patients' impact and protected his patients from their impact on him. Not every case is so lucky. Many therapists do not seek help when they are in danger. Often a therapist may not even know he *is* in danger, even if he already has been partially destroyed. It is easy to suffer partial collapse of the self without knowing it, and to act out destructively, while aiming to do good.

Smith, a gifted, experienced analyst, helped Lois in many ways. Lois lived in a daze. Her previous analyst had had sex with her. Lois had had numerous affairs, but no sustained relationships. The men she liked left her, and she had disdain for those who wanted her. She required hospitalization twice and lived on the verge of hospitalization for many years.

Lois's mother had been psychotically depressed, and Lois had been alone for long periods in early childhood. When Lois's mother was there, it was awful; and when she was away, it was awful. In middle childhood Lois had had sexual contact with her brother, who lost interest in her when he was in high school. In adult life she repeated the pattern of moments of intense connection followed by emptiness. Smith helped Lois feel good enough about herself to get and keep a good job. He also helped her maintain a long-term relationship with her boss.

When Lois tried to disengage with her boss, or voice dissatisfaction with her job, Smith encouraged her to stay with it. He did not want her to withdraw or live episodically. He valued the continuity in love and work he helped her sustain.

As the years went on, Lois became angry and bitter about the relationship with her boss. He was married and was not going to leave his wife. He had his own life; Lois was a side dish. She did not advance in her work as much as she thought she should. She felt held back by her relationship with her boss. She felt discriminated against, as if he feared her going too far. He wanted her around him, not on her own. This went on nearly fifteen years. Whenever she tried to break away or think of living another life, Smith persuaded her not to. He feared she would drop into isolation and promiscuity and end with nothing.

Smith thought she was doing well. She no longer needed hospitalization. She supported herself and had a man. Smith did not take her seriously when she said she did not care for her job, did not really have a man, and wanted more. Apparently he thought this was the best she could do. He was eager to maintain Lois in the life she built, rather than risk gambling on a major change. He seemed to feel that living falsely was better than not living at all.

Smith sought my help shortly before his death. He was a gay man who maintained the mask of a marriage and lived out true sexual currents in episodic relationships with young men. He maintained a high level of professional functioning, but underneath suffered partial somatic and psychic collapse, which he tried not to acknowledge. He was used to paying a great personal price for maintaining status and competency and had urged Lois to do the same.

I have written about Smith in detail elsewhere (1993, see Chapter 9) where I tried to show how Smith was able to let down somewhat and to experience elements of his collapsed self before he died. After his death, I referred his patients to other therapists. Lois stayed with me. I could see how his fight against weakness and fear of breakdown had played a role in Lois's achievements. He had kept her in life the way he kept himself in life: behind a mask, several times removed. He could not let her follow her true desires, anymore than he let himself do so.

True, he saw her when she was younger, when living a life in and out of hospitals was possible. He saved her from that. But he could not take her beyond the splits he cultivated in his own life. What a price for hiding madness!

Within a few years after Smith died, Lois initiated and won a suit against her company for sexual discrimination and harassment. She quit her job, ended her relationship with her boss, and deepened her life as an artist (one of her strongest wishes). With another analyst, she might have freed herself years before. It is also possible another analyst might not have gotten her above her psychosis.

Today Lois is an older woman with physical problems. She has had to get used to not being the femme fatale she had imagined herself to be. She may well suffer now more than she had with Smith. But she can go to the bottom of her experience, not hold herself above it.

Smith identified with Lois's fragility and potential for collapse and fought against it. He helped Lois, but became for her a dangerous therapist because of his need to keep above himself. For years he kept her away from her deepest longings and thought he was doing her a favor. He was afraid of what her giving in to life would do. He knew only too well how dangerous life could be and sought to protect her from going too deep, too far. He built a profession upon his loss of life and taught Lois to do the same. Loss of self in the service of competence can take one only so far. In time, self and life recoil at the disaster one's personality becomes. Sometimes it takes death to set one straight.

I cannot say that Lois was lucky to meet herself, go to the bottom of herself, sooner than Smith did. Lois's bitterness did not end when she tasted the thrill of self-opening. But, at least, her lifelong bitterness no longer stopped this thrill. In old age, she'll know what Yeats meant when he wrote in "Sailing To Byzantium" (II. 1–4).

> An aged man is but a paltry thing,
> A tattered coat upon a stick, unless
> Soul clap its hands and sing, and louder sing
> For every tatter in its mortal dress . . .*

It is soul clapping hands that makes life more than disaster.

REFERENCE

Eigen, M. (1993). *The Electrified Tightrope.* Northvale, NJ: Jason Aronson.

---

*Lines from "Sailing to Byzantium." Reprinted with the permission of Simon & Schuster from *The Poems of W. B. Yeats: A New Edition*, edited by Richard J. Finneran. Copyright © 1928 by Macmillan Publishing Company. Renewed 1956 by Georgie Yeats. Also by permission of A. P. Watt, Ltd., UK, on behalf of Michael Yeats.

17

Winning Lies

A prominent characteristic of the Anita Hill testimony during the confirmation hearings for the appointment of Clarence Thomas to the Supreme Court in 1992 was the suppressed violence that pervaded its tone. Under the veil of polite inquiry and the search for truth, acid sarcasm, ironic ridicule, and opportunistic cruelty held sway. The senators seemed to silently agree on the cast of characters: loudmouth slashers, icy rhetoricians, nice guys bending backward to be gentle and just, quiet omniscient presences waiting for justice to unfold yet fearful the whole thing would backfire, energetic competent underlings feeding information into the clash of monsters.

They did not seem to care what impression they made on sensitive viewers. Or, more disturbing, they cared a lot and felt they made the right kind of impression. They felt that the way they did things was normal, the way one ought to do things. Violence was part of fact finding and truthing. They imagined that most people took verbal aggression for granted, even respected it. There seemed to be tacit agreement that if they did not go on the attack, however crudely or subtly, they would be perceived as weak and lose ratings and status.

I imagine I would be crushed if I were subjected to Congressional hearings. Perhaps I would rise to the occasion and develop resources now lacking. But my tendency to oscillate between positions, seeing many sides of issues and persons, would make me appear unsure and useless, given the public greed for one-sided certainties. I'd need more time for zigzag thinking than the situation allowed and would be too ambivalent about everything.

Is there room for uncertainty, indecision, and self-questioning in public life? The display of such traits seems tantamount to political suicide. This leaves people in the position of having to feign more confidence, zest, rightness, and conviction than they possibly can possess. Social and political life takes for granted a working rift between public presentation and private feelings, a rift that can be inherently violent and lead to violence.

I never got a good sense of who Anita Hill and Clarence Thomas were. They slid through my fingers as persons. There were qualities of each that put me off, yet I could sense each might be engaging in certain circumstances. I did get some sense of what each had to go through, as combinations of senators tried to expose sore spots and weaknesses in each.

Perhaps Anita Hill was more withdrawn and Clarence Thomas more combative. I fell victim to stereotypes, since I could fantasize having a better time with Thomas in a bar and a better time with Hill in a discussion of legal subtleties. Had the wrong one been nominated? I did not see Thomas as Supreme Court quality. But people study and grow and I will be happy to be wrong. Perhaps I would not have a very good time with either person in any place, but that might be my problem.

As the hearings went on, I got sick of people being forceful, sick of the search for facts and truth—a witch-hunt approach to "truth." I believed Hill more than I did Thomas, but was sickened by the whole procedure. Something outside who was right or wrong warped the whole thing. Pursuit of the truth through verbal slaughter, yelling, intimidating, cajoling. browbeating, self-aggrandizement, and cutting sweetness: a sort of seek-and-destroy the lie or weakness mentality, may the best man or woman survive when the smoke clears. Indeed, was truth the object or rather *victory for one or the another side?* Winning and being right were more important than anything. Truth was a plaything of battle. Is this the way democracy must work? Is this the way human beings are when they play for position, for a slice of the pie? Is violence necessarily part of pie slicing? Are the rules of procedure for Congressional hearings a sort of codified violence or control of violence? When I think of this unapologetic, unmodest display, I feel appreciative of talmudic tracts in which the discussion of difficulties inherent in decision making get their due, and contrary to popular belief decisions between claimants are less damaging.

The core emotional tone or impact the hearings had on me could be broken down into five psychodynamic operations or structures.

Hysterical Affect

Part of the drama of these hearings involved an underlying hysterical affect, an affect usually controlled and modulated by schizoid, paranoid, and psychopathic maneuverings. Without this underlying affective surplus, the hearings would have been deadening. It did not take much for the hysterical affective core to come through. Given almost any excuse as an opening, the volume of the hearings would rise. Everything would take on larger-than-life import and then drain away into small-scale backbiting, as if pulling away from affective tidal waves that tested controls. The exaggerated self-importance of senatorial bearings barely disguised the muted hysteria of inflated emotional judgments.

Paranoid Ideology

The intellectual structure of discourse tended to be adversarial, me against you, one side against the other, whatever the sides might be at a given time. At any moment, there did not seem to be room for multi-ocularity or ambiguity. Instead, aggressive one-sidedness was the rule. Implicit in this procedure was support for my side, attack against yours. There was not much intellectual cross-dressing.

The pervasive, if only implicit, hostile one-sidedness in any moment's position seemed akin to paranoid splitting. The other person is trying to get away with something, is lying, is misrepresenting, is wrong. My job is not to let him or her get away with anything. My job is to smoke out the lie, the evil, the error. The Other is somehow the enemy or barrier or threat. I am on the side of the good, the law, the people. I exert a policing function for the public economy and protect society from falsehood and error. The interrogator never questions what is false, incomplete, or duplicitous in his or her position. Suspicion is reserved for the Other, the enemy, the interloper.

The interrogator funnels his capacities into one-sided positions, shorn of ambiguity and self-doubt, whether accusing or defending. It is necessary to be somewhat less or other than fully human, since one must constantly marshal one's resources into a one-sided mold. To an extent, one is an actor playing a role. But an actor funnels resources into esthetic revelation: there is one-sidedness for the sake of being moved and enlightened about the human condition. The interrogator reduces or pinches life into a sour caricature of the detestable. One's aim is not to uplift but to gore. In the paranoid structuring of hysterical affect, one enhances one's position or apparent virtue by exposing the other's flaw, a one-up–one-down style.

Psychopathic (Sociopathic) Manipulation

In the psychopathic attitude, one feels justified in twisting things to one's advantage. Exposing the Other is only incidental to aggrandizing the self. In extreme instances, the goal is to win at any cost. One needs to get ahead, and to hell with anything or anyone that gets in the way. One does not care what becomes of the Other, as long as one scores points.

The paranoid idealist might actually believe he is hunting lies and devoting shark-like capacities to social ecological clean-up. The psychopathic realist is adept at practical manipulation. He uses a kind of empathy to tune into underlying hysterical affect in order to turn it to advantage. He may be sensitive to the Other, mainly to get a sense of how to maneuver him or her successfully. He uses natural empathic cunning in the service of getting one's way.

Psychopaths frequently overextend themselves because they do not realize what impression they make on others outside the subsystems that house them. It is as if they, more or less, blend in with certain environments and feel that no one notices their manipulations. They feel their machinations are somehow oddly invisible. They may feel genuinely surprised if someone is alarmed at what they take for granted. They do not expect to be evaluated by criteria outside their domain of viability.

Many years ago I was accosted on the street by a well-groomed man who was certain he could manipulate me. When he failed in his first attempts, he actually began talking about his ability to get anyone to do what he wanted. He felt convinced of this, and no disconfirmation could dissuade him. He told me that if he put enough into it, he could get me to do what he wanted. He could put on winning, cajoling, and intimidating ways that would con anyone. He really did have the feeling that he could outsmart anyone.

For me, he was a sort of negative angel, a revelation, a quasi-pure slide of a hidden psychopathic megalomania that was part of being human and that challenged humanity. I have seen versions of him in action many times over the years. It was inconceivable to him that someone saw through him just by looking at him, by virtue of being outside the operative image he valued. It was inconceivable that someone could look at him and walk away. He would have enough marks, enough hits, people for whom he would be significant, so as not to have to face the enormity of his irrelevance for those who were wired differently.

To some extent, the conduct of the Anita Hill hearings crossed the threshold of visibility, reached the point of overextension. The grossly aggressive manipulation for political and individual aims, mixed with bad taste, began to ring bells. Of course, the sea of time would swallow the garbage, and the flow of events and media images would provide other preoccupations. But how can our psychosocial stomachs metabolize all the trash that is dumped into them?

Schizoid Lack of Feeling

An uncanny, deadly, unfeeling attitude informed the interrogations. Together with paranoid structuring and the psychopathic manipulation of underlying hysterical affect, there was a cold, detached, untouched, and untouchable spirit or tone. The interrogators seemed immune to the pain they caused, as if dissecting live animals was something they were used to. When I saw them in action I understood more keenly the Torah's injunction against eating the flesh of a living animal.

The hearings were premised on an insensitivity to pain. So much public life shares this premise. The lion can't be too empathic with the deer and get a meal. One thing I love about Judaism is its emphasis on thawing out the heart, turning the heart of stone to one of flesh (circumcision of the heart). It is as if Torah were only too aware of the unfeeling streak in us (Pharaoh's famous hard-heartedness), and did what it could to protect us from ourselves while we worked on becoming human, part of our evolutionary task.

Once a senator got going, nothing could deflect him, except collision with another one-tracked locomotive. Instead of dialogue, there were mono-manic collisions. Yet the mono-mania was not merely blind. A detached, cold, unreachable, unfeeling seeing steered the line of questioning. An interrogator could not be deflected because his one eye was glued to the spot he wanted to get to, and he watched for whatever might help him get there.

I think it important to know that hysterical affect goes perfectly well with unfeeling detachment. Part of the *belle indifference* of classical hysteria may well reflect a certain unreachable, unaffected, unfeeling detachment, even in the midst of hysterical oblivion. We learn from neurotics that the sensitive soul who cannot bear much can be quite insensitive to him- or herself and others. At the hearings, sensitivity is an invitation to be crushed. One must learn to use one's sensitivity to funnel information and promote winning ways. A transcendent, unshakable, unfeeling element enables paranoid-psychopathic manipulation of underlying hysterical affect to be successful.

The Autistic Capsule

There is a kind of *out of it, somewhere else* dimension to our lives that needs acknowledgment. It takes many forms, from spacing out and going blank to vast depersonalization. We need empty, formless moments as respite and to reset ourselves. Blank immersion plays a generative role in creative processes. Voidnothingness has a long history in enlightenment literature and takes touching turns in modern French poetry.

A hollow emptiness can freak people out, be a menacing part of disintegration states. Emotional emptiness is a chronic complaint of many patients and skyrockets in psychotic processes.

The particular sort of blanking out I want to call attention to here can occur on a grand social scale. There was a way in which the entire hearings took place in another time-space zone or warp, as if a veil or caul or bell jar encased them. Yes, they were surrounded by enormous political and media upheaval or hubbub. It was hoped, in some quarters, that the issue of sexual abuse at the workplace would become more a part of public consciousness and discourse and action. The fact that accuser–accused were a professional black man and woman had incendiary potential, especially since they were partly pawns in political struggles between empowered white men. The hearings were afloat in waves that lapped the nation, and depending on how high and rough the waters and where they hit, casualties were unpredictable.

Nevertheless, there was a sense that the hearings took place *somewhere else,* in a world of their own, sealed off, inured, even encrypted, like figures from walls in an Egyptian tomb coming alive at night, enacting ritual, ruthless, blood-curdling murders. They floated in a television bubble, although the consequences might be cruelly real for some of those involved.

To an extent, this out of it, somewhere else, bubble-oblivion element in human life makes murder and many acts of violence possible. We know that murder is involved, since language tells us that various characters were fighting for their political or judicial life. It was a life-and-death matter for some characters involved. To kill someone in full view of the nation on the television screen may not only involve bloodlust but also a certain encapsulation. One must be numb to the suffering one inflicts or act in spite of it. Some murderers enjoy their victim's suffering, but many are obliviously indifferent to the chain of events they set off. Murder has its own time warp or zone.

Medical and theatrical images come to mind. A doctor does what he has to do on the battlefield. If no anesthesia is available, he must partly immunize himself to the pain he causes by cutting as he must. The political doctors did what they thought they had to do. They were also on stage, cutting an image, making an impression, building or losing personal power. In one way, they were intensely conscious of what they did. They had a sense of how to induce, play, and get the most mileage of muted, public hysteria. What I have called paranoid-psychopathic-schizoid operations indicate that a lot of (obsessive) thinking and plotting was going on.

And yet the paranoid-psychopathic-schizoid manipulation of events and feelings, the whole circus show, could not occur without a certain autistic encapsulation, a mindless oblivion (in spite of intense, goal-oriented mental activity) to entire dimensions of experiencing. The autistic bubble includes not only the immediate protagonists or actors but also the entire nation. The media, the viewers, the consumers of autistic paranoid-psychopathic-schizoid hysteria are part of the show. We are all floating in a sort of mindless autistic unit we protest against, feel repelled by, yet feel unable to affect. Whatever we do seems to become part of the enclosure. The bubble expands to include our objections. It is like trying to get out of a surrounding film, but getting more entangled in sticky glue. We are all parts of the same, larger dreamwork.

The fact that we have ritualized a public way of being that requires unfeeling violence and the lack of self-questioning as tools for success needs to be an ever wider part of public discourse, and there are signs this is happening. Such discussion has long been part of political philosophy and serious literature. There have been religious critics of society, including ascetic dropouts, who have felt the need to cleanse themselves from toxic side effects of civilization. Many people have made every attempt to burst the bubble.

Social and religious reforms bring new kinds of violence, new problems to meet. It does not seem we can do anything without inflicting injury or spreading poisons. Will more widespread talking about what we do to ourselves and our planet help? Is there something to gain by treating society as a patient? Psychotherapy puts a lot of weight on talking, the power of words, of words linked with feeling. We may never be able to talk our way out of our bubbles, but by feeling our way into them and listening to each other, we may become a bit less chillingly abrasive.

THE WINNING LIE

The Hill hearings echoed a style or strategy or tone that typified the politics of the nation, from former president George Bush down. The goal was not so much to speak truth. Truth is dangerous, explosive. One cannot control truth: one never knows what its next turn will be. The practical tactic was to find a *winning lie.* One tried to put a spin on things that worked, that brought success (for me, at your expense). That starkly colorful and accurate term, *spin doctor,* lays the cards on the table: everyone knows what's happening.

A winning lie contains no apparent paradox or ambiguity or multiplicity of meanings. The one who proposes it must show no weakness or confusion. One pursues a one-sided track with utmost confidence. The goal is to be on top, with some other people at the bottom. Since it is not possible to be or mean one thing, this method inevitably contains destructive elements: it *is* violent and perpetrates violence.

There seems to be a broad market for winning lies: they work. People eat them up. If expediency demands, former president Bush can change his stance on abortion, take a public position that disowns his private belief, play a shell game with personal truth, act tougher than fits his frame, and become totally unbelievable: yet he wins if he finds the right angle, the right line, or bearing. In time, his bones begin to break through his bubble, and he loses to an apparently more expansive personality, who brings a new bubble with him.

President Bill Clinton's bubble seems to have a lot of openings. He's not one-sided and sealed enough. He oscillates and zigzags too much. Can he turn those qualities into a strength? Does he presage a time when ambivalence and uncertainty can finally be integrated into the public image? Is he a political forerunner of a time when one-sided stances will be dinosaurs? Will one-sided hammerheads strike back with a vengeance, or is it time for further growth in the nation? Can the general population ever become sophisticated and complicated enough to find one-sidedness distasteful?

"Slick Willie" is no innocent. He doubtless shares aspects of the paranoid-psychopathic-schizoid-autistic-hysterical elements of other politicians. But he is less publicly divisive, at least so far. His rhetoric does not inflame hate or go for the jugular of this group or another. Hate-filled elements of the population may find this intolerable: that is, not speaking H-words (hate words) may inflame haters. Clinton does not have a hate bubble; his violent drivenness takes other forms. In spite of his rhetoric of inclusiveness, he may have left too much outside.

Finding winning lies is part of politics the world over. I remember recoiling at the lies that informed Khrushchev's rhetoric years ago and his one-sided U.S. bashing. Being critical or self-critical is one thing, but such blatant, flamboyant distortions, such streams of verbal violence! And people all over the world ate it up, including many intellectuals in our country. Today, tyrannical governments in Africa, the Caribbean, and elsewhere use similar tactics to cover the graves of their opponents. Not even the stunning sum of Stalin's murders could shake many individuals out of their trance. The political violence of a Joseph McCarthy could only find success in a world where violent lies are part of one's daily bread. Senator McCarthy is an exaggerated instance of a style that is still widespread (possibly even a norm?) in muted forms today.

Europeans laugh at Americans for not taking political lying for granted. They see Americans as politically naive. I think the problem is more difficult. Winning lies are part of political expediency. They are an integral part of American politics, as they are everywhere else. But Americans seem to react with more than usual outrage when catching someone with his pants down (at least we are told so by Europeans). Is there some reason or sets of reasons why Americans need to dress practicality and expediency in truth rhetoric? Do we need periodic orgies of unmasking, in the name of truth, in order to let the lying continue in another form, with other persons? We seem to need several orders of violence, practical and moral. But it is oddly provincial for Europeans to think this trait to be mainly American.

ABUSE

A sign of hope is that the rhetoric of abuse is becoming more common. Often, the idea or reality of abuse is abused. Strident, small-minded people use it for political and personal gain. There is always danger of false accusations and deceitful histrionics. Myopic fanatics feed on bits of larger issues. Nevertheless, the fact that various forms of abuse have become an increasing part of public consciousness may reflect and trigger some evolution of sensitivity.

Political maneuverings, cutthroat tactics, and winning lies certainly blunted the impact the issue of sexual abuse at the workplace might have had at the Hill-Thomas hearings. To many people, Anita Hill was discredited or, at least, lost value or effectiveness as a *person*. The systematic sharpshooting and laser-beaming in on her personality, on what made her tick, on who she was or especially was not, were more damaging than anything that was established about what she did or did not say or what allegedly did or did not happen between herself and Clarence Thomas. What was consistently penetrated and attacked was her self-presentation, her television *image* as a person. On top of the possibility of vocational sexual abuse was the reality of visual-aural abuse in front of the whole nation, a sort of political pornography.

The greatest abuse of all was out in the open, like the purloined letter, for everyone to see. But it was almost something that everyone was used to and was part of a procedure that perpetrators assumed was the best show in town: the way democracy works, something to be proud of. The methodological centerpiece involved good old-fashioned smear tactics, using the best available psychological profiles and image research or intuition—an updated version of *character assassination,* a term that is up front about the violence of political surgery. Winning lies seem to grant a temporary immunity or invisibility to the warp of one's own personality and methodology: they make one look good and mask one's abusive style until one's time bubble begins to dissolve or wears thin with shifting conditions.

Still, the phenomenon of abuse is in lights before the nation: child abuse, marital abuse, vocational sexual abuse, ecological abuse, racial abuse. More people may begin to think and talk about the violence that seems to be part of human relationships. It is important that those who have suffered literal, definable abuses speak up or are spoken for. Unfortunately, those who speak up are often punished for trying to make things better for themselves. Trying to have more of a say in one's life, boomerangs all too often. Having to go through judicial or congressional proceedings is punishing itself: what might be called judicial trauma is widespread (Moss 1984).

Yet one hopes, over time, that more people will have more of a say about what is good for them or at least will have the ability to try to find out for themselves, what is good for them—the pursuit of happiness, an "inalienable right." Am I dreaming, or hasn't this happened somewhat over the course of history? Aren't there more democracies, fewer tyrannies? Aren't there more voices, for more peoples? Don't more people over the face of the earth feel that every person *ought* to have legal rights and protections, whatever the prevailing state of affairs?

As a psychologist, I'm in the habit of looking inward and, among other things, finding ways I've been abused and am abusing. There is literal, corporal abuse and neglect, but emotional and spiritual abuse can be more subtle. Once one tunes into abuse one sees it everywhere, including the ways that therapist and patient abuse each other. The abuse virus is quite real and alarming and injurious. It can't be wished away or easily defeated. It may never be defeated. But one grows through working with it, no matter how one fails. There is an abusive gene or virus that runs through human nature, and we must find less destructive ways to live with it. The person who has made an honest attempt to work with the destructive force in him- or herself and others, is not quite the same in fifty years as one who has ignored or indulged it.

In a psychic democracy, there is a cross-representation of voices: I hear you and you hear me, we resonate through each other. One must make inner sacrifices and adjustments to hear another person or really feel heard. As a psychologist, I value this kind of mutual resonance, speaking, listening, feeling, and working imaginatively with the impact of each other's being. I realize that in the world out there a lot of speaking tends to be manipulative, a way of getting the other to obey me, not even caring about the other, as long as I get what I think I want. Since I traffic in words, I know I am implicated in manipulative power needs as well.

One difference is that I know I'll grow if my patient explodes my lie. I've learned this the hard way. I need that back and forth. My patients and I grow through our lies together. We are able to come through many forms of emotional violence together and be better for it.

If I were Anita Hill, the hearings might have strengthened me too; perhaps I would have grown. Living through such experiences must do things for a person. But the public message was: you have to be able to tough it out, not let down; real dialogue is destructive. If the hearings were real life, therapy must be la-la land. If the capacity for open dialogue is valuable, the hearings indict themselves as a macabre caricature of communication; indeed, they gain part of their eerie fascination precisely by putting constructive, personal communication out of play. It really didn't matter what Anita Hill said or didn't say. The matter was settled by forces beyond any impact her words could have had.

I would not want to choose between what takes place in the therapy greenhouse and what life outside therapy offers. I don't want to further the violent split between public–private that seems so necessary for civilization. The rhetoric of polarities has its own awful violence, as witnessed by Congressional waving of the "rationality" banner for this or that cause. My position is rational, yours irrational. Attributions of rationality–irrationality seem to be favorite tropes of public discourse, especially in the rhetoric of accusation. I hope, in time, we become more critical of polarity language and recognize how its boxes can abuse the subtlety and richness of experience (even if providing provisionally handy hangers).

When a senator uses polarity language, there is likely to be a basic similarity, some common ground, between his position and the one he opposes, if only an implicit agreement that it is normal for each to maximize his own position against the other. Polarization tactics above, reinforce them below. Rap songs that polarize men and women, blacks and whites, rich and poor, do more than express the way things are. They are more than personal outcries and signals to the empowered elite. They also reflect ways the elite act. Similar categories govern the minds, beings, styles, tone, and words of those who are running the country. Congressional hearings have their own rap style. As models of behavior, they seem to be more sophisticated versions of what goes on in the street.

Indeed, those on top provide valuable models and messages for those on the bottom. What they teach is that it's important to be on top, to get there whatever way you can, and to use anything you can get away with to extend your power. Don't worry whether what you say is truthful. Find a winning lie and ride it as far as you can go. Trade it in for another, like a worn horse, if conditions warrant. Pick a winner: winning is all. It's natural to go to bat for you and yours. The others don't count as much as you do.

One of the odd things about violence is that the perpetrator, and even the victim, may not be aware of the real impact and consequences of his or her violence. Often it happens in a semi-trance, where one is protected from the feelings one's actions might arouse. The actions reel off, with a momentum of their own. At times, it seems as if someone else is doing it, and that it's happening to someone somewhere else. One may be blown away by an explosive force that has its own logic.

Congressional or presidential or judicial violence may be harder to recognize or do anything about, since it can be threaded through protracted chains of arguments, lines of reasoning, and rational questioning, which depend partly on back-room reshuffling of the cards. In such a situation, it is more difficult to find a murder weapon than in the street, since everyone has a brain and tongue, and there is no law against exercising them.

Therefore, it is unlikely that solving poverty will be enough to "solve" violence. There is the violence of luxury, as well as the violence of poverty. This in no way mitigates the importance of doing what is possible to help the poor or to discover conditions that would make poverty a thing of the past. Even so, it is difficult to see how such a miracle at the bottom would quell the lust for more and more that characterizes the top. In a sense, the right wing of politics is correct in saying that the liberals have the wrong idea. The liberals have wanted to ameliorate conditions at the bottom, but the illness at the top remains pretty much untouched and trickles down.

In light of the enormity of what faces us, a therapist's ambition to become the sort of person someone can talk to seems fragile indeed. So much is needed, yet I don't think there is anything that society needs more.

REFERENCE

Moss, D. M. (1984). Judicial trauma—judicial travesty: a personal encounter with evil. In *Evil: Self and Culture*, ed., M. C. Nelson, and M. Eigen, pp. 181–200. New York: Human Sciences.

18

Boa and Flowers

Within minutes of entering my office Janice told me that analysis had destroyed her. She did not actually tell me, but cried, shouted, screamed at me. Not simply a cry, shout, scream from the heart, the kind that elicits a saving response. Her tone accused, nagged, threatened, demanded. She *knew* what she wanted, she *knew* what had gone wrong, she *knew* what she needed.

"It's the simplest thing in the world," she said. "I need good parenting. Will you give it to me? Can you give it to me? Will you do it?"

Here was a moment of raw appeal. "Yes," I felt. Who could deny the need for good parenting? She was right, and my innermost being responded, but I could not suppress a "but." This "but" was our undoing.

"I don't want analysis shit," she told me. "That's what killed me. I was alive. I know what it's like to be alive. She [Janice's analyst for eight years] told me I was acting out, that my style of being alive was self-destructive. She tried to analyze me away. Analysis killed my soul. Now I'm a total mess. I can't feel anything. Nothing is alive for me. I'm a dead person, a nothing. She was jealous of my life. I went around with rich people, jet-setting, partying, terrific clothes—*my* element, not hers. She was down. She never lived. She couldn't take life. She had no idea of what life could be. I was high on life, and she couldn't stand it. Now I need love, the kind a baby gets, so I can come back, so I can *be* again—so I can have a *self* again. It's the simplest thing in the world. Can you do it? I need to know. No ifs, ands, buts, maybes. Can you do it or not?"

Was an unqualified yes possible? Not by me, no matter how much I wanted to help, no matter how much she may have been right. I did not have a totally unambivalent and certain psyche and could not bring myself to lie about it.

"Have you ever helped people like me before?"

That question I could say yes to. Yes. How good it felt to be able to say yes. I knew if she stayed long enough, there was every likelihood that she would benefit. But there was the catch: probability, likelihood, which to her meant there was a chance that therapy might fail, that I would not be good enough, that she would continue to die. There really is no bottom to this kind of dying. To Janice, if the outcome of therapy was not an absolute certainty, it was a dice roll.

"You wouldn't beat around the bush if your own child was in distress. You would comfort her. You would care for her. No qualifications or doubts. You'd love her and give her what she needs. I saw your book. There was too much Freud in it. You're too Freudian for me. That shit doesn't work. I can tell you it doesn't work. It kills. Did you read Alice Miller? Do you agree with her? She's right. That's what I need. You can give it to me, if you want to. I can sense it. You'd give it to your own child. That's what I need—the same thing you'd give your own child. A chance to come back, to be myself again. That's what I want. Will you do it or not?"

How could I say no? How could I say yes? Her appeal came through the noise of her personality, through her accusations, through her dismissal of the therapeutic medium through which she sought help. Yet her demand for absolute care and certainty of outcome, comprehensible as it may be, acted as a practical barrier to her appeal.

If I tried to comfort her, she attacked me more. I did not find the right spot in just the right way. Moreover, she felt my failures were willful.

"You do not really want to help. If you did, there would be no reserve. You would give me what I need, as you would a child. Maybe you'd warm up after awhile, but I can't wait. I'm dying now."

Perhaps other therapists did not share my limitations. I pictured someone more related and caring than I. Face to face with Janice, I felt my restrictions only too keenly. Whatever was dry, reserved, or removed about me felt exacerbated. I felt how incarcerated I was by my distance, my ungivingness, my unyieldingness. Suddenly I was all Scrooge. What happened to the goodness I liked to feel, the *jouissance*? It was gone like the killed-off life Janice raved (I wish I could say raged) about.

If only I could think of the right person to refer her to, the one who could click. But I learned that I was the eighth therapist she had seen in the past year. The therapy that killed her ended five years earlier. How many therapists could she try?

The death-dealing analyst was known in the field as competent and caring. Janice diagnosed her as suffocating and suffocated, someone who disparaged as manic all life manifestations (in Janice's words). Janice tore herself away and searched for the right situation. This past year, before she came to me, she thought she found it in a male therapist who took command and said he would be the parent she needed.

For several months Janice's dream came true. She felt inklings of the life she lost, moments of hope. He was helping her the way she wanted. He was not afraid of contact. He found and cared for her child self. Then he turned on her. He became impatient and angry and put her down. He told her about difficulties in his life. He wanted her to give him something too. She loved him and wanted him to take care of her, but could not bring herself to give him anything. He let her down, but she liked him better than other therapists she had tried. She felt that he had the right idea, but his craziness and needs interfered. She wanted someone like him, only less crazy and more reliable. "Call him and find out what he does," she told me. "He does it the way I want. He's got the right idea. Call him and find out about it. I think you could do it if you wanted to and do it better."

I could do it and do it better! Wow! Megalomania, here we come! I knew the man she spoke about and liked him a lot. He believed in working with the baby soul like a parent, if need be. But he was a big baby himself and expected the parent–baby business to go both ways. Many of his patients swore by him. But Janice was not ready for reciprocal quirkiness and mutual catering to baby needs. She wanted to be the only baby, the center of someone's universe. She wanted total devotion.

She could not tolerate the idea that any person who tried to do what she wanted must inevitably recoil. There would be a backlash. No personality could bend so thoroughly for so long. Even parents rebel.

Yet Janice's need was real. Her capacity to be alive was deeply wounded. She wanted loving attention. She wanted someone who could give. She wanted someone who could let her be, who would let her be first.

One thinks of primary love or primary narcissism or the need for mirroring of archaic grandiosity. But a self psychologist referred Janice to me. He could not get to first base with her. And an object relations therapist had referred her to him. She ran the gamut. I wondered about humanistic psychologists from the 1960s who did hands-on parenting. There were no guarantees.

I could not help wondering what massive or specific or cumulative failure of parental/environmental provision might underlie such a painful loss of self-feeling. As if reading my mind, Janice said, "I had a happy childhood. My parents were loving and good, and I loved them. It's not my childhood. It was my analysis that killed me. I want the feeling I had before she killed my life off. I want to get back to me."

I have been in the field for over thirty years. I knew analysis could kill. I have seen harmful and helpful effects of therapy. I also knew individuals who idealized their prebreakdown selves. Compared to the horrors of breakdown, their earlier misery seemed like happiness. It could be that Janice's analysis was harmful and that she idealized life prior to it. Or the situation could be more complex. Perhaps Janice felt assaulted by the ambivalence of life and counter-attacked by oversimplification. Perhaps she already was on the way toward break-down when she sought help, and analysis failed to help her. I could extend this list of possibilities, but complexity was certainly something that Janice did not want. She used the word "simple" repeatedly: "What I need is simple. It's simply what you'd give a child of your own. The simplest thing in the world."

I feel that simple thing at the center of my being. It shows in my eyes, my tone, my skin. I live from and through it. It is my home. Yet some people see it, and some do not. To some I may seem cold or distant or reserved and, to others, warm and playful. Some coming near me may feel they are entering the House of Complexity. Where is that simple thread leading to and coming from the heart's center? Where is it when it is lost? How can something I feel so deeply and thoroughly not show? With Janice I felt like a stroke victim who could feel his shining essence unable to break through layers of imprisonment.

Yet she saw something in me. She felt I could help, *if I wanted to*. There was the rub. It was up to my desire. If I wanted to, I could. I could not help wondering what pressure she must be under if she felt desire could do all. How often it was said to me from childhood on: "You can do it, if you want to!" I could not help wondering what disease or deficiency of desire plagued Janice's life. Who wanted her and how? Who did not and how not? What provision was made for loss and limitation? For immersion in experience?

"I can do it myself if you'll just be there for me. I can. I know I can—I know what it is I need and where to find it. But you have to *be* there while I do it. You have to let me do it. I have to know that you can be there, that you *will* be there."

But mere being is inadequate. "You have to take charge. Do you understand? You have to direct it. No analytic bullshit. It has to be real. You have to know what you're doing. I have to be able to lean on you. I have to rely on you to be there and take charge when I am falling apart. You have to put me back together when I fall apart. I have to do it, but you have to take charge. Do you get it?"

Well, Mr. Therapist, Mr. Wise Guy, let us see what you are made of. Put your money where your mouth is. Only true emotional reality will do. The thing itself. Isn't this what you talked about all these years?

Now I think of the picture on the cover of the paperback edition of Groddeck's *Book of the It*—an impish man popping out of a body slit, a mock image of pulsations of the unconscious. Now I picture soul filling body, simple emotional availability, a flow back and forth through surface–depth, person to person. I wish I were one of those people who make you feel good just by looking at them. So many barriers, barriers upon barriers. Janice hated all barriers. I felt as if all I had to offer was the grim prospect of hard work. Psychotherapy—sometimes a feather that tickles, now the Grim Reaper.

I do not have a party line, a dogma about just how I am supposed to be with every patient. I am willing to shift ground, try different styles, try to locate some way of being/experiencing that might work. I do not like getting boxed in to any particular version of myself. Often I have the feeling of my personality regrowing around the impact of a particular O[1]—reshaping itself with the re-

---

[1] O is a Bion notation connoting unknowable ultimate reality; here the ultimate reality or emotional truth of a session (Bion 1970, Eigen 1981, 1985, see also Chapter 4).

quirements of the emotional reality of moment. Such reshuffling sometimes happens rapidly and automatically. Sometimes it takes going through many deserts.

If Janice would give us time, we could try this and that until we became viable. Mothers and infants work at feeding. Each learns to do what has to be done—the mutual adjustments that make a difference. When I suggested that I might learn to work with her, that we might learn to work with each other, Janice replied severely, "If I needed a physical operation, I would not get a doctor who had to learn how to do it. I would get an expert, one who knows."

"I don't know that thoughts and feelings are exactly like brains or livers. Their location isn't so certain." Did I say or merely think this? I already said too much, too little—all wrong.

No uncertainty of locale could be tolerated, and there was no time. Either I was the one who could do it or not, and I had to be the one to say so.

I do not mind contradictory demands of difficult patients. My paper "On Working with 'Unwanted' Patients" (1977) summarizes ten years of work with clinic patients. My book, *The Psychotic Core* (1986), summarizes nearly twenty-five (now nearly thirty) years of work with psychotic dynamics and psychotic-like processes. I am supposed to be something of an expert in the "difficult," and this reputation is why Janice was referred to me. Over the years my practice imperceptibly became weighted with psychoanalysts and psychotherapists. Am I becoming soft? Would Janice have been too much for me twenty years ago? At that time I would have done anything to make contact.

Now all I had to do was say I could do it. The words did not come. I felt more deeply in contact than twenty years ago, a deeper inner sense of being, but outwardly was I more removed? Perhaps Janice was right in thinking she would have to work too hard to get to me.

My patients years ago were not less disturbed, but they tended to latch onto therapy long enough for something to happen. They seemed to take their unconscious, masochistic attachment to therapy more for granted and held on for dear life. They needed to establish a parasitic grip whether via rage, withdrawal, depression, or seductiveness on therapy and were willing to play the game in exchange for being allowed to hang on. They gave me time. They did not seem to mind losing time. The passage of time did not irritate them. Perhaps in those days submission to a doctor was more permissible.

Janice opposed her masochistic desires with brittle interrogation and demands. She wanted to be sure what she was getting into. She could not afford another failure. She knew how to *shop* and what she was looking for. She was examining the goods very carefully. She wanted to be in control; she knew her rights. What did I do, and how did I do it? It was like examining the teeth of a horse. But I did not feel that she would allow herself to *see* me. Her trust in herself had been destroyed. After all, she had given therapy a chance and lost. How *does* one select a therapist?

Janice took what little time we might have had away. She saw me only once and came twenty minutes late. During her twenty-five-minute hour a construction crew furiously ripped up the road in front of my office window. Jung's synchronicity came to mind—how fitting that this noise should happen now.

I could play or be the analyst and establish the frame of silence—the construction crew saw to it that this would not be. Or I could confront or elaborate or empathize or interpret or hunt for a good-enough maturational response. I could tell her how right she was in being circumspect, in trying to find what was right for herself. I could try to be myself. I could be honest, but which profile of honesty, which part of the elephant would manifest the word or gesture that counts? It was clear to me in an instant that I was unable to present myself in the way she wanted and that from her viewpoint I offered no viable alternative. She could only leave, unless she could do precisely what she could not do: give us time to see what might happen, give us time to learn to work together. I could not give her the one thing she demanded: I could not be sure. I could not end time.

Janice and I spoke by telephone for almost two weeks after this visit. She kept calling and leaving long messages. She did everything she could to make me say yes, to be sure, to reassure her that I could do it, that I was the one. Nothing I could find to say and no way that I could find to be were useful. Janice brought me up short against my limits and refused any intersection at or beyond the boundaries. She was fixed on my having to be sure and on her having to be sure that I was sure, that I was the one who could do it, who wanted to and who would. She was very articulate about this position and yielded no leeway.

She did not ask about my fee, and I did not bring it up. I knew my colleagues charged her for their consultations. I did not think that charging or not charging would make a difference. I could not bring myself to charge, perhaps because of the noisy construction crew, perhaps because I was psychologically impotent or because I wanted her to know that the unconscious could be generous even if it did not seem so, that there were ways that time and timelessness could be interchangeable.

She left a vase of flowers in my waiting room one day. They were obviously hand arranged by her, and beautifully so. My self psychologist colleague told me she left him one too. So many flowers, so beautifully arranged. How many flowers she must have left behind!

We spoke a number of times after she left the flowers. She wanted me to speak to a therapist whom she felt really knew her, someone who had been good, a woman in Washington whom she saw years ago when she left college. Perhaps this woman would help me find the right way to be.

Janice contacted this good doctor, who called me. We spoke when she came to the city for a funeral. She scarcely remembered Janice. She had seen Janice briefly. Now she felt Janice needed hospitalization; she feared Janice could not take care of herself. She planned to tell Janice's parents. She asked me which hospitals in the area I thought were good, and I told her. The calls from Janice stopped.

I have worked with people far more collapsed than Janice. Perhaps some doctors would have felt that some of these people should have been hospitalized. Janice's flowers were not even close to the bleeding flowers of schizophrenic dreams. Her loss of self did not have the butchered, bleak quality of psychotic landscapes. She used flowers to finalize loss. Where self had been and might be again, flowers are—not the flowers of the living self, but markers of the place where self disappeared, the place where self was last seen and where Janice is waiting. If only we could both sit at the fishing hole in the ice and wait for spring.

Janice's flowers showed me what I was missing by not saying yes. They were my punishment for my "but." If only I could have taken the leap, what a sensitive being I might have discovered. Her vase of flowers was a token of the flowers to come, the promise of our work together, the promise whose grave they marked.

How many promises, how many graves litter Janice's search and mark her trail? Perhaps the search is more real than the trail. Trail implies movement and direction, implies that someone has been somewhere.

The bread Janice leaves behind is dropped in the same place, over and over. Droppings. Therapists left behind like droppings. More waves of therapists to come. Janice moves from therapist to therapist, searching for Mr. Right, the One Who Can and Will Do It. Her flowers tell me what I am missing, that I am missing Someone Special. She shows me that she is generous, that she forgives my miserliness. But I am not just I. I am all therapists, the therapy field, the barren field in which no flowers grow, the field she hopes to activate.

Why do I feel something in the search is real? It is not a scientific search, a patient testing of hypothesis or imagining of hypotheses, although these are not entirely excluded. It is a search for the flower that is not there, the therapy flower, the flowers outside her that match those within. A search for the flowers she wishes were there, within or without. She shows up to find nothing again, the blank hole in the ice. She will not hold hands or fight or wait it out at the brim. But her flowers say that she could do all that *if* only you were the right one, if only you were good enough, if only you would or could say yes. If only you would do as she says and be as she wants.

I think of Milton's fairest flower "no sooner blown than blasted," a hymn to a dead child. So many dead therapies to mimic the therapy that killed her.

Her search cancels itself out, but is not dead. I can feel aliveness in the intensity of its standstill. It dies over and over until only its drivenness remains. But I can feel this restless drivenness, the scratch of nails that will not let go. I can feel its insistence in how much I am driven to exercise myself trying to enliven the corpse of therapy, how I ache and work to find a way. We both wear holes in ourselves from this mad, soldierly discipline, running in place until feet burn and lungs burst and earth disappears. Our psyches grind themselves to smithereens trying to make contact with nothing, trying to give each other the benefit of the doubt.

Infinite uselessness. I know I will feel exhausted after this brief meeting, which seems to go on forever. I could have remained detached and immune—precisely what Janice might criticize me for. But another psychic force field was at work. I did not find myself sitting back and thinking, "There's nothing I can do. She needs to be hospitalized." I found myself working like a madman, chewing myself up, trying to find the right current—*because I sensed it was there.* There, but not available, not available to me, not available to most (perhaps all) therapists, and not available to Janice.

The good female therapist from Washington feared that Janice was unable to take care of herself. It would not surprise me if I missed the most obvious thing, if I did not see what stared me in the face. Perhaps her breakdown was not a florid kind. No hallucinations or overwhelming panic or depression. Just a kind of scatter and depletion of functioning, a kind of blank breakdown.

I knew Janice was depleted, bleeding to death, running scared, sensitive, and tyrannical. I saw that she could not give me the chance to find a way to reach her, nor could she extend me the courtesy of torturing me for months or years or properly exhausting my repertoire of abilities (she already said she could not give a therapist anything). Perhaps what was most irksome was that Janice did not *really* try me out at all. I was unusable, and perhaps the sense of not being used or usable is what exercised me. Perhaps I was so preoccupied with my own breakdown and the unfairness of not being given a fair audition that I did not see the need for a hospital.

Previous therapists had not hospitalized her. Had she reached a new low in depletion or spinning? Was the therapist from Washington speaking out of her own sense of impotence, or was she right? Am I too used to psychotic and psychotic-like states and dynamics to see a hospital case in front of my nose?

Winnicott (1969, Eigen 1981) has taught us that it may be precisely the capacity to use another person that is unavailable and must be grown in many patients. Is it fair to say I was not being used, or was I and the therapy milieu being used to feel useless? Was precisely this state of uselessness my (our) use? Was the therapist who recommended hospitalization feeling this endless uselessness? Was she hoping a hospital could contain what was beyond personal containment, perhaps beyond containment of the therapy milieu in general? Was any container adequate for this limitless uselessness?

I can picture Janice in a good hospital being nurtured back to aliveness. She rests and finds herself in a setting that upholds her and allows for growth or repair. At last she achieves what she wants, a chance for true self. This growth can and does happen. Would it for Janice? I have learned from hard experience that often I must say something like, "Yes, a hospital stay may do you good. But when you come out, the same problems will be waiting. You still will be you. The world will be the world. The dirty work will be waiting."

One can speculate and question. Did my uselessness reflect the deep uselessness Janice felt or feared to feel? Did she need to make the parent feel useless? In what ways were the parents useless or worse than useless? Would one expect to find distant or controlling parents or both? Was the parental need for a happy child too great, so that emptiness became the inner reality or protective shell? Did the loss of self protect against invasive overstimulation or reflect a lack of inner richness in her once "happy" life? Perhaps there were real elements of richness to her happiness, but the impact of reality after college was too hard to bear. Was the contrast between family and reality too great? One could go on.

In our twenty minutes together Janice hid her history in the gloss of happiness. She would not let me near her past, not in any obvious way. She displayed a wound that was still smarting, a death in process, an accusation, a demand. Actually she did not display it so much as talk about it and berate therapy. She demanded that I be an empathic, usable object who can take charge, who can set direction and let be, who can establish conditions in which she can find herself. How tantalized I was with her sense of rightness, her knowing what was right for her. A knowing that dangled and withdrew the carrot, saying, "I'm sorry. Your dance is not quite right. Please do the right one now. I know you can." And frantically I pressed the jukebox until only whirring remained. That whirring nullity is what I suspected Janice was vanishing into. I looked for the hole in the needle she said was there, but it too was whirring away.

"If only you would treat me like your own child, love me like your own child." God, how I love my children! How I can hate them too! How exasperating they can be. They drive me over the edge, those beastly monsters, those so, so precious beings. But don't you know, Janice, I loved them before they were born. I loved them before they were conceived. They came into a love that was waiting for years. And they ignite new loves, loves I never catch up to. Each child plays on me with his own personality and creates loves with unique tones. I become musical instruments that never were before and never will be again. "Sing a new song to the Lord." New songs, new hearts. My children create in me new hearts and wear my hearts down.

Their life kills me off. I come back. I want to kill them and *fight* for my life. "I go to bed crying and wake up laughing," as the psalmist says. My soul is restored, ready for more. What a battleground the playground is. Is this what the Bible means by slavery in Egypt—*Mitzrayim,* the "narrow strait," the binding limit, cement mixed with blood? Janice, don't you know my children never asked to be loved?

Yes, I think you know or once knew. Somehow it got narrowed down. How this process happened I cannot know, but would like to learn, if you let me. Perhaps someday you will become the kind of person I can love like I do my children. But you are not like them now. They do not tell me that I must be sure I can be a good parent before they splatter themselves all over me. They do not require my certainty that I will not fail them before they run at me and jump on me. I am certain I will fail them. I cannot count the times I have made them cry. But I am certain I will keep on trying, as long as I have breath–at least part of the time, intermittently, as much as I am able. How can they escape my wounds, or I theirs? We each have our inner drummers. We are driven to come through—to live. I look at them and feel my death. I look at them and thrill to life.

Janice, you have closed yourself off to this mixed-up, painful, joyous growth of real life. You have become a purist. You want a guarantee. One of my boys is more cautious, the other more abandoned, but both press headlong into the maelstrom, wound after wound, coming back for more, growing and growing. Who can get enough of life? Who can hold back for long? They can be impossible, conniving, spiteful, and nurse their wounds—but life sweeps them up, moods change, things happen, currents flow every which way from hidden springs to the seas.

I suspect I am wrong in saying you closed yourself off. It is more accurate to say that closing off or narrowing happens. You did not plan psychic deadness any more than a flower plans what happens to it when rain does not fall or light does not shine. Perhaps this is why control is so important to you now— so much is out of control. You want me to will you into life, for will has failed.

Yet you say you had plenty of sunshine and enough watering—until analysis. Analysis took away the conditions of life. Now you want therapy to restore what analysis has taken. Justice. I cannot judge. I do not know what happened. I only know that Something Went Wrong, Something Wrong Happened. Help is needed, but seems more on the way out than in.

The child is not dead. You are there, Janice, beating down therapist after therapist with your raw appeal. I believe your appeal. I picture you as my child, crying angrily, "You broke your Promise!" The world is a broken promise. Every therapy knows that. Yet in spite of brokenness, every therapy is a promise (no matter what the therapist says), a promise linked with an unconscious as "no-less" as it is timeless. Now you cannot say yes to any real therapist, Janice, nor can you say no to the promise.

You ask *if* I want to see the documents. You have written it all down. I can learn from your writings who you are and what you want. From your written words I can see what needs to be done and gird up my loins to do it. As you speak, your inner being slips through the words. You cannot hold it all. You cannot give it to the Other. In your aloneness you have written it. The paper holds it. The Other cannot steal your reality away. You can show it at will, and if I read it, I will know. The self psychologist has the writings. You will bring them to me and hope that by my reading them I will know if I can do it.

Janice never brought them over. I would certainly have read her testimony, her plea, her fury, her poetry, her analysis, as many before me did. But the problem would have remained: I would not be able to say that surely I was the One. The reality of my disability must have hit her, and I imagine she found her way into another sector of the therapy field to continue her fall.

Bion (1965, p. 101) writes of a force that continues after the last point of personality has been annihilated and existence, time, and space have been destroyed. Janice had not yet reached utter pointlessness and loss, but she was on her way. Alice Miller didn't help. Freud, Jung, Winnicott, Bion, and Kohut didn't help either, nor did my training or experience. My very life and personality were useless. I survive my annihilation just as Janice in one way or another partly survives hers. But, like a boa, the force molds itself around the victim's breathing and now and then gently squeezes with the intake of a breath.

In Bion's vision there is no end to annihilation. We move from one heart of darkness to another—heartlessness beyond heartlessness. Just as our eyes become used to the dark, it becomes darker. There is no end to the darkness to explore. The force is on a permanent search-and-destroy mission, a Pac Man feeding on every sign of life. And after life is destroyed, it will continue to feed on death, nonexistence after nonexistence. Surely such a force cannot be real—its existence is a contradiction in terms. But it is precisely this impossibility that gives it power.

Janice, if you saw me today, could things be different? Would I do better? How I wish so. How I wish I could explode myself and become the kind of presence or presence—absence balance that would do it. I know about getting the right distance–closeness balance—how I tried! Where is the me–not-me self you could work with? Where is the I you could say yes to, or say no and fight it out? The missing link is all. It is cuddled in the boa's caress. Each breath it dares to take brings it closer to its undoing. We both know the link is there, but cannot escape our own constrictions.

Please, Janice, let us agree to fail for as long as it takes. I believe the force can be outflanked. There is something deeper, something more. You sense it, or you would not be here at all. It is afraid to breathe now, but perhaps it will wait for us. It will feel "our" breathing. I understand that it is buried under the collapse of the entire earth, that all existence has become the killer. You see, I know the force well; I am part of that constriction. I write too, like you. I am writing you this testimony. For I too slip away when we speak. I am telling you, from my aloneness to yours, writer to writer, that I believe you. I believe in the flowers you gave me. We are those flowers, the missing links. I believe in writing, the writings you never gave me. I am writing to you, Janice, any Janice, who may read this testimony and respond with the next-to-last breath. I have breathed my last breath many times and want to go with you to that place. Between the words, breathing starts up again.

REFERENCES

Bion, W. R. (1965). *Transformations*. London: Heinemann.
——— (1970). *Attention and Interpretation*. London: Tavistock.
Eigen, M. (1977). On working with "unwanted" patients. *International Journal of Psycho-Analysis,* 58:109–121.
——— (1981). The area of faith in Winnicott, Lacan and Bion. *International Journal of Psycho-Analysis,* 62:413–433.
——— (1985). Toward Bion's starting point: between catastrophe and faith. *International Journal of Psycho-Analysis,* 66:321–330.
——— (1986). *The Psychotic Core*. Northvale, NJ: Jason Aronson.
Winnicott, D. W. (1969). The use of an object and relating through identications. In *Playing and Reality*. New York: Basic Books, 1971.

Epilogue

How much aliveness can one take? Susan Deri[1] told a story, near the end of one of Bion's seminars, about a man she worked with for many years, a man she had all but given up on. One can't exactly say she supported him in life, because he wasn't very alive to begin with. But she supported him in whatever he could do.

In those days (three decades ago), many patients who seemed psychically limited, impoverished, and on the dead side were dumped into a category called "chronic schizophrenia." They did not have florid hallucinations or intense affective storms, but seemed rather vacant, emotionless, with little mental flow. Yet a good number of these individuals could be helped to hold undemanding jobs (at least periodically), sometimes keep their own apartments, and even maintain primitive object ties. Without help, they would become vegetative, with chronic institutional care almost inevitable (I wrote about my inability to help one such individual in *The Psychotic Core* (1986), pp. 105–108, and *The Electrified Tightrope* (1993), pp. 238–241).

Occasionally, a therapist experiences the miracle of such an individual growing more and more alive. In such cases not only is an individual helped to function better but also his or her emotional life evolves, becomes less stunted, more varied and intense. This is what Susan Deri experienced with her patient. He refused to give up on himself. She was loyal, devoted, and committed to him, but her expectations were lower than his. She was realistic, but as he came alive, he wanted everything.

---

[1] I heard Susan Deri tell this story on more than one occasion, the first time at this seminar, where part of it was captured in print by Francesca Bion's transcription (*Bion in New York and Sao Paulo.* Perthshire: Clunie Press, 1980: 69–74). Obviously, it exercised Ms. Deri, and was something she shared to be helped with. In retrospect, I wonder if it also did not serve as a vehicle to express unconscious premonition of her own untimely death, not long on the horizon.

Over the course of decades his productivity increased. He more than managed work, felt pleasure in what he did, got a better apartment, and, in general, enjoyed a higher level of existence. Then the unspeakable happened. He fell in love—and his love was reciprocated. I remember Ms. Deri describing her disbelief, her amazement: how could this happen? She credited her patient. It was he who kept going from level to level, wanting more, wanting whatever life could give. She was behind him, with him, each step of the way. But now—he was getting something Ms. Deri could not get for herself. She never thought he had the capacity to support life at its fullest. She worried for him, like a mother worries that a child might run recklessly into oncoming traffic.

He was joyous, ecstatic; his dreams were coming true. He married and took time off for his honeymoon, aiming to return to therapy for help with his next step—having his own family. It was never to happen. His wife called to inform Ms. Deri that he died of a heart attack on their honeymoon.

There is no doubt that Ms. Deri felt his aliveness was too much for him. She felt guilty for—what?—not taking more care that he not get too alive? Surely, he had decades of help to build up to it. How can one call his leap into life precipitous? Yet Ms. Deri felt the final burst of aliveness was too much for his physical being. His heart could not take its own opening.

Which is worse: an individual so addicted to high levels of stimulation and tension that even slight dips in arousal level are felt as deadening, or an individual so used to a quasi-comatose or numb existence that the slightest hint of affective quickening is threatening? To be sure, one cannot tell ahead of time whether a high- or low-stimulation individual feels more alive. I have met many individuals who live high-stimulation lives, yet feel numb. At the same time, there are people who cannot take much stimulation, because every bit sets off more waves of aliveness than is bearable. The possibilies are myriad.

It is hoped that one outcome of immersing oneself in problems and obstacles this book works with is growth in sensitivity to the complex, heterogeneous play of deadness–aliveness in every therapy. In some situations it matters more, in some less. In some, it is a life-and-death matter. There are individuals for whom a sense of fluctuating deadness–aliveness is a radical discovery, whereas others scarcely notice anything else. As therapists, we need to learn how to become better partners with our mixed or double capacity for aliveness–deadness, so that we, our patients, and this precious, dumbfounding, and maddening capacity can evolve together.

Credits

The author gratefully acknowledges permission to reprint the following material:

Chapter 1, "Psychic Death," originally published as "Psychic Deadness: Freud" in *Contemporary Psychoanalysis*, vol. 31, no. 2, pp. 277–299. Copyright © 1995 by the William Alanson White Institute. Reprinted by permission of the William Alanson White Institute.

Chapter 2, "The Destructive Force," originally published as "The Destructive Force Within" in *Contemporary Psychoanalysis*, vol. 31, no. 4, pp. 603–616. Copyright © 1995 by the William Alanson White Institute. Reprinted by permission of the William Alanson White Institute.

Chapter 3, "Goodness and Deadness," originally published in *Melanie Klein and Object Relations*, vol. 13, December 1995, pp. 43–53. Copyright © 1995 by O. Weininger. Reprinted by permission of *Melanie Klein and Object Relations*.

Chapter 4, "Bion's No-thing," originally published in *Melanie Klein and Object Relations*, vol. 13, June 1995, pp. 31–36. Copyright © by O. Weininger. Reprinted by permission of *Melanie Klein and Object Relations*.

Chapter 5, "Moral Violence," originally published in *Melanie Klein and Object Relations*, vol. 13, June 1995, pp. 37–45. Copyright © by O. Weininger. Reprinted by permission of *Melanie Klein and Object Relations*.

Chapter 6, "Two Kinds of No-thing," originally published in *Melanie Klein and Object Relations*, vol. 13, June 1995, pp. 46–64. Copyright © by O. Weininger. Reprinted by permission of *Melanie Klein and Object Relations*.

Chapter 7, "The Area of Freedom: The Point of No Compromise," originally published as "Winnicott's Area of Freedom: The Uncompromiseable" in *Liminality and Transitional Phenomena*, ed. Nathan Schwartz-Salant and Murray

Index